REPRINTS OF ECONOMIC CLASSICS

W AGES & C APITAL

Also Published in

REPRINTS OF ECONOMIC CLASSICS

By F. W. Taussig

International Trade [1927]

The Tariff History Of The United States [1931]

In *Honor of* F. W. Taussig

Explorations In Economics [1936]

WAGES AND CAPITAL

AN EXAMINATION OF THE WAGES FUND DOCTRINE

BY

F. W. TAUSSIG

[1896]

Reprints of Economic Classics
AUGUSTUS M. KELLEY PUBLISHERS
New York 1968

First Edition 1896

(New York: D. Appleton & Company, 1896)

Reprinted 1968 by

AUGUSTUS M. KELLEY · PUBLISHERS

New York New York 10010

_____

Library of Congress Catalogue Card Number

67-28293

_____

PRINTED IN THE UNITED STATES OF AMERICA
_by_ SENTRY PRESS, NEW YORK, N. Y. 10019

PREFACE.

I HAVE divided the present volume into two parts: a first, of five chapters, containing a statement at large of my own views on the relation of capital to wages, and on the wages fund doctrine; and a second, of nine further chapters, in which the history of the wages fund discussion from its beginning to the present time is followed. At the close, a final chapter gives a brief summary of both parts. In this arrangement I have departed from the traditional plan, and perhaps from the strictly logical plan. It has been customary, in critical and historical inquiries as to one or another phase of economic theory, to begin with the history and criticism, and to close with the statement of the author's final conclusions. But criticism and comment proceed inevitably from the thinker's own point of view; and to weigh the conclusions of others, without having explained one's own, necessitates either an incidental and thus unsatisfactory statement of the grounds of an opinion, or a considerable anticipation of views whose full exposition is nevertheless postponed. I have accordingly adopted the reverse order, and trust I have been able thereby to make at once a briefer and a clearer presentation of my opinions.

I am sensible that in the first part, in which my own views are stated, there is some elaborateness of exposition and some liberal reaching-out to related topics. I have endeavored to make my meaning clear not only to those who have already given some attention to economic theory, but to those who are new to such discussions; and hence I may have been prolix, and may have explained at needless length matters that to many readers will seem very simple. The historical and critical discussions of the second part are addressed more particularly to special students of economic theory. While not essential for following the reasoning or for weighing the conclusions of the first part, they yet consider aspects of the wages fund controversy not to be neglected by those who would reach an opinion on the subject as a whole.

I have to express my warm thanks to Professor Maffeo Pantaleoni, who generously put his well-stocked library at my disposal in Rome during the winter of 1894–95; to Mr. James Bonar, of London, who read the manuscript of some of the earlier chapters, and greatly aided me by his criticism; and to my colleague Professor W. J. Ashley, who has read all the proofs of the volume, and offered many helpful suggestions.

Two chapters have already appeared in print. Almost the whole of Chapter III was published, under the title "The Employer's Place in Distribution," in the *Quarterly Journal of Economics* for October, 1895. Chapter XIII, on the wages fund at the hands of German economists, was published, in essentials, in the same journal for October, 1894.

F. W. TAUSSIG.

HARVARD UNIVERSITY, *November, 1895.*

CONTENTS.

PART I.

CHAPTER I.

PRESENT WORK AND PRESENT WAGES.

CHAPTER II.

CAPITAL AND WAGES.

CHAPTER III.

THE MACHINERY OF DISTRIBUTION.

CHAPTER IV.

THE ELASTICITY OF THE WAGES FUND.

PART II.

CRITICAL HISTORY OF THE WAGES FUND DISCUSSION.

CHAPTER VI.

BEFORE ADAM SMITH.

CHAPTER VII.

ADAM SMITH.

CHAPTER VIII.

THE IMMEDIATE FOLLOWERS OF ADAM SMITH.

CHAPTER IX.

RICARDO.

CHAPTER X.

FROM RICARDO TO JOHN STUART MILL.

CHAPTER XI.

JOHN STUART MILL.

CHAPTER XII.

LONGE—THORNTON—MILL—CAIRNES.

CHAPTER XIII.

THE WAGES FUND IN GERMANY.

CHAPTER XIV.

CONTEMPORARY DISCUSSION.

CHAPTER XV.

GENERAL SUMMARY.

WAGES AND CAPITAL.

PART I.

CHAPTER I.

PRESENT WORK AND PRESENT WAGES.

THE subject of the present volume is the wages-fund doctrine and the immediate relation of capital to wages. To discuss adequately this topic it will not be necessary to consider every part of the theory of wages or of capital; yet some parts of the economic field will need to be traversed that may seem at first sight to lie beyond the limits chosen. More particularly, it will be necessary to begin with some description at large of the process of production, and of the manner in which the exertions of men yield them an enjoyable result. In the active controversy on the wages-fund doctrine which has been going on during the last quarter of a century, the question has gradually come more and more into the foreground whether wages come from the current product of labor or from a past product. This fundamental question must be disposed of before any real advance toward the truth of the matter can be accomplished.

In large part we are here on familiar ground, and might pass over it quickly and lightly. Yet the question is so important, and its bearing on the wages-fund controversy so vital, that no pains should be spared to set it in a clear light. The inquiry will therefore begin, in the present chapter, by considering with care and in detail what is the relation between the laborer's immediate exertions, the laborer's immediate product, and the laborer's immediate reward : between the work of to-day, the output of to-day, and the pay of to-day.

The work of to-day and the output of to-day go to-gether. Taking a survey of the varied activity of a great civilized community, let us see what the laborers now do and what they now produce. Evidently the most diverse things. Some laborers are at work in mines digging out ore and coal. Others are at work conveying coal and ore, which had been brought out days or weeks before, to the spot where they are to be used. Others, again, at that spot are engaged in converting materials of still earlier extraction into pig iron. Elsewhere, men are at work fashioning tools and machinery from iron and steel; or using the tools or machinery for spinning or weaving; or making up cloth into garments wherewith to protect us from cold and wet, and to satisfy our vanity or caprice. Or, to take another phase of production : at the moment when some laborers are at work digging out ore and coal, and others are transforming ore and coal of earlier extraction into iron, trees are felled at one spot, timber hewn and sawed and fashioned at another ; ploughs are made of wood and iron, fields are tilled, grain is in pro-cess of transportation from granary to mill, other grain is ground into flour, flour is carried to the bakery,—bread, finally, is baked and sold.

We naturally picture the various sorts of productive effort, as they have just been sketched, as taking place in succession : the ore is first dug, the ploughs then made, the field next tilled, the bread comes at the end. In fact, looking at the work and the output of to-day, these oper-ations are all taking place simultaneously. If we follow the history of a loaf of bread or a suit of clothes, we find them to be the outcome of a succession of efforts, stretching back a considerable time in the past. But if we take a section, so to speak, of what the world is now doing and now getting, we find that at any one moment all these various sorts of work are being done together, and all the various forms of wealth, from ore to bread, are being made simultaneously.

It was suggested long ago that production can be best described as the creation of utilities. Human effort can not add or subtract an atom of the matter of the universe. It can only shift and move matter so as to make it serve man's wants,—make it useful, or create utilities in it. Matter reaches the stage of complete utility when it is directly available for satisfying our wants; when it is bread that we can eat, clothes that we can wear, houses from which we can secure shelter and enjoyment. The object of all production is to bring matter to this stage; or, to be more accurate, to yield utilities, whether embodied in matter or not, which give immediate satisfaction. But a great part of our wealth—indeed much the greater part of it—consists of things which are but partly advanced toward the final satisfaction of our wants. Consider the enormous quantities of commodities which are bought and sold, and which constitute huge items in the wealth of the community, in the form of plant and materials: coal and iron and steel, wool and cotton and grain, factories and warehouses, railways and ships, and all the infinite apparatus of production that exists in the civilized countries of our day. All this is inchoate wealth. It serves as yet not to satisfy a single human want. It is not good to eat, nor pleasant to wear, nor agreeable to look on, nor in any way a direct source of enjoyment; unless, indeed, we make exceptions of the kind that prove the rule, for the cases where ships and railways are used for pleasure journeys, cotton soothes a burn, and grain yields the pleasure of feeding a household pet. Virtually, all the utilities embodied in such commodities are inchoate. These things, or others made by their aid, will in the future bring enjoyment; but for the present they satisfy no need and yield no pleasure. We are so habituated to the *régime* of exchange and sale, and to the continuous disposal of these forms of wealth by their owners for cash wherewith anything and everything can be bought, that we think of them ordinarily in terms of money value, and reckon them as equivalent to the possession of so much completed and enjoyable wealth. But, obviously, for the community as a whole, there is on hand at any given time a great mass of inchoate wealth which as yet can satisfy no want. And, at any given time, a great part of the labor of the community is devoted to making inchoate wealth, of which no part is directly of use or pleasure to any human being.

On the other hand, part of the labor of to-day is given to the close and immediate satisfaction of our wants. The baker bakes bread, the tailor makes clothes. The shopkeeper sells us things necessary or convenient or agreeable, and so brings them to the point where they finally meet our desires. The servant waits on our needs or contributes to our ease. In a multitude of directions it is the housewife through whom the last stage toward satisfaction is reached. Her labors have been celebrated less by economists than by poets; yet they play a very large part in that final activity through which a long series of past efforts is at last brought to fruition.

Compare now for a moment these two things: on the one hand, that part of the work of to-day which is given to inchoate wealth or uncompleted utilities; on the other hand, that part which serves directly to give satisfaction. Clearly the former is much the larger in volume. It must be remembered that commodities serve to give real satisfaction only when they reach the hands of those who use and enjoy them. That iron and stone, factories and furnaces, raw wool and cotton, grain in the bin, are not available for use or consumption, is obvious enough. It is equally certain, though not so obvious, that flour and cloths and boots are no more available, when simply carried to the stage of completion in the mill or factory. To reach the consumer, they must first pass through the hands of one or two carriers and two or three sets of middlemen, whose labors form part of the operation of production quite as much as those of the tillers of the soil and the workers in the factories. It is hardly worth while to lay down any hard-and-fast line in matters of this sort, or to try to define with precision where the very last step comes which brings completion of the products, and so satisfaction to the body of consumers. Ordinarily this stage would not be reached until the goods had been disposed of to purchasers by the retail dealer. While in the shopkeeper's hands, arranged by him and cared for by him, kept and stored in supply large enough and varied enough to meet regular and irregular demands, they are still to be considered as possessing only inchoate utility. Under the conditions of a complicated division of labor, those workers whom in common speech we call producers, as distinguished from the merchants and traders, advance matters a step nearer the end, but usually bring nothing to fruition. The small producer who deals directly with the consumer has not indeed disappeared; but in the communities of advanced civilization the consumer satisfies most of his wants by going to a shop where he finds commodities that have left the factory weeks or months before. The stores of goods that are accumulated in the warehouses of merchants, both of the large dealers and the petty tradesmen, are still on their way to completion, and still form part of the great mass of inchoate wealth. And, to repeat, this mass of inchoate wealth, in any moment, forms much the largest part of the possessions of the community.

It follows that most of the work which is being done at a given moment is work of no immediate service to any one. A few laborers are engaged in putting the finishing touches to commodities on which a complicated series of other laborers have been at work for years, or even decades, in the past. These few alone work to supply our immediate wants. The great mass of workers are engaged in producing tools, materials, railways, factories, goods finished but not yet in the place where the consumer can procure them—inchoate wealth of all sorts.

All this is part of the division of labor; it is, in fact, the most important form of the division of labor. While a few men put the finishing touches, the great mass are busy with preparatory work which is parcelled out among them in an infinity of trades and occupations. It is conceivable that some such apportionment of labor might have developed without a corresponding division of the different stages among different individuals. The same man might first mine the ore, then smelt it, then fashion his tool, then use it, and finally make his own clothing or secure his own food. But historically, the process by which so preponderant a part of the labor going on at any one moment has been devoted to preparatory work or inchoate wealth, has been accompanied by a corresponding growth and diversification of the division of labor. It may serve to make our subject clearer if we consider it for a moment in this aspect.

The division of labor may be classified, for the present purpose, as of two sorts, contemporaneous and successive. We may designate as contemporaneous that division by which one man does all the work of getting the food, another all that of making the clothes, a third all that of providing shelter, and so on; each carrying out all the steps, from beginning to end, involved in the production of his particular commodity. Under such an arrangement each worker would become expert in his trade and would work at it uninterruptedly. It is conceivable that in a primitive community, where all work was devoted to securing a finished commodity at short order, and few steps intervened between the beginning and the end of production, the productiveness of labor might be considerably increased by such a division of it. But vastly more important in the history of the arts and of civilization is that division which involves a separation of successive related acts—the division in which various steps in production are carried on, one after another, by different hands, and through which each commodity becomes the product of the complex and combined labors of a great number of men.* A set of porters, making a profession of carrying packs, develop their muscles and wind to an extraordinary degree, and become capable of carrying those heavy burdens which astonish the traveller in backward countries. Yet their achievements are as nothing compared with those of the successive divisions of labor. When one set of men attend to the making of roads, another to the rearing of horses, another to the procuring of iron and timber, others to wheels, wagons, harness,—we get in the end, through transportation by wheeled vehicles, an enormous diminution in the labor required for a given result. The contrast is still more striking if we consider the successive division of labor in the last form to which the art of transportation has been carried in the present

* This distinction is effectively brought out in Menger's *Grundsätze der Volkswirthschaftslehre*, chapter i, § 5. Compare what is said below, Part II, Chapter XIV, of the services of the Austrian writers in this part of economic analysis.

century. The operations extending over a series of years
for cuttings, embankments, tunnels, bridges, not to mention the tools for these, which engaged the energies of a
still earlier series of workers; the making of iron and
steel, of engines and cars, of the endless variety of railway apparatus,—all finally bring that extraordinary
cheapening of transportation which has so completely
revolutionized the industry of modern times.   To find
out how much labor has been given under these methods to any one wagon load or any one car load, we should
need to consider, in due measure, all the successive steps.
We should need to assign some slight fraction of the
labor given to the making of the wagon-road or roadbed
of the railway; a fraction, less small, of the labor for
making the wagons, or the cars and engines; the whole of
the labor of those, like the drivers of the horses or the
trainmen of the railway, who are engaged immediately in
transportation.   To carry out directly a calculation of the
labor involved in the carriage of a single ton or wagon
load would be impossible; but an infallible test,—the
price at which the service can be rendered,—shows how
enormously more effective is the more extended and complicated mode of doing the work.

It would be difficult to find an historical example of
the bare and uncomplicated use of the contemporaneous
division of labor.   The earliest form doubtless was more
or less of the successive sort, and the two have developed
hand in hand with the progress of the arts.   The contrast
between the primitive porter and the railway is obviously
a contrast not between the contemporaneous and the successive division of labor, but between two phases of the
successive division.   The transporting of goods means only
that materials are carried to those who are to manipulate
them, or tools to those who are to use them, or enjoyable
goods to those who are to consume them or sell them to

consumers. It means but one step,—sometimes an early
step, sometimes a late one,—in the successive division of
labor. But it illustrates the contrast between shorter and
longer ways of attaining a given end, and the mode in
which the progress of invention has caused a long stretch
of time to elapse between the first step and the last
toward the satisfaction of human wants.

So overpoweringly great have been the results of the
successive division of labor, that it is natural to think
of its extension as a cause, or at least as a necessary incident, in the increase of the powers of mankind and the
abundance of enjoyable goods. In a great number of
striking cases we see the progress of the arts taking a
direction similar to that which has just been sketched as
to the art of transportation. The spinning wheel and the
hand loom, easily and simply made, have given way to
the jenny and the mule and the power loom, fixed in a
great building, and moved by complicated machinery ;
all involving a longer stage of preparatory effort, and
yielding the enjoyable commodity in the end on easier
terms. Savages grind corn by rubbing it between two
heavy stones which nature happens to have provided in
something like the needed shape. The grist mill, with its
hewn stones and its simple machinery, serving its own
limited neighborhood, represents a considerable extension
in time of the productive process, and a great increase
in its efficiency. The modern steam mill, with its huge
plant, its warehouses and machinery, with the enormous
apparatus of railways and steamers for bringing the grain
from the four quarters of the globe and transporting the
flour to distant consumers, carries both consequences
still further. Hence it has been laid down as a general
proposition, by one of the ablest and most ingenious
writers of our own day, that every increase in the efficiency of labor brings with it an extension in time of

the process of production.* But it may be questioned whether anything like a connection of cause and effect can be traced, or anything more than a fact of usual experience found. In the past, those inventions and discoveries which have most served to put the powers of nature at human disposal have indeed often taken the form of greater and more elaborate preparatory effort. The railway, the steamship, the textile mill, the steel works, the gas works and electric plant,—in all these, invention has followed the same general direction. But that it will do so in the future, or has always done so in the past, can by no means be laid down as an unfailing rule. The railway, the telegraph, and the telephone, have served to shorten many steps in production; and elaborate machines, though it takes time to make them, do their work, once made, more quickly than simpler tools. Invention in the future may dispense with steps now thought indispensable; or it may enable elaborate plants to be dispensed with, as would be the case if the success of flying machines made the costly roadbed of the railway unnecessary. It would be rash to say that the productive process, under the successive division of labor, is likely to be either lengthened or shortened; for the ferment in the world of invention, and the glimpses of new processes in almost every direction, make either outcome possible. But it is in the highest degree

---

* Professor Böhm-Bawerk's brilliant analysis, in the opening chapters of the *Positive Theory of Capital*, has done more than any other single discussion to emphasize the significance of the lengthened period of production. It is due to this able thinker to note that he describes in these chapters the connection between the extension of production over time and its increasing efficiency as a simple fact of experience, not as part of the nature of things; but in the corollaries drawn from the proposition in his later reasoning it is treated as if universally true. Compare, however, what he has said, in reply to some American critics, in the *Quarterly Journal of Economics*, for January, 1896.

improbable that any changes the future may bring will affect that feature of the industrial situation which is important for the subject here under discussion.   Under any methods of production, considerable quantities of materials will be provided in advance, tools will be made with much labor, and consumable commodities will be brought to completion at the end of long stages of productive effort.

The beginning and the end of the process of production have been just spoken of; but clearly these are limits more easily described in general terms than fixed with precision in a particular case.   The end of the process of production is indeed not difficult to fix.   It comes when enjoyment begins, when the consumer gets the wherewithal to feed, to clothe, to shelter himself, to minister to his satisfaction or pleasure in any way.   Ordinarily this stage comes, as to tangible goods, when they pass from the shelf of the retail dealer into the hands of the purchaser.   But it is by no means easy to put the finger on the point where the process of production has its beginning.   Bread is made from flour, and flour from grain; the sowing of the seed is our starting point in the process of production; but seed was grown a season before, and comes from an earlier stage of effort.   The plough, too, was provided before the seed was sown, and that plough was made with tools which came from still an earlier application of labour.   The mill in which the grain was ground into flour was erected years before, and the railway which carried the grain to the mill stands for another previous application of labour.   Where shall we say that the process of production begins?   If we would be mathematically accurate, we should need to carry it ages back, to the time when the first tool was made; for tools are made with tools, and each is in some infinitesimal part the result of labor applied to its predecessor of a thousand years ago. For practical purposes, to be sure, we can in large part dismiss this consideration. The labor given fifty years ago to smelting iron that was made into tools, which again served to make other tools, is so infinitesimal a part of the labor involved in producing the consumable commodities of the present, that we may say, *De minimis non curat lex.* But the complications of the labor of the present and of the immediate past are no less puzzling. The carpenter works one day at the frame of a steel mill, which will turn out steel beams to be used in buildings or ships; years may elapse before the first completed commodity emerges. The next day he makes a piece of furniture,— or, rather, does his share in the making of it,—which conduces to the comfort of a householder within a week. The railway carries ore which represents a very early stage in the process of production; it carries wool, which may be made into a coat and may warm its wearer within three months; and passengers who at the moment are enjoying a pleasure jaunt. To measure exactly where the labor which builds and operates a railway stands in the process of production is practically impossible.

Hence it is practically impossible to measure how long the average process of production is,—to say how long an interval has elapsed between the time when all the consumable commodities now available were begun and the time when they were completed. We can, indeed, conceive of the meaning of such an average. We can say that the labor of the domestic servant issues in enjoyment very quickly; that of the operative in a woollen mill, after a few weeks or months; that of the farmer, after a year; that of the ship carpenter or steel worker, after years or even decades. If we could take the balance of short processes and long processes, we should ascertain how long, on the average, it had taken to make our present

enjoyable possessions. We can even do more than picture to ourselves this possible grouping and offsetting of
the various processes. We can say, from general observa-
tion, that the tendency of invention has been to lengthen
the average. The process of production, as a whole, has
probably tended to become longer; and if invention follows the same lines in the future as in the past, the process, on the average, will become still longer. But it is
impossible to say how long it now is, whether two years
or five or ten. The complications of the case make any
statement in figures out of the question. When we consider the immediate history of the most common sources
of satisfaction,—food, clothes, shelter; and reflect how
long a time has elapsed, even after the needed tools
were on hand, since the grain and cotton were sown, the
sheep raised for the wool, and the cattle for the leather,
the bricks made, the trees felled,—we may be sure that
the average period of production must be stated in terms
of years. And this vague conclusion, unsatisfactory as
it would be for statistical purposes, is sufficient for the
purpose now in hand. It is clear that production is
spread over a period of years; and it is clear that the
greater part of present labor is given to production at
stages preceding by a longer or shorter interval the attainment of the enjoyable result.

Before leaving this subject one further circumstance
may be noted in regard to the length of time over which,
under the modern division of labor, the operations of
production extend. One part of the period, the last of
all, is perhaps susceptible of measurement. To repeat
what has already been said, the work of the merchant and
trader is as fully productive as that of the artisan and car-
rier. Each does his share toward bringing commodities to
the stage where enjoyment finally begins. It would doubtless be possible to ascertain how long the last stage en-

dures ; to find how long a period elapses, on the average, between the moment when goods pass from the hands of the manufacturer and artisan into the hands of the dealer, and that at which they pass from the last dealer into the hands of the consumer. The great mass of commodities pass through the hands of two or three middlemen ; they go first to the wholesale dealer or agent, then to the jobber, finally to the retailer. Each of these keeps them a space. Barring perishable commodities, like meats and vegetables, a turn-over of more than six or eight times in the year is unusual; as to many articles, one of three or four times a year is common. The inference is plain. Months elapse, on the average, between the time when goods are finished, in the everyday sense of the word, and the time when they reach that stage of enjoyment which is the real aim and end of all effort.

So much as to the first part of the inquiry undertaken in the present chapter,—the relation between the work of to-day and the output of to-day ; an inquiry which has proved to involve some consideration of the work of yesterday as well. Whether as to the work now being done, or the work which yields the consumable goods now available, we have the same result. The work of to-day is applied preponderantly to inchoate wealth, to preparatory stages in production ; and the output of to-day consists mainly of goods not yet in enjoyable form. Most of the labor being done at the present moment will bring consumable goods at some time in the future ; while the consumable goods now available are mainly the product of past labor. The whole process of production is extended over a period not, indeed, to be measured with accuracy, yet certainly to be stated in terms of years.

We may turn now to the second part of the inquiry : what is the pay of to-day ?

The answer here is simple, and could be given in the

briefest terms. The immediate reward for the exertion of labor consists of completed and enjoyable commodities. Food, clothing, shelter, things that satisfy our needs and our desires,—these are the pay of to-day. The laborer's bread and meat, his tobacco and his whiskey, his house and his clothes, things that may do him good or harm, but are at all events desired by him, constitute the reward he now gets.

This is so simple that it would seem not to need another word of explanation. Yet on the subject of wages, as on many others in economics, it is the failure to bear in mind very simple and obvious facts that most frequently causes error. In discussions of wages, of the source whence they are paid and the factors that affect their amount, nothing has been more common than to consider only the machinery by which laborers are enabled to get their real wages. The cash paid them by an employer, or received by them in direct pay for their product, has been mainly thought of. The obvious distinction between real wages and money wages makes its appearance in every book on the elements of economics, but it is too often forgotten when the causes determining wages come to be examined. When a question arises as to the relation between the laborer's output and his pay, it is common to speak of his product and of his pay in terms of money. When it is asked whether the laborer is paid out of capital or out of product, the first impulse is to think of capital as money funds in the hands of the employer and of product as the money value of what is being turned out. In answer to the proposition, attributed more or less justly to the older English economists, that laborers get their wages from a rigidly predetermined source, it is often said that the wages which employers can pay may be increased by quicker sales or by the use of credit,—which obviously refers to money wages. The inquiry as to the direct relation between laborers and employers, and as to that first step in the apportionment of wages which comes through money payments from one to the other, is important and fruitful, as will elsewhere appear. But on the crucial question of the cause of general high wages in the sense of general real prosperity among laborers, it leads only to confusion. If we would learn what makes wages high, in the sense which is mainly important for the workmen as a class and for the community as a whole, we must bear in mind that real wages alone are to be thought of,—things consumable and enjoyable.

What is true of the laborers is true of all classes in the community. All, whether idlers or workers, get their real reward from the same source—the completed commodities which satisfy human wants. These, as they appear in recurrent supply, form the net income of the community. Whether there can be any possibility of separation of this net income into parts destined for any one set of persons, or appropriated to them; whether one part of the available supply can be said to constitute a wages fund, another a profit fund, a third an interest fund, a fourth a rent fund,—these are questions that will engage our attention at a later stage. Here we may content ourselves with the simple and unquestionable proposition, that all real income of any sort comes in the form not of money, but of goods and wares that minister to our wants.

Still further to emphasize this elementary yet all-important proposition, we may consider for a moment where we should find, in any given community, this immediate reward of the laborer. It must proceed chiefly from the stocks in the hands of the retail dealers. Their wares are in the last stage which production goes through, and are on the point of ripening into full completion. A good part of wages, no doubt, must come from elsewhere.

House shelter, partly a necessity and partly a source of comfort and luxury, is ordinarily already on hand, needing no further labor toward complete fruition than occasional repairs. If owned by another person, as is commonly the case with the house occupied by the hired laborer, that person is in possession of the source whence so much of real wages is derived. If the laborer owns his own house, he spends the money received for present labor in other ways. The shelter and comforts of the house he owns form no part of his real reward for the work of to-day; they are the reward of past labor, or past claims or rights of some sort, and no more form part of his pay for present work than the enjoyments which the idle rich buy with their money incomes form reward for any present exertion. His wages for present exertion are what he buys with the cash which, under a money *régime*, he receives for the day's or week's work ; and questions as to the sources of his real wages, their limits, their flexibility or predetermination, are questions as to limits and determinateness of the stocks or forthcoming supplies of goods now chiefly in the hands of shopkeepers, which he will buy with his money wages.

We are now in a position to give an answer to one part of the question with which this chapter opened : whether wages are or are not paid from present or current product. The answer to the other part of the question,—whether or not they are paid from capital,—must still be postponed, requiring, as it does, some further consideration of the definition and function of capital. But wages are certainly not paid from the product of present labor; they are paid from the product of past labor. Present labor produces chiefly unfinished things ; but the reward of present labor is finished things. Real wages are, virtually to their full extent, the product of past labor. At this moment, or within a few days, the last touches

toward completion have indeed been given to the commodities now being enjoyed.   But the great bulk of the
labor whose product all of us, whether laborers or idlers,
now enjoy, was done in the past.

This fact is obscured, in our everyday thought, in two
ways : we think of the product in terms of money, and
we think of the laborer who gives the finishing touches
in production as the " maker " of the article.   When we
want to compare the amount which a laborer produces
with the amount which he receives, the simplest and most
obvious way is to compare the money value of the two : a
method the more tempting because for many purposes,
not least for the business ends of the individual employer,
it is all-sufficient.   Thus we think of product and wages
as similar things, and of product as preceding wages ;
forgetting that in concrete reality they are different things,
and that present real wages must be on hand long before
present product is completed.   On the other hand, the
baker is said to make bread, the tailor to make clothes,
the carpenter to make furniture ; though, with the incon-
sistency characteristic of that early stage of classification
which is crystallized in common speech, we never speak
of the merchant or shopkeeper as "making" anything.
In fact, the baker and the tailor do no more than their
small shares in the making of bread and clothes ; a long
series of farmers and wool-growers, manufacturers, merchants, and carriers constitute with them the complete
chain of the producers of the articles.

There is a sense, it is true, in which we may speak
with accuracy of wages as coming from current product ;
and it is one which deserves attention, because it brings
out the relation between some older speculations on
wages and capital and the more recent turn of the discussion.

The classic economists were in the habit of speaking

of the commodities consumed by laborers as a fund or stock, described in a way that implied a great store on hand, ready and available at once, likely to be replaced after a season by another similar store. This, at least, was their practice when they described the wages fund as a concrete thing, made up of commodities which would yield real wages. Too often they spoke and thought of funds and capital in the money sense, and of wages as coming from the employing capitalists' money means, thereby introducing a confusion which runs through almost the whole of the century's literature on the subject. Ricardo, however, and the abler of Ricardo's followers, usually kept to the first conception, of a wages fund made up of commodities, not of money. In the Ricardian system, again, wages were measured in terms of food, and especially of grain or corn ; and the wages fund consisted of a stock of food. For shortness of reasoning and of statement (too often with the result of confusion in both) this stock was reasoned about as if it were owned by the immediate employers and handed over by them directly to laborers who ate it. The miller and the baker were put aside ; and, what was more dangerous to accurate thought, it was assumed for brevity that the capitalists who employed the laborers were the individuals who owned the grain. The source of wages was then easily conceived as a fund stored up, all ready for use, controlled by employers, limited in amount for the time being, and entirely the product of past labor. The seasonal harvesting of the crops made it impossible this year to procure more than had been sown and harvested ; and the real wages fund had nothing to do with current work and product.

The error of this view is one of degree rather than of kind, of insufficiency rather than of inaccuracy. It is no grievous departure from literal truth if we speak of grain as consumable by laborers, omitting for brevity, the operations of transporting and grinding and baking it. And we may perhaps fairly think of the grain on hand this season as fixed in amount, incapable of being increased or diminished. Doubtless there are here some elastic limits : a heavy crop may be carried over in part to another season, and a lean one consumed at once to the last bushel in anticipation of better times soon to come. This sort of averaging of the yield certainly could take place under modern methods of storage and preservation, and may have taken place even in the days when Ricardo wrote. It is more important to correct the older view in other directions. Food is not the only article consumed by laborers; none of the various commodities that make real wages, not even breadstuffs, exist in the shape of accumulated stores of finished goods. Further, the capitalists who directly employ laborers have usually no ownership of the commodities which make real wages. If these real wages come from capital, the capital is certainly not in the hands of the employers.

Considering both of the last-mentioned facts in the situation,—the variety of the commodities which go to make real wages, and the widely distributed ownership of these tangible commodities,—we reach the conception of a flow rather than a fund of real wages. The community possesses at any given moment a quantity of goods in all stages of completion : some just begun, some half finished, some very nearly or quite finished. The last touches are being given at every moment ; enjoyable commodities each day are consumed, new commodities advance each day to take their place. We have no great stores of completely finished goods, but, as Professor Marshall has happily said, a steady flow of accruing real income.

No doubt the old conception of a fund fits the facts of the case in some regards quite as accurately as the new one of a flow. The distinguished Austrian writer who has contributed so much to the clearer understanding of this part of the machinery of production, has suggested that all the possessions of the community may be reduced to an equivalent in terms of subsistence or other finished goods. What he calls the general subsistence fund is made up of all wealth whatsoever,—machines, materials, completed goods. Its volume may be measured by ascertaining how much labor is embodied in this sum total of wealth, and how long the wealth, completed and enjoyable, which so much labor could produce, would continue to satisfy the wants of the community at its habitual rate of consumption. In this sense we may say that the community owns at any given time a subsistence fund for, say, five years; meaning not that there are stores of finished goods which will last five years, but that the wealth on hand has embodied in it five years of the community's labor, and, simply carried to completion without the initiation of a stroke of new work, would last for a long period.* Here we have a statement of the case, useful for some purposes, which looks to a fund rather than to a flow. And from still another point of view the conception of a fund has its justification. The stock of available finished commodities, if a flow, is affected in its volume by sources which possess some of the characteristics of a reservoir or fund. The number of loaves that can be put forth from day to day depends on the season's stock of grain; that of clothes, on the wool and the sheep on hand,

---

* As to the relation between the amount of the subsistence fund, measured by the quantity of labor embodied in it, and the number of years over which it may enable production on the average to be spread, see the *Positive Theory of Capital*, book vi, chapter v, and the appendix at the close of that volume. The refinements of this calculation, however, are not likely to lead to results useful for the explanation of concrete phenomena, and at all events are not important for the purposes of the discussion in the text.

and on the machinery available for manipulating the materials; that of boots, on the hides and the cattle and the available machinery. How far the volume of consumable goods now obtainable is limited by such conditions; how far determined once for all by the materials and tools of past making; how far capable of enlargement or diminution by changes in the labor of the moment,—these are questions which may engage our attention at a later stage. For the present it is necessary only to get a clear conception of the sense in which there is on hand at any given time a supply or stock of finished goods for the consumption of laborers and others. It is a flow of finished goods from goods partly finished, constantly wasting away and constantly renewed; greatly affected, perhaps determined once for all, by the mode in which past labor has been given to tools and materials; yet certainly not without some degree of flexibility at any given moment, and certainly not an accumulated or rigid fund.

We can see now in what sense it is true that wages,—or any other form of income, for that matter,—are paid out of current product. The goods which laborers get, or, to be literally accurate, the goods which they buy with their money wages, in a sense are made from day to day; they are current product in the sense that the last touches are given them from day to day. Something of this sort has doubtless been in the minds of the writers who have maintained that wages are derived from present or current product. Unquestionably a confusion between real wages and money wages has also had its share in the adoption of their view. Current money wages obviously do come largely from the money value of the present product, and the proposition that wages are paid from the current yield of industry in this sense is as undeniable as it is immaterial so far as the source of real wages is concerned.

We may now summarize the results of this chapter by a graphic representation of the course of production and enjoyment in a modern community. A diagram showing the relation between the work of to-day, the output of to-day, and the pay of to-day may be constructed thus: let A represent the workers who stand in the earliest stage of production, say the miners and lumbermen; let B represent those in the next stage, say the makers of pig iron and of sawed timber; let C designate those who carry on operations in the next stage toward completion; D, those in the next; and E, finally, those who give the finishing touches and bring to market a consumable commodity. The same letters may indicate the products turned out by the different producers, A standing for the iron ore, and E for the bread and meat. A, B, C, D, E may represent the workers and their output in a first year; A_i, B_i, C_i, in a second year; and so on. We could then array the operations of a series of years in this fashion:

In 1890................... A	B	C	D	E
" 1891.................. . A_i	B_i	C_i	D_i	E_i
" 1892................... A_2	B_2	C_2	D_2	E_2
" 1893................... A_3	B_3	C_3	D_3	E_3
" 1894................... A_4	B_4	C_4	D_4	E_4

In each year all the various operations are going on simultaneously. A, B, C, D, E are at work on their separate tasks, and are turning out all shades of products, from the crudest material to the ripened commodity. In successive years the A's and the E's continue alike to repeat their work: the miners remain in the mine, the shopkeepers serve their customers in the shops. In any one

year the community, while producing all the products A,
B, C, D, E, has at its disposal only the commodities E.
These alone are consumable and enjoyable; these alone
can constitute real wages or real profits or real income of
any sort. In the year 1890 E would be available; in 1892,
E_2. The question whether wages in 1894, which must
come out of E_4, are the product from past or present labor,
can be answered by inquiring what labor produces the E
commodities of any one year; say E_4 of 1894. If we suppose present labor, then E_4 will be the product of the work
indicated by the horizontal line A_4, B_4, C_4, D_4, E_4. If past
labor, or chiefly past labor, then E_4 will be the product of
the work indicated by the diagonal line A, B_1, C_2, D_3, E_4. It
needs no argument to show that the workers E_4 can not
be completing the material which A_4 are bringing forth at
the same time. Each stage in the successive division of
labor requires time. E_4 must be at work on products
which came from D of an earlier period, say the D_3 of
1893; D_3 got them, partly advanced toward completion,
from C_2 of 1892; the first steps were taken five years ago
by A of 1890. The diagonal line marks the labor which
yields the enjoyable commodities of 1895—labor mainly
of the past, and only in small part of the present.

It hardly needs to be explained again that a simple
scheme of this sort is far from corresponding to the complexities of real life. The earliest and the latest stages
of production are so interwoven that any brief statement
or simple diagram can give no more than a crude and inaccurate picture. The commodities which we have typi-
fied in the E's, and which are represented as lately finished,
after having gone through a regular series of previous
operations, are sometimes made very largely with recent
labor, sometimes very largely with past labor. Personal
or domestic service is an important source of enjoyment;
as productive of satisfaction, and therefore of wealth

in the important sense, as the labor that makes bread and wine. Here exertion and satisfaction are coincident; there is no chain of successive producers. On the other hand, the shelter and comfort which are now yielded by a dwelling are in greatly preponderant proportion due to labor exerted in varying stages of progression in the past. And at the other end of the scale, commodities in the early stages of unripeness may reach fruition by a longer or shorter route. Pig iron may be made into a stove and may serve to diffuse grateful warmth within a month; or it may be made into a machine which will be used in making another machine, and may not issue in a cosumable commodity for years. Any scheme, or diagram, or classification of the stages in production must have a rigid and arbitrary character, and can not conform to the endless complexities of the living industrial world. None the less, it may bring into distinct relief the general truth which underlies all the variety of detail,—that production proceeds by successive stages, and that the community at present is supplied with necessaries and comforts made mainly by the labor of the past.

CHAPTER II.

The fact that present labor gets its substantial reward from a product made chiefly by past labor was the basis of the reasoning of the classic economists. The products of the past which served to support and remunerate laborers they called capital. They inferred—indeed, assumed as a thing so obvious as hardly to need inference—that wages were paid from capital. In the second part of the present volume we shall have occasion to note how briefly and inadequately they presented this cardinal proposition. Here we shall proceed at once to consider how far it is sound; how far the products of the past are to be called capital, and how far the proposition that labor gets its reward from past product is equivalent to the proposition that wages are paid from capital.

The question of phraseology and definition, which we are thus compelled to face, is from one point of view indifferent, from another very material. From the first point of view any definition can be made to serve, provided it is used consistently. The term capital can be used in any desired sense, if only it be always remembered precisely what it is to connote. Thus a writer may freely use the term capital in a sense different from that of the older economists; only, if thereupon he should deny that wages are paid from capital, he would not squarely meet the question presented in the traditional theorem.* Yet—and here is the other point of view—something more than simple consistency is involved in the choice of phraseology. The object of definition and of classification is not fully achieved if we fail to group together under one head things that are alike, and to distinguish by different terms things that are unlike. One sort of labor, for example, may be designated as productive, and another sort as unproductive; the distinction has its solid justification only if it appears in due course that some propositions hold good of the one sort which do not hold good of the other. The difficulty with the much-disputed terminology which Adam Smith and his successors adopted in their use of the phrase "productive labor" was of precisely this sort; it did not and could not point to substantial differences in regard to that satisfaction of human wants which is the object of all labor. And, to come closer to the present subject, one form of wealth may be called capital while another may be called non-capital; no logical difficulty will result if the terms are always used in the same sense. But the object in view,—an understanding of the phenomena of wealth,—will not be effectually achieved unless we succeed in grouping under each term things that are alike, and as to which the same propositions hold good.

The mode in which these simple general principles bear on the subject in hand can be best illustrated by sketching the historical development of the conception of

---

* A neat example of this sort of procedure is furnished by Mr. Henry George in *Progress and Poverty*, who gives a meaning of his own to capital, and then denies with vigor that wages are paid from capital. The fact that his own definition of capital, when carefully considered, is not so different as it purports to be from the traditional one, does not redeem the operation. Compare what is said below of George's position in the wages controversy (Part II, Chapter XIV).

capital. Adam Smith, with whom the whole modern discussion begins, defined it as the wealth which yielded a
revenue to its owner. This definition had a vogue for a
while, and has not been without its adherents in our own
time; and for some purposes it may still be used with
advantage. To the individual, capital is that which he
uses not for the immediate satisfaction of his own wants,
but for securing in the future a revenue wherewith to satisfy them; whether the capital be in the form of ships
and warehouses, materials or goods in stock, cash ready
for investment or a dwelling let to a tenant. But for the
community as a whole, and with regard to the mode in
which different sorts of wealth bear on general prosperity,
such a distinction is far from satisfactory. The dwelling
owned by A and let to B is capital, under Adam Smith's
definition; but if bought and occupied by B it ceases, under the same definition, to be capital.* The place which
it has among the possessions of the community does not
change by its sale and transfer; it still forms part of the
apparatus for shelter and enjoyment. Again: the horses
and carriages of the stable-keeper would be capital, in
Adam Smith's sense, since he uses them as a means of securing revenue; but the equipages maintained by those
rich enough to own such a luxury for themselves would
not be capital. Here, too, both forms of wealth clearly
belong together, so far as their position and effect in the
welfare of the community are concerned. Since the causes
that affect the prosperity of the community, and not those
that affect the prosperity of the individual, primarily come
within the scope of economic science, it is inadvisable to
use a definition which, like Adam Smith's, gives different

---

* Compare, however, what is said below, in Part II, Chapter VII,
page 147, of the manner in which Adam Smith qualified his definition in
regard to these forms of durable wealth.

names to things that have the same relation to the general welfare.

The next generation of the classic writers, under the lead of Ricardo, did not usually fall into the error of considering economic phenomena from the point of view of the individual rather than of the community. Indeed, their greatest errors often arose from an excess in the other direction : they regarded things so much in the mass that they neglected many important details. So far as capital was concerned, they gave up Adam Smith's definition, and substituted one in more general terms : capital was the wealth used for the production of further wealth. What was to be included under capital was explained more explicitly by the retention of the division of capital into fixed and circulating. Adam Smith first applied this distinction and the words for indicating it ; but the later writers adopted a different line of division from that of the originator.* Fixed capital consisted of tools and implements used in a succession of operations. Circulating capital consisted of things that could be used only once and then were gone ; it was divisible into materials on the one hand, and means of support for laborers on the other. Gradually there developed the tradition of separating capital into three constituent parts,—fixed capital, raw materials, and wages fund ; an enumeration which gave point and precision to the vague phrase that capital consisted of the wealth used for producing more wealth.

The part of the later classic definition of capital which is pertinent for our purpose is the wages fund. For two generations no one thought of doubting that the food and

* For the history of this phase of economic speculation, which is touched here in the briefest way, the reader is referred to Mr. Cannan's thorough and accurate *History of the Theories of Production and Distribution from 1776 to 1848.*

other goods which supported laborers were part of capital. Even in the first attacks on the wages-fund doctrine there was no disposition to proceed to a revision of the conception of capital. Yet no satisfactory solution of the controverted questions about wages is possible without some overhauling of the older classification and definition of capital.

Bearing in mind still that our point of view must be not that of the individual, but that of the community as a whole, we can readily see how the commodities which form the wages-fund part of the capital of the classic writers, in some ways at least, are of a different sort and perform a different function from the other constituent parts. Food, clothes, boots, house-room, ornaments,—any and all the commodities consumed by laborers,—constitute the wages fund. These are enjoyable and consumable commodities. Plant and materials, whether called fixed or circulating capital, are inchoate wealth. The former are real income—the latter are not. The question on which economists in our day differ, and in regard to which there are serious difficulties, is whether the enjoyable form of wealth called the wages fund is so like the inchoate as fairly to be grouped under the same general name of capital.

On the one hand, it may be urged in favor of the old-fashioned view that the laborers must have the wherewithal to live and to keep themselves in working condition in order that productive operations shall be continuous and effective. The succession of efforts which was described in the last chapter, and the extension of the working process over a long stretch of time, make it necessary that a considerable stock of commodities should exist in completed or partly completed form. In order that the successive division of labor may achieve its wonderful results, there must be not only tools, machinery, and materials, but bread, meat, and clothing for the active workers. Some such supplies there must be at once, for the needs of to-day; others must be ready, or nearly ready, for the morrow. A stock of enjoyable goods is as essential for effective and abundant production as is the array of inchoate wealth through all the stages of productive effort. The necessary enjoyable commodities are thus like the inchoate wealth, in being indispensable parts of the provision essential for any production advanced beyond the most rudimentary stage.

The view that such enjoyable commodities are to be regarded as capital was strengthened by the belief of the older writers as to the quality and quantity of real wages which laborers were likely to get. In the days when the wages-fund doctrine and all that went with it held full sway, the laborers were usually thought of as getting "natural" wages and no more. This, again, was rather assumed and implied than expressly and carefully stated. It was the result partly of a very old tradition; for before the days of Adam Smith and of the classic school the common statement in regard to wages, and indeed almost the only statement, was that they depended on what was needed to maintain the race of laborers. It was partly due to the conditions of the time when the wages-fund doctrine got its hold, day-laborers' wages being doubtless little above the minimum in the early part of the century in most European countries. It was in good part due to the indelible impression which Malthus's writings on population made on two generations of thinkers. At all events, for one reason and another, laborers were commonly described as getting "natural" wages, and no more; only so much as in the nature of things they must have.

Here, again, there was a curious intermingling of very different trains of thought. The "natural" wages, which

Ricardo said laborers must have, were not stated to be the simple physical necessaries. They were the wages which habit and custom rendered necessary; the wages without which the laborers would not marry and rear children, and which, if exceeded, would lead them to marry earlier and have more children. In this sense, necessary or natural wages, as fixed by the standard of living, might be a great deal more than the bare necessaries of life. But while Ricardo and his followers of the wages-fund school said explicitly that natural wages were determined by the standard of living, not by the physical minimum, they thought of that standard as universally low. Any general statement they might make at the outset as to a possible high standard was usually forgotten or put aside as they went on. Half unconsciously, they converted the original conception of habitual "necessaries" into a conception of physical necessaries. Largely for this reason the wages which laborers got were thought of as needed in their entirety to maintain working strength. Thence it was a natural step to think of them as necessary for the maintenance of productive effort, and therefore as capital.

So much as to the grounds, and the reasons for the former easy acceptance, of the view that commodities indispensable for the workers are to be called capital. But that view is open to objections for the purposes of almost any economic inquiry, and to very serious objections for those of the inquiry here in hand.

In the first place, the situation of the laborers in general is not so desperate as Ricardo and his followers were apt to assume. Even at the time when they wrote there were great strata among the workers who got more than the minimum needed to keep them in working condition. In our own more prosperous days the large majority of laborers are in this better situation. Hence only part of the commodities which they get could be considered capital in the sense of being indispensable to production. Only what the older writers called "productive consumption" could be so classed,—the consumption without which the maintenance of efficient production was impossible. It would follow that, in the great majority of cases, wages must be regarded as paid in part not out of capital but out of some other source ; the unproductive consumption having no resemblance to tools and other effective apparatus of production. The proposition that wages are paid from capital, stated and limited in this way, would be a different one from that of the classic school; for this school, to repeat what was said a moment ago, regarded all wages as paid entirely from capital. Modified as the proposition must be in view of a more prosperous condition of laborers, it makes an unexpected division, and on the face of things an illogical one, of real wages into two parts, derived from different sources.

This difficulty becomes even more serious if we enlarge the meaning of the terms "laborers " and "production," in the manner likely to find acceptance among most economists of our own day. The older English writers, when speaking of wages in general and of the wages fund, commonly thought of those engaged in manual work alone as "productive laborers." In every direction the conception, if it is to be consistent and satisfactory, must be enlarged. Not only those who work with their hands, but those who work with their heads, are productive ; not only those who turn out a tangible product, but all who serve human wants. This is not the place for a disquisition on these much-disputed questions of terminology. It is clear that the engineer and the business manager are as productive as the hod-carrier and the mechanic. It is clear, too,—though not so universally admitted,— that there is no ground for real distinction between those whose labor does and those whose labor does not issue in a "material" commodity. The actor and the painter, the maid-servant and the maker of table linen, alike minister to the ease and enjoyment of life, and in this essential sense are alike productive. In neither of the directions here suggested did the older writers think of applying their reasoning as to capital and the wages fund. The income neither of the active business man nor of the house servant was thought to have anything to do with the payment of wages from capital. Yet the "productive" consumption of these, as well as of manual laborers, is essential for the procuring of the community's enjoyable revenue. It may be a question how far we should extend the term "productive" as applied to labor; and some would doubtless not be disposed to go as far as the present writer.* But it would be impossible to

---

* If a distinction between productive and unproductive labor is still to be made, it would seem that it could be done only on the lines of separating that labor which is essential and effective for the processes of production as now organized, and that labor which is only an incidental and perhaps dispensable adjunct of them. No one would deny that the merchant whose activity serves to bring together commodities and then to despatch them where needed, is productive. But side by side with him is the speculator who but watches the tricks and turns of trade; indeed, the merchant himself is often, in half his activity, no more than a speculator. The banker, again, aids to put capital into the hands of those likely to make good use of it, and so is productive; but who would say that any and every "banker and broker" in our great cities performs functions really serviceable for the community? No doubt it is difficult to draw the line in all such cases between the activity which contributes to social welfare and that which does not; and some allowance must be made for the inevitable useless hangers-on in every occupation. Yet, when every allowance is made, it is difficult to believe that all the work of the crowds of speculators, brokers, "business men," in the cities of modern times, is in any solid sense helpful for the organization and direction of industry. Much of it means simply that the conditions of a complicated division of labor make it possible to pick up, by

stop, as the older economists did, with manual laborers. What is needed to maintain the active manager of industry and the merchant, the engineer and the inventor, the physician and lawyer (so far as the services of such are needed to keep laborers in health and business affairs smooth-working),—all this is surely capital in the same sense as the indispensable food of the ploughman. We thus should get a conception of capital and the wages fund applicable not to all the income of a part of the laborers, but to a part of the income of all of the laborers.

Once this conception is reached, however, it becomes more and more difficult to maintain that there is a real resemblance between wages-fund and other capital, and a real distinction between one and the other part of real income. After all, the commodities which go to one and another sort of laborers, whether necessaries or comforts or luxuries, are immediate sources of satisfaction. They are consumed, not to enable work to be done, but as the result of work being done. They represent, not a stage in the production of wealth, but the consumption and enjoyment of wealth. Men are not to be regarded as cattle, fed and tended as a means toward an end. Their con-

---

shrewdness or by luck, large or small shares of income that represent no contribution to general welfare. Something of this sort doubtless underlies the distinction between unproductive and productive labor (and capital as well) which has been laid down by one of the most ingenious and suggestive of the theoretic writers of modern times,—Professor Loria, in the *Analisi de la Proprieta Capitalista.* Exaggerated and often forced as are the attacks on "unproductive" labor and capital by that writer, they yet seem to point out the way to an instructive line of distinction. Much of the activity of lawyers, of financiers, of those who buy and sell on 'Change, can be said to be but incidental to the really effective work of modern industry, not essential or even perceptibly helpful.

sumption is the object of all production.   Therefore it is
to be regarded as income, and as single and indivisible
income.

The total flow of enjoyable goods and services which
is regularly coming into the possession of society is thus
best considered as one great mass of homogeneous income, different from the inchoate wealth which is on all
hands admitted to be capital.   The members of the community, whether capitalists or landowners, headworkers
or handworkers, idle or industrious, all form one body
of consumers.   There are, indeed, differences in the causes
which bring income to one set or another; and even
among those whose income is only a return for labor, there
are important differences both in the forces affecting the
size of the income and in the machinery by which it gets
into different hands.   But all together constitute the community, and the whole fund or flow of enjoyable things
constitutes their real income.   If we conceive the community to be organized on a collectivist basis—a procedure which often helps to bring out the essentials of social
life—we readily see that the total of enjoyable things secured in any one season would be regarded as its real
available income, apportionable among the various members in any desired manner, partly necessary for life and
strength, partly luxury, but not to be called part capital
and part non-capital.

It would seem best, therefore, to let the term capital
stand simply for inchoate wealth : for all the possessions
that do not yet serve human wants.   Tools and machines,
factories and warehouses, raw materials and half-finished
and nearly finished goods,—these all go together as being not directly conducive to enjoyment; while all forms
of finished commodities,—food, houses, clothes, ornaments,—belong together as enjoyable wealth and as income.   The successive steps by which inchoate wealth is

finally converted into enjoyable wealth were described in the last chapter; the same description would serve now to distinguish capital from wealth in general. Hereafter capital will be used in the sense indicated: the tangible apparatus for the production of wealth, and so all the goods still in the stage preparatory to final enjoyment.*

These questions of terminology and classification, however, happen to be of less importance for the purposes of the present inquiry than for some other parts of economic analysis. In whatever sense we use the term capital, it will still appear that current wages, considered with reference to any but a very short period of time, are derived in the main from capital. The grounds of this statement, apparently in contradiction with the outcome of the preceding discussion, need some detailed explanation.

In the last chapter it was pointed out that flow rather than fund was the word appropriate for describing the mode in which the community's income of enjoyable commodities becomes available. If this is true in regard to the process by which productive labor yields its regular return, it is still more true in regard to the accretions of real income which form current wages.

---

* Whether or no the term capital should be used in the narrower sense to which preference is given in the text, or in a wider sense to include the things needful for workers, it seems to be agreed that some phraseology should be adopted for distinguishing the two parts which in some regards are so essentially different. Thus Professor Marshall, many years ago, in his *Economics of Industry*, suggested the terms "auxiliary" and "remuneratory" capital; and in the third edition of his *Principles of Economics* uses the phrases "production capital" and "consumption capital." Such a practice may cause ambiguity when the word capital is used alone, and, on the whole, does not seem to me indispensable in order to bring out the fact that some supplies for the workers are needed for the operations of production.

Doubtless some of the enjoyable goods now available possess the characteristics of a fund rather than of a flow. Those of a more durable sort exist rather as a fund, those of a more perishable sort rather as a flow. Houses and house furniture are fully finished and ready, available now and likely to remain available for a considerable space to come. Food stands at the other extreme, being usually perishable, and existing in no great stock. Grain in the bin, flour in the merchant's stock, cattle on the fields,—various half-way stages,—these are the more typical forms in which supplies of food available for the early future exist. Clothing stands midway : a present stock is immediately available, and will last some little time, yet needs constant renewal at comparatively short intervals. The difference clearly is one of degree, not of kind. One of the important commonplaces which the classic economists insisted on was that all wealth is being constantly consumed and reproduced, the differences in durability being simply differences of degree. But these differences are very great ; so great that we may speak of the commodities of which dwelling houses are the familar and typical example as being for considerable stretches of time a present and permanent fund of enjoyment.

If these more permanent sources of satisfaction, now existing and available, were the things from which the real income of current work were regularly and mainly derived, they would have some resemblance to the " fund " of which the older writers spoke. But, in fact, they are usually the reward of the labor of the past. They have played their part in distribution, and are now the established possessions of those whose former labor, or other source of income, has enabled them to be bought. Clothes, household furniture and implements, food in the larder,— these have been bought with the money income of former days, and now are the settled property of their owners. They have nothing to do with current wages or profits or rents. No doubt they can be sold, though usually at a disadvantage. But when sold, they merely pass from one hand to another: what one gains in the way of fresh real income another loses. The total available for the community becomes no more or less. Moreover, since their sale rarely causes them to shift from one class in society to another, the real income of the several classes becomes no more or less. They belong to the distribution of the past, not of the present.

It may be remarked, incidentally, that commodities of the sort now under discussion have sometimes been called capital in a sense different from any yet noticed, and perhaps deserving a moment's attention. They are durable sources of satisfaction. While they may be described as a fund, because not needing prompt renewal, they may be also described as yielding a continual flow of utilities. The utilities which they yield can not all be enjoyed at once; they are of necessity distributed over some stretch of time. The house or suit of clothes may be considered as throwing off, so to speak, successive instalments of satisfaction. They are thus analogous to machines, which may also be considered as continually throwing off utilities, embodied in the enjoyable commodities which they serve to produce. Hence various thinkers, of curiously different schools and tendencies, have come to the conclusion that the durable sources of immediate satisfaction are capital, like machines and other means of providing utilities; and, since duration is only a question of degree, have concluded that all material commodities of any sort are substantially capital.* But there remains an essential

---

* See Hermann's *Staatswirthschaftliche Untersuchungen*, 2d edition, pp. 221 *seq.*; Jevons's *Principles of Political Economy*, 2d edition, pp.

and indeed all-important distinction between the commodities of which the dwelling house is the type, and
those of which the machine is the type. While both may
be said to yield successive utilities, the one does so without further human exertion, the other only after more or
less of labor. The dwelling house is a completed enjoyable thing, available, until the moment for repair or
renewal comes, without further labor. So are clothes
and boots and household effects in their several degrees.
They are in this important sense income, and so distinguishable from wealth still inchoate; even though they
are income that from its nature stretches necessarily over
some space of time.

To return from this digression to the main course
of the argument. It has been said that durable sources
of satisfaction usually belong to the distribution of the
past, being secured and realized wages or profits or rents.
To this general statement there is at least one important
exception: in the case of dwelling houses occupied by
others than their owners. Such houses are paid for by
the tenants out of their current money income, and the
shelter which they yield is thus a constituent of their
current real income. They therefore play a part in the
process of distribution which is going on in the present.
The exception is particularly important in regard to those
classes with whom we usually associate the word wages
and with whom the wages-fund doctrine is supposed more
especially to deal. Hired manual laborers are more
often tenants than owners of their dwellings. Their

280–287 ; Cohn's *Nationaloekonomie*, § 147. In general, I have endeavored to avoid cumbering this first part with literary references, re-
serving such matters to their appropriate places in the second part. But
this particular phase of the discussion on capital will not again be
touched.

clothing, household furniture, and some stock of food on hand they usually own, these having been bought with income of former days. But their dwellings are not commonly their own property. The shelter and comfort which their houses yield are thus paid for out of current income, and are part of current real wages. The dwellings themselves, being enjoyable at once without further labor, are part of the community's real income and not of its capital. The source of this part of current wages is, then, not social capital, but social income.*

More commonly, however, the commodities which constitute real wages are, at the time when the work is done, still in the last of the inchoate stages: they are just on the point of emerging from capital into income. They are in shopkeepers' hands, awaiting purchase. The last step in production is not completed until they reach the hands of the consumer whose wants they satisfy. Until that moment they are still strictly to be considered as

---

* It may indeed be contended that the final stage in the work needed for full enjoyment is not reached until the letting of the house is accomplished. As the labor of the shopkeeper is the last step in the long series of efforts which bring his goods to the consumer's hands, so the house agent or active landlord does his share in the work of bringing the dwelling at last to serve the tenant's wants. The relatively high rent of the tenements occupied by the poorest laborers, which require much care and repeated attention in the business of letting them and collecting the rents, is the concrete expression of this fact. The dwellings hired by tenants might thus be said to emerge from the stage of capital into that of enjoyment and income by successive slight acts of exertion. But it would be a mistake to make anything of refined reasoning of this sort. Substantially, the dwellings, whether hired or owned, may be regarded as available and enjoyable, and as present sources of real income.—For another case in which substantial truth is reached, even with some violation of theoretical nicety, compare what is presently said in the text, at page 42, of the purchases of household tools by retail buyers.

capital. Hence, the source of real wages exists, in the main, in the form of capital at the time when the work is done.

This is more obviously and more completely the case if we consider not a short period, but any considerable stretch of time. It is not to be doubted that the wages of such a longer period exist now mainly in the form of goods not yet enjoyable. The bread for the coming season must come from the grain now in store; the clothes from the cotton and the wool, the yarns and the undyed stuffs; and so on. Whatever our conclusion as to the income of this day or this week, it is certain that the income of the current year is to be derived mainly from what has been capital during its course.

Lest there be misconception, some further aspects of the sources and constituents of real enjoyment may be briefly considered. It has been tacitly assumed in the preceding paragraphs that real income is secured, and enjoyment begins, when commodities pass from the counter of the retail shopkeeper into the hands of the purchaser. In literal strictness some modification of this assumption would be needed. Flour in the larder, though owned by those who are to enjoy it, is not yet a source of enjoyment; and a cooking stove or sewing machine belongs to the class of inchoate wealth as much as a baker's oven or a spinning mill. Not a little apparatus is thus beyond the last stage in buying and selling, and yet still in the stage of inchoate wealth. In a strict enumeration and classification of the community's income and capital, such apparatus would need to be put in the latter class. But for the purposes of everyday life, it may be questioned whether anything is gained by following the division between capital and non-capital beyond the last stage in the processes of exchange. The retail purchaser considers the commodities which he buys as serving for the direct satisfaction of his wants from the moment they pass into his possession. Even though they serve, like the cooking stove or the sewing machine, for an ulterior purpose and a later satisfaction, they do not stand in his mind side by side with the tools of his trade.

It often happens, indeed, that current income is intentionally used in a manner to postpone satisfaction: when it is saved and invested. Saving may take the form of a direct purchase of inchoate wealth, as when the manufacturer buys more machinery and materials out of his current gains. Quite as often it takes the indirect form of the purchase of securities and obligations, whence a fixed future income is expected. In either case there is a conscious postponement of enjoyments which might now be had. Some of the effects of this sort of postponement on the problems connected with the wages fund will receive attention at a later stage. They are referred to here by way of contrasting them with the postponement which is, so to speak, unconscious. For all practical purposes, real satisfaction and real income may be said to begin when the consumer buys goods or services for his own direct use; whether that use yield him enjoyment at once, or only after some further labor has been applied by himself or his household. The things so procured, bought ordinarily over the counter of the retail shopkeeper, may be considered, without sensible departure from the substantial truth, as real income; and that income does not emerge finally from the stage of capital until the moment of purchase.

In this sense, then, we may lay it down broadly that wages are derived from capital. In terms, the proposition is very similar to that which the classic writers had maintained; but the terms are used in different senses. Wages mean all the income of all laborers; capital means that supply of inchoate goods, in all the stages toward com-

pletion, from which the steady flow of real income is derived. In the main, the commodities from which the
labor of the immediate present and the early future gets
its reward exists not as a store of already enjoyable
things, but as a varied assortment of things nearly finished.
Those from which the labor of the present season—a
longer stretch of time—gets its reward, exist as an assortment of things less nearly completed. Some of the more
durable forms of enjoyable wealth, such as houses, furniture, clothing, do indeed form rather a store or fund, not
needing still to be brought to the stage of fruition; but
these are usually possessions in hand, the reward of past
labor or the realization of past income, secured in a form
which continues to yield satisfaction for a longer or
shorter stretch of time. The case of house shelter presents an exception, where houses are hired and current
income is spent for the use of a durable source of direct
enjoyment. Bearing in mind such exceptions, it may be
said in general that the labor of the present and of the
near future, still more the labor of the current season
or cycle of production, get their reward in some part
doubtless from commodities which are now so fully finished as to be virtually enjoyable, but in much the larger
part from commodities still in the inchoate stage, and
therefore capital.

The proposition that wages are derived from capital,
in the sense in which it has been developed in the preceding pages, evidently has a different meaning from the
same proposition as it would be understood by one having in mind the relations between capitalists, employers,
and hired laborers. Indeed, in any sense of the word
"capital" which has regard to functions essential for the
community, employers and hiring are of no consequence.
Whether in the old sense of a stock of food and other
necessaries, stowed away and essential for supporting

laborers, or in the sense of a supply of inchoate wealth gradually being carried forward to the stages of fruition and enjoyment,—capital must refer to real and tangible things. It must mean food ready or soon to be ready, clothes in hand or soon to be in hand. It has nothing to do with money or with money wages, or with the hiring of laborers by employers, or with the wealth of the individual capitalists. The relation of wages to capital, as described in the preceding pages, would be the same under any social organization: whether under one where capitalists and laborers were completely separated and laborers got earnings only in the form of payments stipulated between them and their employers; or under a *régime* of co-operative production, where groups of laborers owned their own tools and materials and shared their earnings; or under a system of complete collectivism, where the community owned the inchoate wealth, and apportioned among the members only the accruing increments of enjoyable commodities. In all, production would be spread over a considerable stretch of time, and the reward of present work would have to come, for any longer period, mainly from goods still in the making.

But the payment of wages from capital has been closely associated, in most of the controversy on the wages fund, with the direct dealings of employers with the laborers whom they hire, and so with the organization of society typical of modern times. It has been supposed to be the result of the separation of capitalists from laborers, and of the payment of wages by the former. This association began almost with the first stages of the discussion. The classic economists started with a conception, incomplete though not without a solid basis in truth, of the relation between present labor on the one hand and product and capital on the other. But their conception was not only incomplete; it was vacillating. Most of them spoke,

more or less often, of the funds in the hands of the immediate employer as capital whence wages were paid.
The capital was sometimes described as food, clothes,
and quantities of things consumed by laborers; but quite
as often it was enumerated in terms of money and of
millions sterling. This double use of the term, and the
recurring confusion which ensued, will receive abundant
attention in the second part of the present volume. But
it may be well at this stage of the discussion to show how
great is the confusion to which it leads, and how impera-
tive is the need of keeping to a consistent use of the term
capital: which can best be accomplished by considering
one or two typical cases as to which it has been debated
whether or in what way wages are paid from capital.

Perhaps the commonest case that has caused per-
plexity is where the employing capitalist sells his wares
before he pays the wages to his laborers. Wages may
be paid monthly or fortnightly; meanwhile the employer
sells a part of the product, and so secures funds for paying the laborers. How, it is asked, can wages in such a
case be said to be paid from capital? Clearly they are
not paid from capital, if we mean by that term money
funds on hand and accumulated when production begins,
or if we think of capital as necessarily owned by the individual who pays wages. But it need hardly be pointed
out that all such reasoning and questioning does not
touch real capital or real wages. What is real capital?
Under any rational conception, not money or funds, but
things tangible or usable; under the definition accepted
in these pages, tools, machinery, and materials, and all
things not yet in enjoyable form. What are real wages?
Again, not money, but the enjoyable commodities which
the laborer gets. These he buys with his money wages;
and the important question is the relation between real
wages and the commodities, enjoyable and on the way to

enjoyment, which form respectively income and capital for the community.

Another case may be mentioned. The question whether the source of wages at any given time is an elastic quantity or a rigid and predetermined one, has played an important, almost a decisive part, in the wages fund controversy. In discussing it there has been a constant tendency to run off to questions of the employers' means and the direct money wages which employers pay to hired laborers. What the bearing of hiring and of employers' activity is on the controverted questions, we shall presently consider. But it would never be denied, though it has often been forgotten, that the real and important question as to the elasticity or rigidity of a wages fund must refer to real wages, not to money wages. Larger payments by employers would not avail, unless there were more commodities ready for purchase. Whether there are more commodities; whether the supply of enjoyable goods, available or soon to be available, is settled by causes that have worked in the past, or is easily swelled by causes working in the present; these are the substantial questions. Whether employers can pay more or less, is only one step, and by no means the crucial one, in answering them. Still more inadequate for a satisfactory answer is the consideration whether the individual employer's means for paying laborers are fixed or elastic. Of all this, to repeat, more will be said in one and another part of the pages to come. At present let the reader bear in mind that real income, real wages, and real capital are the essential things, and that any propositions which we may lay down must be applicable to the relations of wages and capital in this sense.

It has already been suggested that the conclusions of this chapter, as to the relation between capital and real

wages, have a wider application than the old doctrine of
the wages fund. The reasoning, while directed to wages,
applies equally to every other form of income. Not
only laborers, but all classes in the community, get their
present remuneration from the now accruing increments
of enjoyable goods. That these enjoyable goods form
the total income of the community was, in fact, the first
step in the reasoning. Hence everything that is true of
wages is true of interest, and rent, and business profits.
All are derived from capital in the same sense. Interest
or rents received some time ago may have been put into
durable forms of enjoyable wealth, and may still exist, as
mansions or cottages, perfect works of art or primitive
ornaments ; and these things are not capital. But the interest and rent received from day to day are nearly all
spent from day to day, and are spent, in the main, on
commodities which do not reach the stage of enjoyment
until the purchase is accomplished. In this sense all
forms of present income alike, while made up of enjoyable goods, were capital but a moment before. If any
law of wages has been reached, it is a law equally applicable to all present rights and claims. It is but a statement of the fact that all the enjoyment of to-day comes
from commodities which are the product of past labor,
and have ripened to-day, or yesterday at best, into the
finished form which makes enjoyment possible.

Herein, again, certainly we have a conclusion different
from that of the classic economists. They never dreamed
of applying to profits and to rent the same reasoning that
was applied to wages. Wages, according to them, came
from a different source and were determined by different
causes from those that affected the other sorts of income
which are usually associated with prosperity and wealth.
According to the views just developed, all alike come
from the same source and are determined by a chain of

past events whose general influence is the same as to all.

Not only are interest, rent, and wages to be considered together from this point of view, but the different sorts of wages also go together. It is immaterial what the machinery is by which wages are turned over to the laborer: whether in the first instance in the form of money wages by an employer, or in the form of money received directly by the laborer for a product sold by him; whether daily wages to an unskilled workman, or a yearly salary to a high official. All get their real wages from the same source and in the same way, by spending their money receipts on consumable commodities. This was, again, by no means the scope of the older wages-fund doctrine, which was declared more or less explicitly to refer to hired laborers only, and was always stated and applied in a manner to show that, even among these, only manual laborers were thought of. Whether or no the old doctrine was meant by its authors to be limited in its scope to hired laborers, the important truth which has been set forth as underlying it holds good in the much wider sense which has been explained in the preceding pages. Past product, existing for any season mainly in the form of unfinished goods, is the source whence all laborers, hired or not hired, and all capitalists, and all the members of the community, get the income of the present and of the immediate future.

And yet there is something more to be said of wages and capital, and of laborers, hired or other, than this general proposition as to the source of the whole community's income. It is obvious at the least that there are differences in the machinery by which this income reaches one hand and another. Hired laborers get the money incomes which constitute their claims to the accruing real income of the community in one way; independent workmen in another; rent receivers and interest receivers in still another. The unmistakable differences in the mode in which the various members of the social body get their share of the general income bring some important consequences, both as to distribution at large and as to wages and the wages fund. The examination of these differences and the consequences which flow from them will form the subject of the next chapter.

CHAPTER III.

THE MACHINERY OF DISTRIBUTION.

THE conclusions reached in the preceding chapters, if not of universal application, are at least of very wide application. They hold good of any community which has got beyond the most primitive stages in the arts, and in which the development of the arts has brought any complicated series of productive acts. They would hold good of a socialist community as well as of one maintaining the *régime* of private property. They are conclusions as to real income and real wages, which have nothing to do with the ownership of capital or the inequalities of wealth, or with the money incomes and money wages which are such important elements in the existing machinery of distribution in modern communities.

In the present chapter we have to do with precisely this machinery. Here money and money income play a vital part. Money wages, money interest, money rent, are the only avenues to the real income of consumable commodities. We can make our conclusions concrete, can follow them out in all their ramifications, only by following the actual working of the intricate money machinery of exchange and distribution. In doing so we shall find, as is the case with every investigation that goes beyond first principles, new premises, new points of view, new conclusions.

For the simplification of the inquiry, let it be assumed

at the outset that the money *régime* has reached its complete development; let it be supposed that the division of labor, and its consequenes of exchange, money, and sale, have been carried so far that no one consumes any of the things he produces. Every article produced comes to market and is sold. This is so largely the case in the advanced communities of modern times that conclusions reached on the assumption of its being universally the case can not diverge seriously from the truth. It follows that the total product or output of the community is sold for money. It follows also that all income of every sort appears first in the form of a money receipt. All real income is thus derived from the use of money income. The inquiry as to money income becomes an inquiry as to the first step, and a most important step, toward the final receipt of consumable goods.

But while real income under these conditions is derived only by the expenditure of money income, the total money income of the community is by no means the same as the money price of the real income. This total is much greater; it is the money price of the entire output of the community. Real income is the flow of consumable goods which are regularly reaching completion, including also a due fraction of the value or utility of the stores of durable finished goods. The output of the community, while including this real income, includes in addition all the inchoate wealth or capital which is being steadily produced. But this clear distinction between output and enjoyable income does not appear either in the case of the individual's money income or in that of the community's total money income. Here income and output, in the first instance certainly, run together. Whatever is produced, no matter in what stage it may be with reference to the final emergence of enjoyable wealth, is sold. Every form of output is measured by its owner in terms of money, and

is reckoned as a receipt.   The gross money income of all
the individuals in the community is thus the money yield
of the total output.   Each producer's net money income
is some part, possibly the whole, of the receipts from the
things he happens to make and sell, irrespective whether
those things do or do not belong to the real net income of
the community.

Let us now suppose a simple case, perhaps never to be
seen in the actual world, yet largely typical of what goes
on in it, and at all events serviceable as a first step toward
understanding its complexities.   Suppose a capitalist, active in the conduct and management of a productive enterprise, to own all of his plant, and to start at the outset
with funds sufficient to pay all laborers and buy all materials until sales are made.   Such a capitalist buys for
cash and sells for cash, pays laborers out of funds in his
own possession, and has his assets always under complete
and ready control.   His product, whatever it be, whether
an article nearer or farther removed from completion so
far as the community's real income is concerned, yields him
an available income as soon as sold.

That income he is free to spend as he pleases.   He
may spend the whole of it for his own immediate pleasure ;
he may reinvest the whole of it, or, rather, may reinvest
everything over and above what is necessary for his support and the support of those whom he cherishes as part of
himself.   If he reinvests, he devotes this gross money income to the purchase of more materials, the enlargement
of plant, or the payment of more laborers.   If he spends,
he devotes it to the purchase of real income, of enjoyable
wealth, for himself and those dependent on him.   The
mode in which he shall apportion his money income between these different objects is a matter at his discretion.

We should not usually think of such a person as unfettered, or as free to spend for immediate enjoyment as

much or as little as he pleased of his money receipts. We think of him as committed to maintain his capital intact. Even if he has not borrowed, and so is under no obligations to provide out of his receipts for principal and interest of a debt, he is expected to keep his own principal unimpaired. The habit of maintaining accumulations intact is so strong in the social strata to which the managers of business belong, that we forget that it rests on the steady and recurrent exercise of a choice. The capitalist would ordinarily set aside out of current receipts enough to replace the funds which he has spent for wages and supplies, and to repair his plant or accumulate in due time enough to replace the plant when it had worn out. Only the excess over what is needed to maintain the principal intact is thought of as free income, available for expenditure on enjoyable things. In reality, however, it is all free. The fact that a choice is usually exercised in a particular way does not prove that no choice exists. If the man is not prosperous for a season, he may very likely fail to keep up his plant or to replace in full his working capital, trusting that better times will come. He then exercises his freedom in such a way as to trench on his capital and get a share of the community's real net income, even though he has secured no net income in the sense in which that term is used with regard to an individual. On the other hand, if he has been prosperous, he may add to his capital, and spend for the necessaries and luxuries of life less than his private net income would bring within the bounds of prudence. On the average, the latter is the typical case. As a class, the active men of affairs get as net income more than they spend for enjoyable wealth. They exercise their freedom in such manner as to add to capital, or, in the everyday phrase, make money : a fact which is of no small importance in the working of the machinery of distribution.

Let us now stretch still further this supposition of simple conditions. Let it be assumed that all the capitalists of the community are of the sort just described: that there are no idle investors, no bankers or other lenders, and that all buying and selling are for cash. Every active producer owns his own plant and materials, and every shopkeeper and every merchant his stock. All these persons collectively own the capital of the community: that is, the real capital of the community, the inchoate wealth which is to be advanced by successive stages to fruition. Further, let it be assumed that all laborers are hired by these capitalists. None work on their own account, or sell anything but their labor. None own capital, or have any source of present income, beyond pay for the labor of the day. They may have some accumulations in present enjoyable form, such as houses, furniture, and food in the closet; but these must have been derived from income of the past. Their income for present work comes exclusively as pay from the capitalists. The older English writers constantly assumed, by implication if not explicitly, that such was the situation of all laborers. The assumption may be used advantageously as a point of departure in reasoning about the social conditions of modern times, if only it be not forgotten that the complications of real life and their divergence from the simple assumed conditions must receive in due course a careful consideration.

In such a society, then, the total money income would flow in the first instance entirely into the hands of the capitalist managers. All things produced, whether real capital or real income for the community, would be their property. Under a completely developed division of labor, all things produced are sold; and the money yield of all the output would be the gross income of the capitalists. That income they can use as they please. They may spend it all for themselves, or invest it all. They may spend only their net income, i. e., the excess over what they must use to keep intact their capital (and so the community's capital) ; or may spend less than their net income, and so cause capital to be added to.

The laborers, on the other hand, would be dependent for their present income on the manner in which the capitalists chose to spend their gross income. If the capitalists were frugal, spent little for personal pleasure, and added much to their accumulations, then more money income would go to the purchase of plant and materials, and more to the hire of laborers. If they chose to spend much for present enjoyment, less money income would go to the laborers. There is, indeed, a case, of no small importance in actual life, in which it would be immaterial to the laborer, at least for the time being, whether the capitalists turned their income to enjoyment or to investment. This is where the enjoyment of the capitalists takes the form of abundance of personal service : where they take their pleasure not in food, clothes, and adornments, but in footmen and maids. Here the alternative is not whether more shall be spent on goods and less turned over to laborers as wages, but whether wages shall be paid for one sort of work or another. The tendency in modern times, however, is for luxurious expenditure to take the form of personal service less and less. In the main, an increase of expenditure for enjoyment means proximately that a smaller part of money income is turned over to laborers ; while an increase of investment and a disposition to add to capital mean that more is turned over to them. At all events, what the laborers get under the conditions here assumed would be determined by the use which the capitalists made of the money income.*

---

* What is said in the text applies, of course, to the immediate effects of a change in the direction of the capitalist's expenditures. After the

It will be observed that money income alone has so far been spoken of. That money income, to serve its real end for laborers or capitalists, must be spent on commodities. But if we examine in what manner capitalists can spend the gross income which has just been described as freely disposable by them, important limitations to the conclusions just stated appear.

Real income, to repeat, is enjoyable commodities; and if the capitalists wish to enjoy, they must buy the finished goods which alone constitute the real income of the community.* The quantity of such real income existing at any time is limited; for the moment it consists of the finished goods now purchasable. For the season, it consists of such supplies of partly finished goods as can be got to the stage of completion within the season. It is limited by the quantity of materials, worked up in part or in whole, which may be on hand, and by the tools and machinery existing wherewith to carry on operations. The total real income available in any season is obviously less than the output of that season. In a community which has reached a high stage of industrial organization, which has spread the operations of production over a considerable stretch of time, and in which a large part of labor is steadily given to the earlier stages of production, the output is very much larger than the real income.

---

first stage, the change from investment to enjoyment means simply that laborers are employed in one way rather than another. The later effect is on real income : laborers make commodities for the enjoyment of the potential capitalists, rather than for the enjoyment of other laborers.

* Strictly, an expenditure on servants would need to be considered, this being a case where immediate satisfaction and immediate real income are secured. It is a case in which the quantity of real income available for the well-to-do happens to be peculiarly elastic, and forms an exception to the general reasoning of the text. Quantitatively, the exception is in modern times probably of no great importance.

But the total money value of the output is the total money income of the capitalist, in the case now assumed. The real income which they can buy is therefore, in its normal money value, very much less than that total income which has been described as freely disposable by them. Even the whole of the real income available for the community is not, in any substantial sense, at the disposal of the capitalists. They can get enjoyment only from finished commodities of the kind and in the variety that their tastes and needs call for. A large part of the commodities now on hand would not serve their turn. The supply of bread and flour and grain at any moment is adjusted to the expected needs of the whole mass of consumers; and after our capitalists had had their fill, the rest of the breadstuffs would be virtually incapable of giving them any satisfaction. Other commodities would be too coarse for their tastes, or would pall long before the total available quantity was used. The effective choice which the capitalists would have as to the disposal of the gross money income which was freely theirs, would then be confined, for the time being at least, within limits not very elastic.

Limitations of the same sort appear as to the real wages and real income of the laborers. Like the capitalists, they can get for the money turned over to them only such consumable commodities as exist or will be ready within the season. We may suppose, for example, that the capitalists have been moved to abstain from personal expenditure, and have reinvested largely and heavily, the process involving a transfer of an increased part of their money income to the hired laborers; or we may suppose—to put a case that has played no small part in the history of the wages controversy—that a general trades union of all the laborers has put the capitalists in a position where, under pain of ceasing investment entirely, they

must raise money wages. Whatever the ultimate outcome
in this much-debated case, it may be averred without hesitation that the laborers' combination might win a victory in the first step in their campaign,—the advance of
money wages. That step is the only one of which laborers or capitalists usually think, and, it must be confessed,
is the step with which alone economists have too often
busied themselves. But the real gain (apart from the joy
of victory) for the laborers must come in the purchase of
more commodities in the way of food, drink, clothes, shelter; and of these no more can be bought than there are.
How elastic the inflowing supply of such commodities is
for any season, how great and rigid are the obstacles to
an immediate or rapid change in the available real wages,
we need not yet discuss. What is plain is the existence of
some limits in the nature of the available supplies of finished and half-finished goods. The capitalists, in the case
supposed, can turn the money income in any direction
they please: keep it all for themselves, or turn more or
less of it over to laborers; but the real income which can
be secured and enjoyed is in some degree predetermined
in quantity and quality.

All this means simply that the machinery of production at any given time is arranged for the supply of the
habitual and anticipated wants of the community. Each
individual capitalist produces the commodities which he
has sold before, and which experience leads him to expect
to sell again. The pig-iron maker has a reasonable faith
that his iron will be bought by the maker of machinery,
and he again that his machinery will be bought by the person who means to use it in making one product or another.
That process of investment and accumulation by which
existing capital is maintained and new capital is added, is
thus prepared for and virtually accomplished before the
individuals commit themselves to the decisive step of

turning their money income to investment rather than to enjoyment. The producers of luxuries go their way in the same fashion. Some create or maintain machinery for silks and satins, others prepare the raw material, others finally buy the products from the manufacturer and arrange them in the shops of the cities for the expected purchases of the consumers, who will presumably do as they have done in times past,—spend part of their inflowing money receipts for enjoyment. Not least, the makers of the commodities for laborers continue to produce these on the accustomed scale, anticipating the transference of money income by capitalists to laborers in the course of that continuance of investment of which the purchase of machinery and materials is the other part. The output of the season, produced and owned under our supposition by the capitalists as a body, is sold again to these capitalists as a body. They own the whole output at the start, and get the whole money income. A part of the output they buy directly, either as plant and materials for further production or as commodities for enjoyment ; a part is sold to them indirectly through their transference of money income to the hired laborers. But the assortment of goods, finished and unfinished, that is on hand at any time depends, not on the apportionment of their money income which is then made by the capitalists as spenders, but on the apportionment which these same capitalists as producers have been expecting and planning for during a considerable stretch of time in the past.

So much as to the nature and the causes of the limitations by which the capitalists would find themselves fettered during any one season in the really free disposal of their incomes. Over a longer stretch of time the case would be different. Here their choice would be effective not only as to the disposal of money income, but of real output and real income as well.

The steps by which this real control over the product and the income of the community would be exercised need no elaborate explanation. Assume that there is a sudden change in the manner in which the capitalists choose to use their money income; for example, that they become more frugal and more disposed to invest. Less of luxuries and comforts will be bought by them; the merchants who deal in such commodities will find trade dull; the series of producers who make them will in turn feel the depression. Eventually less will be made, and the constitution of the real income of the community will in time conform to the new apportionment of the money incomes of the capitalists. On the other hand, the money formerly spent on the luxuries and comforts will be turned in other directions. The makers of machines and materials will find a brisker demand for their products. More money income will be turned over to laborers, and the makers of the commodities consumed by them will similarly find trade good and profits "satisfactory." A shift will eventually take place in the direction in which the productive apparatus of the community is turned. In the long run it is thus true that not only the money income of the community is freely at the disposal of the active capitalists, but that its real income and its real output exist in such forms and in such apportionment as their choice determines. Allowing for the time needed to enable the productive apparatus to accommodate itself to demand, we shall find so much real income for capitalists and laborers, and inchoate wealth in such quantity and variety, as the capitalists' use of the total money income calls for.

Before going on to the next stage in the analysis of the machinery of distribution, one corollary from the preceding proposition may be noted. It is true that the supposed simple community of completely independent employing capitalists and completely dependent hired laborers is still under consideration here. As to the complex phenomena of the actual world, we shall find hereafter occasion for much qualification of the preliminary results. But one part of the conclusions holds good for any community in which the institution of private property exists : it is, that the maintenance and accumulation of capital depend on the disposition and the will of those who become recurrently the owners of the money income and so of the real output of the community. This was what the old economists had in mind when they said that it depended on the will of the owner whether a commodity should be capital or not capital. They sometimes spoke as if his will could become operative at once ; as if by magic he could convert a pack of hounds into a cotton mill. But the truth which underlay their dissertations on this topic is an important and solid one. In every community in which private property exists there are inequalities in wealth; in almost all, great inequalities. The money income of every season flows first, in very large part, into a comparatively few hands, and is directed by them at their discretion into one channel of purchase or another. The inequality in possessions may be regrettable, and the stewardship which it involves of the community's capital may be well or ill administered ; but the facts are not to be gainsaid, and must be faced if we would get a true understanding of the industrial world. The importance of this force, as of others that are constant and familiar in their operation, is often forgotten. The recurrent exercise of the choice of the capitalist takes place habitually in much the same way : changes in the direction of greater or less expenditure, or greater or less (usually greater) accumulation, come slowly and gradually. The motive power which thus drives and controls the apparatus of capitalistic production works in the

main so steadily that we forget that it consists of the col-
lected volition of hosts of individuals, each and all of
whom are free to do as they will with their own.

We may now proceed to make our conclusions fit more
closely to the facts of real life, by introducing, step by
step, the complications which appear in the actual organization of the machinery of production and distribution.

In the first place, no active capitalist is in that position
of complete independence which has been assumed: of
neither borrowing nor lending, of buying for cash and
selling for cash. He buys on credit, and thus is under
obligations to turn over part of his money income, as it
flows in, to his creditors; while those to whom he has
sold on credit are under similar obligations to him. As
between the direct managers of industry, the obligations
which thus follow each one do not change the case for
the mass. Collectively, they are still free and uncon-
trolled as to the disposal of the general money income.
But quite as important as their relations *inter se*, are their
relations to the great body of bankers, brokers, money-
lenders, middlemen of all sorts and degrees, whose business it is to make advances to the more immediate directors of business affairs. The banks of discount and
deposit find their chief function in such advances, and
are the great types of this factor in the industrial world.
Side by side with them are to be found, in every considerable centre, other parts of the same credit organization.
Brokers negotiate loans whenever they find funds offering
for investment over those short periods for which the
regularly recurring debts of the business manager are
contracted. The great wholesale houses play a most important and effective part. They buy on credit, make advances on consignments, nurse this producer and drive
that one to the wall; they themselves meanwhile borrow
largely from the banks. Their action goes far in settling

when and how and where money income shall flow into
the hands of those who are in the more direct and obvious
sense the directors of production and the employers of
labor. In other words, the body of persons whose judgment and discretion determine how the gross money income shall be used, and what part of it shall be turned
over to laborers, is much larger than the group of the
immediate employers. In the discussion of the wages-
fund doctrine, and indeed in most academic disquisitions
on wages and business management, this has been often
lost sight of. The immediate employers are thought of
as the only persons who decide primarily how and where
laborers shall be hired, and whose resources determine
what direct advances of wages shall be made them. In
fact, the immediate employer is controlled, in greater or
less degree, by his relations with this large and complex
body of lenders and of middlemen. He can sell rapidly
to the merchants who are his first customers, if their
judgment approves of his wares, and he can get advances
from them if they have faith in his capacity and integrity.
Similarly, he can borrow from the bankers and brokers
according to his repute for success and character. If a
long career of successful ventures and of punctual probity
has given him not only large means of his own, but a high
standing in the business world, his immediate resources
are almost limitless; he can secure at a moment's notice
the command of millions. On the other hand, a rumor of
disaster, a revelation of dishonesty, may practically wipe
out his means.

Thus we must consider the resources of a large and
varied body of persons, if we would examine the immediate source of the money wages of hired laborers.
Such an examination at best is incomplete ; the inquiry as
to the source of real wages remains the important one in
the background. But the questions as to the machinery

of immediate money wages are important enough ; and, to repeat, they are to be answered only by examining the doings of the whole array of employers and middlemen and lenders who collectively form the active managers of industry. In recent discussions as to the source of wages, it has been asked not infrequently whether the funds of the immediate employers, available for paying money wages, are predetermined or limited. If any question of this sort is to be raised, it should be, not whether the funds or means at the disposal of the individual employer, but whether those of the whole complex body, are limited. The answer will be considered in the next chapter : it may be said at once that the degree of elasticity and indeterminateness is much greater for the individual member than for the whole group. However this may be, it is clear that the control of the total output of society, and so of its gross money income, which was assumed at the outset to be entirely in the hands of the immediate producers and employers, is exercised in reality by a much larger and more varied body.

Next we have to consider another difference between the real world and assumed conditions—one of far-reaching importance for many questions of social organization, but less important for those here under review. The employing capitalists,—we may now mean by that phrase the complex body which directly or indirectly is active in business management,—were supposed to own all the capital. But in fact we find, separate from them in the main, a great number of investors, who own capital and derive an income from it, but take no direct part in its management.

The investors have made loans to the active business men. They have received an engagement for the payment of interest at stated terms, and for the eventual repayment of the principal. They may be conceived, for many social purposes, as the owners of a great part of the community's capital. When a plant is erected with borrowed capital, the lender is in so far virtually its owner. While legally but a creditor, in the eye of the economist he may often be regarded as an owner of real capital. As it happens, however, the legal relation fits exactly the economic relation, for the purposes of the present inquiry into the working of the machinery of distribution. If it is asked, who, in the end, owns the capital of the community? the answer must be, the idle investor as well as the active business manager. But if it is asked, who controls the capital of the community and first becomes owner of its total income? the answer must be, the active manager, indebted though he may be to his creditor. The output became his as it goes to market and is sold, and the gross money income passes first into his hands. He must simply pay the stipulated interest to his creditor. In so far only is he subject to a direct and immediate limitation in his control of the inflowing money receipts.*

It may be suggested that the business man is subject to a further important limitation in that he must repay the principal when due. But while this is clearly the case so far as the individual is concerned, it is not the case for the whole body of active managers. Investors usually spend for enjoyment only their income, not their principal. The principal, as it falls in, is reinvested—that is, the funds are

---

* Investments of what may be called the "productive" sort are chiefly referred to in the text. Those large loans which are made to states present, in the main, a different chain of phenomena. The money income is here promised the investor by a public body, which in turn gets its funds by taxes; these funds being again derived, if the taxes are indirect, chiefly from the money receipts of the active capitalists, and, if the taxes are direct, from any and every source of money income. Where the proceeds of the loan are used for public works yielding an immediate money revenue, the situation is more like that described in the text.

turned back into the hands of one or another active capitalist, to be again at his free disposal. Substantially, therefore, it remains true that the existence of a separate class of investors affects our supposed case only in one point—the money income which the capitalists get is not wholly at their disposal, but is subject to periodic drafts for interest payments to investors.

It may not be amiss to refer for a moment to the mode in which the operations of the investors are connected with that determination of capital through the choice of its owners, which was the subject of some of the preceding paragraphs. At any moment the investors have put their principal beyond control ; it has been turned over to the active capitalists, who have spent it for plant and materials or have paid it out in wages.* Usually, funds borrowed for a considerable time from investors are spent for plant and other durable forms of capital, while loans for purchase of materials and for wages payments are obtained from the bankers and other middlemen who are the active co-operators in business management. The plant lasts a long space; the investors have put their means beyond control. This irrevocable commitment of the investor's means finds its other side in the irrevocable commitment of part of the community's gross income to the form of

---

* The reader conversant with economic theory will readily carry the reasoning here in another direction, and will remark that ultimately all the funds are found to have been directed to hiring laborers. Tools and materials are made by labor, and (under the supposition that laborers are hired) represent in the end nothing but advances to laborers. This point of view is the one to be taken if we were to consider the whole series of operations which intervene between the beginning and end of production. For the inquiry carried on in the text, however, the operations of a single season only are pertinent ; and for a season the funds turned to hiring laborers should be treated as entirely separate from those turned to the purchase of tools and materials.

capital. As time goes on, the plant wears out and is renewed, the loan falls due, and the principal is reinvested.
These two operations go on side by side; not in the sense
that the renewal of actual capital and the reinvestment of
investors' funds coincide in individual cases, but in the
sense that, for the community at large, they form two
aspects of the one process by which capital is maintained.
Here again the actual making of concrete capital,—of
buildings, machines, apparatus, materials,—does not take
place as the direct consequence of the investor's decision
to keep his principal intact.   It precedes the decision, or
takes place *pari passu* with it, in anticipation of that habitual reinvestment which goes on as a matter of course
in modern communities.   Like other habits, it rests on
the repeated exercise of volition in the same direction; the
effect, while almost invariable, being none the less caused
by the exercise of a choice which, time enough being given,
is unfettered.

What has been said of interest payments holds good of
rent payments.   Important and fundamental as is the difference between interest and rent, the machinery by which
they reach the hands of their owners is the same.   If the
business man uses for his operations a site which enables
him to achieve a given result with less outlay than his
competitors, he will pay the price of the advantage to the
fortunate owner of the site, in the same manner as he
would pay interest on borrowed capital. If he happens to
own the site, the inflowing receipts are so much the more
completely under his control; precisely as, if he owns all
his capital, he is not fettered in his expenditure of the gross
receipts by the obligation to pay interest.   In neither case
is there a distinguishable part of the total income, appear-
ing at the outset as separable interest or separable rent.
Both represent, so far as they are distinct payments at all,
obligations which the active business manager has incurred

for a specified diversion of a part of his total money income. They are independent of what may in fact be received by him in consequence of his possession of the capital or the site; they are often different from that usual or " normal " gain accruing from their use, which economists call true interest or true rent. They are simply money payments which the business man has promised to make out of the general inflow of his income.

The reader will readily follow the same line of reasoning in other directions—to monopoly receipts, royalty payments, and other sources from which the idle well-to-do and the prosperous business men get accretions of income. So far as the business man is owner, he gets in these ways additions to his unfettered means; so far as he has borrowed, he has undertaken stipulated payments to others. The business corporation of modern times presents all possible varieties of the relation between active manager and idle investor. Nominally, the stockholders are a group of associated active capitalists. Practically, they range from shrewd managers to the most helpless of inactive investors. Throughout, in all the complexity of the meanings and final causes of these various payments, we find the machinery for effecting them to be the same. In the last analysis, the payments may be regarded as interest, or interest plus earnings of shrewdness, or rent, or monopoly extortion; but they all come from gross receipts flowing first into the hands of the active capitalists, who may then be under bonds to make the payments to other persons.

So much as to the mode in which the simple conditions assumed at the beginning of this inquiry are affected by the varied and scattered ownership of capital and other instruments of production. A different modification, and a more important and instructive one, comes in another direction. At the outset, as all capital was supposed to be in the hands of active business men, so all laborers were supposed to be hired by them. It is time now to consider how far laborers in fact are in this condition, and how far the conclusions derived from the analysis of the simple case need to be modified in regard to the laboring classes.

Clearly, in almost every country great numbers of persons who are usually spoken of as laborers are not hired by capitalists. It happened that in England, at the time when the classic economists were developing their system, a larger proportion of manual workers were in this situation than has been the case in any other time or place; hence, the easy assumption of such conditions by these writers, and hence (in good part) their easy acceptance of the wages-fund doctrine. But even in England there were and are unmistakable exceptions. Cobblers, carpenters, cabmen ply their trades independently, either owning or hiring their tools. In other countries the exceptions are more important and numerous. The tillers of the soil, who in England are employed by capitalist farmers, elsewhere are very commonly owners or tenants. In countries like France or the United States, millions of men whose work is mainly hard, monotonous manual labor, are owners of plots of land, and as independent of hire and of stipulated wages as any great employer. On the continent of Europe generally, production on a large scale has not permeated manufacturing industry as much as in English-speaking communities, and the independent artisan holds his own in larger degree against the capitalist producer. The blacksmith, the carpenter, the shoemaker, the weaver, have nowhere been entirely crowded out by the factory, with its *régime* of hired workmen. In many countries such laborers still form a large part of the body of persons whose income is essentially reward for physical exertion.

The question may be raised whether such independent

workers can be said to get simply wages. They usually have some capital; indeed, they must have some small possessions of their own in order to maintain their position of independence. They may perhaps be described as capitalists, and as receiving something different from wages; this term being confined to the hired workmen who get stipulated sums from employers. Any one who is familiar with the traditional plan of economic text-books, inherited as it is from the classic days, will see with how uncertain a voice most writers have spoken on this topic. Distribution is usually set off under the rubrics of wages, interest, rent; profits being sometimes added of late years as a fourth independent constituent. Wages are described to mean any reward for immediate exertion, regardless of the mode in which the reward comes. In the detailed discussions of wages, however, the case of the hired laborer and of what the employer will pay him occupies the chief place. In everyday speech, too, this is the person whom we think of as receiving wages; and the large array of persons who get a return for labor in a different way are left without any distinctive designation.

The same question of classification and nomenclature appears in the suggestion that the independent workman is not a laborer but a business man,—an *entrepreneur*. So considered, he would be said to receive, not wages, but that mixed and vexed income which Mill called wages of superintendence, and which in our own day is entitled sometimes business profits, sometimes profits simply, sometimes managers' earnings. And certainly a good degree of justification for this course is to be found. The gap between the poorest independent craftsman, and the great employer whom we think of as primarily a capitalist and as earning something different from wages, is filled by a series of different workers, among whom it is hard to find any sharp line of division. Where do business profits cease and mere wages begin?

We need not stop for any prolonged consideration of this question, which involves not only matters of terminology, but very substantial problems. Probably the best plan for the exposition of distribution at large is to describe all reward for exertion as wages; thereafter pointing out, however, how various are the forms of exertion, and how different the causes which affect the reward of different forms; and in the end going so far as to give a special name, such as business profits or managers' earnings, to the wages for some peculiar kinds of work. Certainly for most purposes of classification we should not be consistent if we drew the line between wages and not wages according to the bare independence of the workman. The cobbler who works alone in his petty shop gets, in the main, a return for labor as much as the workman in the shoe factory; the peddler and the shopkeeper's assistant, the small farmer and his hired workman, all earn an income by labor. No doubt the shrewdness and judgment of the farmer or peddler affect his income, as the skill and capacity of the hired workman affect his. No doubt, too, the class of which the farmer and peddler are types own some of the instruments of production, capital or land, and get their earnings in the course of using such instruments. But the earnings come, in a multitude of cases, without that conscious consideration of the income-yielding possibilities of capital and land which accompanies the work of the large capitalist and large landowner. Theoretically the earnings may be parcelled off as partly interest, partly rent, partly wages. Practically they come in as the return for so much work, shrinking or swelling with the fortunate or unfortunate use of such labor and capital as the individual may have at his disposal.

But in one important respect the receipts of the independent laborer, even though they be regarded for most purposes as wages, are to be put in the same class as those of the well-to-do capitalists who were supposed at the outset of the present inquiry to be the only owners of capital and the employers of all laborers. The independent workman gets a primary and not a derivative share of the total income of society. With regard to the machinery by which distribution is accomplished, he belongs in a different class from the hired laborer, and belongs in the same class as the active capitalist. He becomes legal and absolute owner of a part of the output of society, and so comes into direct control of part of the gross money income. He may be fettered by debt, as his fellow on a large scale may be; but he is dependent on no fixed bargain for the money income which will serve him to procure a share in society's real income of consumable goods. Herein his situation differs essentially from that of the hired laborer, and herein the phenomena of real life differ essentially from those assumed at the beginning of this inquiry. The hired laborer gets his money income as the result of a bargain by which he sells his working power for a space. The independent workman gets his money income directly from the sale of what he makes. The situation is not always advantageous to the latter. The peasant proprietor and the petty craftsman do not necessarily prosper more than the hired mechanic. But the hired workman is directly dependent for his money income on an employing capitalist; the independent workman is not.

For an understanding of the machinery by which distribution is accomplished in modern times, the classification of sources of income should thus be different from that to be adopted for an explanation of the fundamental causes. For the latter purpose the different sources of income may still be appropriately divided into wages,

interest, rent, with possibly business profits as a fourth
term.   But so far as the concrete mode in which money
income (and this is the first step to real income) reaches
different hands, we must put on one side all the independent producers, whether they conduct operations on a
large scale or on a small; on the other side, all receivers
of stipulated interest or stipulated rent, and all hired
laborers.   The former get a primary, the latter a derivative share of the total income of society.

Both the primary and the derivative shares, as they
appear in fact, may or may not be what the economist
would analyze as simple incomes.   The independent producers may be great capitalists, and their net receipts,
separated into the constituent parts which are important
for the permanent explanation of things, may be made up
of interest, and rent, and wages ordinary and extraordinary; or they may be small fry, in whose earnings wages
for very common sorts of labor play so large a part that
the other constituents may be dropped from consideration.
The other dependent persons may similarly get mixed or
simple incomes.   The interest paid by a corporation may
stand in part for natural advantages which have been
capitalized and converted into a bonded debt; that which
is interest in form being thus rent in substance.   On the
other hand, the payment which, in ordinary parlance, is
rent for building or for a plot of land, is usually a mixture
of the rent and interest of the economist.   Concrete wages,
too, may be a complex return, including in the case of a
highly trained workman not only wages for labor but
interest for the capital sunk in his education.   Thus distribution, as analyzed in its last elements, is an abstraction: its demarcations rarely correspond to the actual receipts which are seen in the industrial world.   It may
explain the situation, and in that larger sense describe it;
but it does not describe with accuracy the direct phenom-

ena. On the other hand, the analysis of distribution which has formed the subject of this chapter presents the literal facts of the case. The incomes of independent producers, large and small, are the primary sources of distribution ; interest payments, rent payments, wages of hired laborers, are derivative, and their recipients may be described as dependent.

The point has now been reached where we can observe the differences, in their relation to capital, between the wages of the hired laborer and those of the independent workman. The hired laborer is undoubtedly dependent on capital, and gets his wages from capital, in a sense in which the independent workman does not. His money income, the first and the essential means toward getting a real income, is turned over to him by capitalists. It comes from funds in the possession of a body of which his immediate employer is a member, and which includes all the active co-operators in the management and control of industry. Except in so far as he has made a contract covering some length of time, his wages depend recurrently on their disposition to use for productive operations their inflowing money receipts. In this sense his earnings depend on a wages fund—on the sums which the employers judge it expedient to turn to the hire of labor ; and in this sense the independent workmen evidently do not depend on capitalists or on a wages fund.

In another sense, all workmen, whether hired or independent, get their wages from capital and are dependent on a wages fund. This is in the sense that all real income is derived from consumable commodities ; that these are the product of past labor ; that the supply of them available for fresh use at any time is small ; and that the supply for any considerable stretch of time exists mainly in the form of inchoate wealth. The real income of all classes in the community comes from past product, and in the main from real capital. This is a very different wages-fund doctrine from the other. It will hold good under any conditions of society, so long as the arts are carried on in such manner that a long stretch of time elapses between the beginning and the end of the successive steps in production.

These two things have been curiously interwoven and confounded in the long controversy over the source and measure of wages. The wages-fund doctrine, in the form in which it so long held sway, was supposed to apply primarily to laborers hired by capitalist employers. It was supposed, rather than explicitly stated, so to apply, for the limitation was more often tacitly assumed than pointed out in terms. Adam Smith's brief but pregnant paragraphs had directly connected the payment of wages from capital with their payment from the funds of employers. Scarce one workman out of ten in Europe, says he, is an independent artisan; hence the wages of the great mass depend on what the masters can and will pay them. Later English writers had the same organization of industry in mind, though they did not often say so. While their theories were stated in general terms, they were framed with an eye to the conditions and the needs of the England of that day, where, as it happened, the great mass of laborers were of the hired and dependent class. At a later stage in the discussion it was more often pointed out in express terms that hired labor alone was meant to be within the scope of the wages-fund doctrine. When the whole subject then came to be overhauled, it was seen that this assumption had been more or less overtly made, and the avowed scope of the doctrine was accordingly limited. Its advocates set forth that it pretended to do no more than explain how the wages of hired laborers were determined. Its opponents accepted the limitation, and retorted either by pointing out how large was the number of cases so left unconsidered and unexplained, or by questioning whether it could be maintained even within the chosen limits.*

Yet, in fact, for the solid truth which underlay the doctrine as to real capital and real wages it was not necessary to exclude from its pale all other than hired laborers; while, on the other hand, so far as these hired laborers were concerned, the support which it got from their relations with their immediate employers was a treacherous one. None other than these direct employers were usually referred to as the holders of the funds on which laborers were dependent. When it began to be asked whether the money funds which they could pay laborers were rigid or elastic, the only possible answer was that nothing in the nature of a predetermined fund existed, and that the sums

---

* In his direct discussion of wages, the younger Mill said that "wages depend on the demand and supply of labour, or, as it is often expressed, on the proportion between population and capital. By population is here meant the number only of the labouring class, or rather of *those who work for hire.*" (The italics are mine.) *Political Economy*, Book II, ch. xi, §1. Much the same sort of expression appears in the chapter on Profits, Book II, ch. xv, § 6. Yet, in his first consideration of capital, Mill had pointed out that "when the labourer maintains himself by funds of his own, as when a peasant farmer or proprietor lives on the produce of his land or an artisan works on his own account, they are still supported by capital—that is, by funds provided in advance." Book I, ch. iv, § 2. Compare what is said of Mill below, in Part II, chapter xi. Cairnes, in commenting on Mill's statement of the wages-fund doctrine, remarks parenthetically that "the question at present is exclusively of *hired* labor." (Cairnes himself puts the word "hired" in italics). *Leading Principles*, Book II, ch. i, § 5. Hence Sidgwick remarks, at the beginning of a chapter on general wages, that "since other economists generally denote by 'wages' (when used without qualification) the remuneration of labour hired by employers, it seems convenient to adopt this meaning in the critical discussion [of the wages-fund doctrine chiefly] which will occupy the first part of this chapter."—*Principles of Political Economy*, Book II, ch. viii, § 1.

which they had at command, whatever causes might affect them, were not in the nature of an accumulation that was fixed once for all when the bargain between them and their workmen was made. With this negative answer the whole traditional mode of dealing with wages and capital was given up. It was forgotten that in an important sense hired laborers are primarily dependent for their wages on the funds which the whole body of active capitalists can and will turn over to them; and that in a still more important sense all laborers, hired or independent, get their real remuneration from that product of past labor to which the earlier economists had given the name of capital.

One further topic may be touched before this lengthened inquiry is brought to a close. So far as the machinery of distribution is concerned, the receivers of rent and interest payments and the hired laborers have been described as alike getting derivative incomes, and as in that sense alike dependent. It may be asked whether there is any greater degree of dependence for the laborers than for the others.

In one respect the laborers are certainly more dependent. The engagements with them are usually for a shorter period of time. The active capitalist often binds himself for years with those to whom he pays rent or interest; for weeks only, as a rule, with those to whom he pays wages. This is not always the case. The growing strength of organization among hired laborers has led in modern times to more permanent engagements, in which both sides bind themselves for months or a year. Usually, however, the contract with the hired laborer covers a brief period. He is liable to be called on at short notice to show his strength in bargaining with the employer.

The longer term over which the *rentier* (to use that convenient Continental term) makes his bargain is not al-

ways to his advantage. He commits his principal irrevocably for a series of years, and takes his chances that
his debtor, the active capitalist, will repay it when the
loan falls due, being meanwhile powerless so long as the
interest instalments are met. That investor whose stipulated income would be called by the economist rent is
indeed usually in a more assured position. The natural
site or resource which enables him to get the business
man's promise of stated payments is likely to endure in
another's hands as well as it would in his own ; and if his
rent does not appear punctually, he usually finds its source
unimpaired when he retakes possession. But so far as the
investor of capital proper, the recipient of true interest,
is concerned, the advantage which he may have over the
laborer from the more permanent nature of his contract
with the business manager, is conditional on the care and
judgment with which he selects his debtor. Economic
history, ancient and modern, presents a plenty of cases in
which the greater security of the investor's position over
short periods has proved his ruin in the long run.

Much has been said of late years in regard to another
phase of the hired laborer's dependent position : the importance of his strength in bargaining. Recurrently,—as a
rule at short intervals,—the contract on which his income
depends must be renewed. If he stands alone; if he has
no savings from past income which would enable him to
wait and see what the market offers; if he is ignorant and
generally helpless,—he bargains at great disadvantage. If
he is banded with his fellows, if he possesses the wherewithal to make a trial of strength, and if he has shrewd
and well-informed leaders, he bargains to the best advantage. The strength which the trades union gives
the hired laborer in dealing with his employers was not
doubted even in the days of greatest faith in the natural
laws which were supposed to regulate economic phenom-

ena in general, and wages in particular. No one would question it in these less conservative times. The bargaining of the outside investor with his active debtor is not affected at bottom by factors so very different from those just mentioned. Usually he can wait a bit for his income : therein his ordinary position is better than that of the hired laborer. He is often, but by no means always, reasonably shrewd and intelligent, and knows what the general market affords. He gets advice, which may or may not be good, from the large class of bankers and brokers who make a business of placing investments. As to his legal position and the mode in which the machinery of justice enables him to enforce his claims, he may have been in former days better cared for than the hired laborer who is also a creditor of the active capitalist ; but the mechanics' liens of modern legislation give the workmen much the best of it here, apart from the fact that the more rapid recurrence of his stipulated payments diminishes the sum which at any one time is at stake.

This brief notice of some aspects and effects of the hired laborer's dependent position will serve to explain the sense in which the term dependence is to be understood. We may keep far from that pessimistic view which finds its expression in the turgid description of the laborer as the slave of the employer, without going to the opposite extreme of concluding that the laborer is no worse off than the investor, because both alike are dependent for income on what the active business manager has promised or will promise to pay them. Neither the helpless widow and orphan, nor the down-trodden laborer,—two familiar figures confronting each other in the literature of social controversy,—are really typical of the practical outcome of this dependence. As to the hired laborer, his position does indeed show that the ownership of wealth in modern societies is very unequally divided, and in so far is not consistent with that ideal organization which, under ideal conditions, would doubtless bring the maximum of human happiness. But it is consistent with a steady improvement in his condition, in his place and power in the community, and in his sources of happiness; and therefore we need not despair if, men, manners, and morals being what they now are, it is perhaps the only position he is likely to have for a long time in the future.

CHAPTER IV.

THE ELASTICITY OF THE WAGES FUND.

THE results reached in the preceding chapters, while different in important respects from those usually associated with the wages fund doctrine, have yet been largely conservative. It has appeared that all wages are paid from the products of past labor, and that the supply of products of past labor exists mainly in the form of real capital. It has appeared, too, that the class of hired laborers not only derive their wages from capital in this sense, but that they are dependent, for their share of the real income into which capital steadily ripens, on the funds which the employing class find it advantageous to turn over to them. It remains now to consider another aspect of the old doctrine,—whether the capital from which wages come is rigid, or elastic; predetermined, or easily adjusted to present demands. This question may be considered as to both sides of the doctrine : as to the sources of the real income going to all laborers, and those of the money income going to manual laborers, and more especially to hired manual laborers.

It will be convenient to begin by inverting the former order, and to consider first the case of the hired laborers. Are the money funds which employers can turn over to them limited ? Are they so determined by previous happenings that a given sum must go to laborers, and no more can go ? Or are they elastic, swelling easily when employers are led by competition among themselves or by pressure from their workmen to advance wages, and shrinking promptly when their niggardliness or ill fortune leads them to retrench ?

One part of the answer has already been given.* As to the direct employer, considered by himself, it is clear that there is no rigidity or predetermination. He sells and borrows, adjusts his payments and receipts, and nurses his bank account. Within limits that are certainly not narrow, he can make his available funds fit new conditions and new demands. In the language of Thornton, who was among the first to face squarely this phase of the problem, it sounds like mockery or childishness to ask if the funds which he can apply to wages are limited or predetermined.†

Consider, however, the whole employing class, as it was described in the last chapter. For the hired laborers as a whole, the money wages of a season came from the large body of active capitalists : from the merchants who buy goods or make advances on them, from the bankers who discount and lend, as well as from the immediate employers. Is the total of funds which they can pay in wages limited ?

No doubt there are some limitations here. There is a general limit of some sort, in the total of money means which the sale of output or product brings into the hands of the managing class. There are more specific limits within this general one. Contracts of long standing and duration compel the payment of certain sums to investors, in the way of interest or rent. Further, the funds directed to production must be apportioned with regard to existing methods and existing supplies. That workmen may

---

* See pages 62–64.
† See what is said of Thornton below, at pages 246–255.

be employed, machinery and buildings must be on hand,
and materials must be provided. In other words, a large
part of the gross money income of the season must go to
purchases which may indeed in the last analysis be resolvable into a succession of advances to laborers, but
which involve no present payments to laborers. This
was what one of the last defenders of the old doctrine had
in mind when he divided capital into the three constituent
parts of plant, materials, and wages fund, and pointed out
that only the wages-fund part was available for paying
laborers.* While the individual employer, supported as
he is by the multiform apparatus of credit and connection,
is not compelled to make any hard-and-fast apportionment of his directly available means between these different uses, the body of employers must divide their purchases and advances in a manner which is determined in
its main lines by the state of the arts and the succession
of the productive operations.

But, with all this admitted, it still remains clear that
nothing in the nature of a predetermined and rigid wages
fund can be found. While the payments due to outside
investors for interest and rent may be fixed for the moment, the sums which the active capitalists can set aside
for their own enjoyment are flexible. The apportionment
of those sums, again, which go to the maintenance of the
settled course of production can not be said to be rigorously predetermined for the different channels of advances
to labor on the one hand, the purchases of tools and materials on the other. The limits are elastic. Even the

---

* Cairnes, *Leading Principles*, Book II, ch. i. Compare what is said
below at page 257. Cairnes apparently had in mind, when making
this division, the money funds of the direct employers, which go to the
one destination or the other; not the division of the actual possessions
of the community into finished and enjoyable goods on the one hand
and inchoate wealth on the other.

total money income at the disposal of the capitalist class
can not be described as a fixed thing. It has been spoken
of as the total price of the output; and such it is.   But
that total price depends on the relation of the circulating
medium to the whole volume of things sold.   The modern machinery of credit as a substitute for money makes
prices and total money payments for commodities vary
under very short-lived influences. Banks of deposit and
issue, which form so important an element in the whole
body of the active managers of industry, can swell their
loans, and so can add effectively to the total of money
funds received in exchange for the industrial output and
available for fresh operations.   In almost every direction
the causes which determine the advance by the active
capitalists of a part of their funds to laborers, operate in
the rough, and with no machinelike precision.

If therefore we put the case of a general trades union
embracing all the hired laborers, and a general strike by
them for higher wages,—a case which, improbable and unreal as it may be, has rightly been made to play a prominent part in the theoretic controversy,—the answer must
be that nothing in the proximate conditions of industry
stands in the way of their success. Success, that is, in the
sense which alone is here under consideration : an advance
in money wages. A larger share of the total inflowing
receipts of the active capitalists might be diverted into
the hands of the hired laborers.   Possibly those total
receipts would be simply swelled by an increase of the
bank credit part of the circulating medium. Possibly
the employers might be compelled to submit to a reduc-
tion of their net profits. Possibly a diminution of the
funds applied to the purchase of materials and plant
might shift the shrinkage of profits more particularly to
those who happened at the time to be in largest part the
holders of these forms of inchoate wealth.   The outside

investor, though usually shielded by the length of his contract from the contingencies of the season, might yet feel in some degree the effects of the general pressure; here and there he would encounter defaults, reorganizations, new and harder terms on old loans falling due and on fresh funds seeking investment. At all events, there are no cast-iron obstacles to the attainment of the immediate end of the universal strike: higher money wages.

As to the eventual outcome, the situation doubtless might be different. The forces which permanently determine distribution would come into play. To follow their working is not within the scope of the present inquiry, and is called for the less because economists are here much more nearly in agreement than they are on the machinery by which the result is brought about. The general rise in money wages (which may be assumed not to be offset by any corresponding change in general prices) would bring down the returns of the capitalist class. How the loss would be divided among the different members of this class, temporarily and even permanently, would be hard to foresee. Among the active capitalists, some would be at first hit harder than others; and the distribution of the loss among them, through the transfer of capital and the working of competition, would be no simple or certain matter. As between active capitalists and lending investors, in the course of the recurrent renewal of their loans and contracts, there would again be a tendency to distribution of the loss, whose outcome could not be clearly foreseen. At bottom, the mode in which these two classes would act in face of the loss would depend on whether the business men had been getting, before it set in, just enough to induce them to undergo the labor and risk of production; and whether the investors, in their turn had been receiving just enough to induce them to forego immediate expenditure and enjoyment.

On these limits the last word has perhaps not been said. The minimum which the two classes of capitalists, under a real dilemma between cessation of operations and submission to a smaller income, would accept, probably goes lower than is suggested in the usual expositions of this part of economic theory. But wider questions are here touched than those connected directly with the proximate sources of money wages, and it is not necessary to attempt to go further in their consideration. Some aspects of them will be touched again in the next chapter; and, at all events, enough has been said to indicate that they carry us far from the wages fund controversy proper.

From this digression we may return to the main subject, and summarize the results of the investigation up to this point. Briefly stated, the main conclusion so far has been, that for a season the resources immediately available for capitalists in their employment of laborers, while obviously not indefinitely extensible, are not limited or predetermined, and that the money-wages fund which goes to hired laborers is not a rigid one.

Next comes the question as to the source of real wages —the important and essential question as to the welfare of laborers. An increase of money wages is of no advantage unless there are more commodities to be bought. Are the commodities available at any given time predetermined in amount?

As to the source of real wages, it will be recalled, no distinction can be made between different classes of laborers or between different classes of the community. All alike, whatever the channel through which their money incomes are derived, get their real reward from the finished and enjoyable commodities which appear at the end of the lengthened processes of production. To this general proposition there is, indeed, an exception of some interest and importance. When savings are made, purchases for

immediate enjoyment do not take place. The proximate
source of real income is then not found in the flow of consumable commodities. The consideration of this case,
however, may be postponed. Let it be assumed that the
whole of money income is devoted to the purchase of
presently enjoyable things. On the elasticity or predetermination of the real income thus available for the community at large two sets of questions may be raised : one,
as to the limits of the total available for all ; the other,
as to the limits of the share which can go to wages.

First, as to the total real income of the community.
That this is at least in large degree predetermined, is obvious from a consideration of the form in which at any
moment it exists and the mode in which it recurrently appears. The form in which that part exists which is most
immediately available, is in the stocks of the retail dealers. It is here, in the great mass of cases, that money
income is converted into real income. The stocks which
the dealers possess are a given quantity. The reserves
of things ready for sale which are held by the wholesale
dealers and the manufacturers are again so much, and no
more. New supplies can be got only by working up more
materials ; and the materials on hand, as well as the tools
and machinery for working them up, are for the time
being unchangeable. Machinery can indeed be made to
work more or less quickly, and this suggests at once an
elastic rather than a rigid limit. But materials, such as
wool, cotton, hides, grain, timber, are usually dependent
for the variation of production on the return of the seasons ; and some considerable time must elapse before the
existing supplies can be substantially changed. What is
now available, and what will be available for a year or two
to come, has been determined once for all. If all the active
members of the community work harder or more effectively, they may secure more enjoyable things after a

space; but present income depends on the manner and the extent to which the earlier preparatory stages of production have been carried on.

Not only are the present available supplies so predetermined, but the tendency must be to arrange them in such manner as simply to meet the habitual rate of consumption, and leave no great margin or reserve. It may be suggested that in the stocks of merchants and producers there is a reserve fund which can be drawn on more or less rapidly, and which can be replenished from further reserves of half-finished goods and materials. Unquestionably such a reserve exists. The whole series of goods, from those barely begun to those almost finished, constitutes the stock from which the necessaries and comforts of the period must come; but the tendency of every individual holder of the stock is to have no more than is needed to meet the usual demands from consumers, or from the producers who stand next in the order of transmission to consumers. Every dealer keeps enough in stock to meet current demands, and tries to keep no more. It is to his advantage to diminish his holdings to the minimum consistent with satisfying his customers. For every business manager, whether merchant or manufacturer, a needlessly large stock similarly means a needlessly large committal of his funds. The nature of the trade and the accident of individual choice and judgment must affect the extent of the holdings in the different storehouses which contain the community's varied fund for more or less immediate enjoyment and subsistence; but the drift in all must be to accommodate the supplies to habitual and expected demands, and to keep no excess. If, therefore, a very rapid increase of consumption were suddenly to take place, a corresponding deficit would ere long appear. An increase in the productive power of the community can issue in a real increase of the sources of satisfaction only by giving the lengthened methods of production time to work out the result. It can not be anticipated by making immediate larger drafts on the existing supplies, for these are adapted only to meet the usual rate of consumption.

So much is in general true; but it is equally true that we can speak here only of tendencies and drifts, of limitations that hold good against great and rapid changes, but are not of a rigid and unalterable sort. The habitual stocks of dealers may be purchased by consumers a bit faster or a bit slower. Commodities on the way to completion may be hurried forward somewhat. Materials on hand may be drawn on more rapidly, and a period of scanty holdings may be tided over by some straining and ingenuity until fresh supplies can be made to appear. An increased satisfaction to consumers may be yielded by more elaborate manipulation of the materials already on hand. In various ways of this sort some stretching of the existing store of available goods is possible. That it has unmistakable limits, and not very distant limits, is not inconsistent with its being elastic within those limits. How great the degree of elasticity is, can not be stated in exact terms or measured by any conceivably practicable mode of statistical investigation.

On this topic, then, as on so many others in economics, we must be content with conclusions stated in general terms. The real income of the community for any season depends mainly on forces which have operated in the past. It is settled and predetermined, in the sense that it can be no greater than is made possible by the past labor given to machinery, to materials, to all the earlier stages of production. It is not made elastic by any great stocks kept in reserve beyond what the usual rate of consumption makes necessary. Yet it is not rigidly predetermined. It may become in some degree larger or smaller under the influence of forces coming into operation to-day; it is elastic within limits which, if not great, are not so small as to be safely set aside as of no practical import.

The second and narrower part of this question, as to the elasticity of that portion of the real income of the community which goes to wages, has been largely answered in what has been said on the broader topic.   Real wages are limited and predetermined in general as much as other sources of income, and no more.   Any force which is to bring about a substantial advance in the real remuneration which laborers shall get must bring about its effects through the slow-working machinery of production.   Like other classes, they may get some immediate increase of real enjoyment by a defter use, a better combination, the temporary bridging over of gaps, in the existing resources ; but a considerable advance must begin at the beginning, and go through the orderly stages of the successive steps which lead to the final attainment of a consumable commodity.

In this regard it is immaterial what is the form of the remuneration of the laborer : whether he gets his wages from an employer once for all, or earns an independent income which is substantially all of it return for present exertion, or gets a mixed income which is in good part resolvable into interest or rent.   Whatever the channel through which his income in money first comes, it is spent on an elastic but by no means indeterminate mass of finished commodities.

Still a further question presents itself : Is the share of real income which the laborers can get, as compared with the total available for all classes, more flexible than this total itself ?   It is conceivable that though the whole income of the community were predetermined within narrow limits, the part of it which some members got might be very flexible, swelling or diminishing according to forces of immediate operation.   Something may be said as to the situation of the laborers in this aspect of the case.

The first step in such a changed division of the total income must be an advance in money wages. This we may suppose to have been effected, as to hired laborers, within the limits already set forth as to the possible money advances which they can secure from their immediate employers; as to others, within the limits made possible by the conditions of demand for the things they have to dispose of. The money wages, in whatever manner obtained, go to the purchase of commodities the whole mass of which is not susceptible of rapid enlargement. If, now, among the mass, the commodities which they can buy and will buy are of a particular kind, of different materials, and of different fashioning from those sought by other classes, their share is as much predetermined as the whole supply. If, on the other hand, they buy very much the same sorts of things that their employers and other supposed betters buy, they can get a larger slice of real income at once.

Evidently a great existing inequality of wealth, and a great disparity of tastes and habits, would make the substantial change more slow and difficult of accomplishment. More democratic conditions would make it more rapid and easy. As between the great mass of manual laborers and the well-to-do, the disparity of tastes and habits is in most communities considerable, and a great shift of the real sources of satisfaction from the one to the other could not easily take place. There is, to be sure, a large constituency among the well-to-do whose members do work for their living and get a return which, while euphemistically termed salary or income, is as clearly wages as is the pay of the day laborer. As between these and the prosperous receivers of interest and rent there can be nothing in the way of a predetermined separation of the real sources of income. Even as between the manual laborers with whom the word wages is usually associated, and the well-to-do classes who are separated from them by habits of greater ease and usually higher culture, the line of cleavage as to commodities bought is not unmistakable. There is some margin of interchangeable things, broader or narrower according to the more or less democratic character of the society. The staples of food are alike for nearly all the members of the advanced communities of our day, and many materials forming a large part of the available supplies of a season can be worked up in one fashion or another to meet at short notice the tastes of the eventual consumers.

Thus we find again limits that are elastic, not rigid. The total real income of the community, while predetermined in the rough, has some degree of elasticity. The share of real income which shall go to wages in general, or to wages of the great mass of manual laborers, is to a certain extent predetermined by the character of the commodities on hand or in the making. But in no small degree it is indistinguishable and inseparable, forming part of a mass of things that may be diverted to one set of persons or another according to their command of money income for the time being.

The question has sometimes been raised, in the course of the controversy over the wages fund, whether laborers can get an immediate or early benefit from the results of improvements made at the time when their wages are earned. On the one hand, it has been maintained that a general increase in the productiveness of labor, due to advance in the arts or to greater strenuousness or intelligence among the workmen, inures to their advantage at once. On the other hand, it has been denied that they can secure an immediate gain. In essentials, the reasoning of the preceding pages clearly supports the negative answer. The solid effects of greater efficiency in production can appear only after the interval made inevitable by the complex and slow-working machinery of production. Improvements now made do not inure to the benefit of present real wages: always subject to what has been said as to the degree of elasticity which does exist in the sources of real income. But this holds good of wages, simply because it holds good of all real income. It is the total volume of ripening real income which is determined by the causes of the past. Advances in the arts increase the total more or less rapidly, according to the point at which they take effect in the successive stages of production and the extent to which they require a larger supply of supplementary tools or materials for their full fruition. It would be a rare case in which a considerable interval must not elapse before a sensible effect on the flow of consumable commodities could appear. If the extreme case of a sudden doubling of all productive efficiency be supposed, it may be said with confidence that laborers and others would not receive at once, or for some little time to come, a double portion of real income.

There is another possibility, and a significant one, of more practical importance in regard to other forms of income than those usually called wages, but not without its importance for wages also. It has been assumed hitherto that money income is spent as soon as received, and goes at once to the purchase of consumable commodities. But purchases may be postponed and savings made: a modification in the assumed conditions which we may now proceed to consider.

The simplest form of saving is hoarding; and it is an easy matter to trace the modifications which would ensue from hoarding. The real income for labor comes when the money income is spent. If it is spent a year after the work is done, the consumable commodities then existing are the source of real income. In the meanwhile, some of these commodities may have become more abundant and cheaper; in which case wages, as to the part postponed, are subject to the conditions of supply of the later date, not to those existing at the time when the work was done. So far as the conversion of money wages into real wages is put off, the laborers thus have a clear field for participation in the results of improvements going on while they work, or in those of greater strenuousness of their own labor.

But the usual form of saving in modern communities is investment, not hoarding. Investment means, not a postponement of all purchases, but only a postponement of direct purchases for immediate enjoyment. Through one or another of the many channels which modern society offers, the funds saved are turned over to the active managers of industry: through the savings bank of the poor, or the purchase of securities by the well-to-do, or the operations of life-insurance societies. By the active capitalists who thus get control of the funds, they are used for the purchase of materials, plant, labor, as their judgment suggests. They are additions to the funds that would in any case be turned in these directions for the maintenance of existing capital. They go in part to wages; and in so far they are not abstracted from the money income which goes for the season to the purchase of finished commodities, but simply shifted from hand to hand. In the long run, indeed, not the part only, but the sum total of the invested savings, goes to wages, by a succession of advances to labor; but this holds good only of the operations of a lengthened cycle. For any one season, the process of investment means, in large part, the purchase of inchoate wealth, or real capital. Such inchoate wealth is usually on hand to meet the new demand. Not only is enough being produced to make good the waste of existing capital as it wears away or becomes useless, but additional supplies of real capital are constantly being made in our modern communities, in anticipation of the fresh accumulation of individual capital. New investment, as well as reinvestment, takes place so regularly that the concrete change in the community's possessions has usually taken place before the decisive committal of his means to accumulation has been made by the individual investor.　Saving thus usually means a transfer of purchasing power from the immediate receiver of money income to other hands.　Partly it means a transfer to the laborers whom the managing capitalists may employ with the additional funds, and thus a simple shift in the demand for consumable goods; partly it means the buying of tools and materials, and so a real postponement, for the time being at least, of any purchase of enjoyable things at all.

As to the individual saver, the postponement is usually permanent.　He does not ordinarily avail himself of the recurrent opportunity for spending which comes as the loans made to the active managers fall due.　He reinvests, repeating the decision to save.　He spends only the money income handed over to him as interest on his accumulations.　With this he becomes each year (assuming that he does not again save out of income) a purchaser of real income, and a sharer in the inflowing supplies of consumable goods.　The quantity and quality of these supplies may vary from year to year, and the possibilities of his real income may thus vary.　But so far as the reward for his labor is concerned, he is independent of those present limitations on real income which we have found to exist for such as spend their whole money income at once for the satisfaction of immediate wants.

How great is the importance of this additional element of elasticity in the real reward of labor must depend on the extent to which savings are in fact made from money wages. As to the great mass of hired laborers, and even the great mass of those independent workmen, in agriculture and in the crafts, to whom also we commonly apply the term wages, the savings are probably very small as compared with their total earnings. More especially is this the case with hired laborers. It is true, the accumulations in the savings banks of the more advanced countries form an imposing mass; but they are to be compared with the much more imposing mass of the total earnings of the laborers. They come only in part from savings by receivers of wages; and in any case they are small as compared with the whole sum which is paid in wages. It can not be far from the truth to say that virtually the whole of the wages of hired manual laborers is spent at once on consumable commodities, and therefore is subject to the causes by which the supply of consumable commodities is so largely predetermined.

The class in society as to whom the fact of saving is of most importance is that of the successful managing capitalists or business men. It is from them that the largest habitual accumulations of capital are derived. Hired laborers may save a bit from their wages; independent laborers, when prosperous, may save a bit more. The investor, again, getting his fixed income from a capital which is expected to remain intact, is likely to put aside only a small part of his receipts. The professional classes of lawyers, physicians, and the like, do indeed usually save some considerable proportion of their income. But the active managers of industry, more than any other set of men, find the main object of their ambition and the one test of their success in "making money"; in acquiring larger money rights than they spend; in accumulating, and in adding to their possessions. The prosperous business man sets aside for the enlargement of his wealth a greater proportion of his income than any other member of society; and of the total accumulations of fresh capital for the community, the greatest part probably comes from the eagerness of this class to acquire permanent wealth. While he is still in harness, the possessions of the active capitalist usually consist in large part of inchoate wealth directly owned, and of claims against fellow business men, offset more or less by cross-claims; the whole having an uncertain value, depending on the outcome of the operations still in progress. Each one, as he reaches the point (if ever he reaches it) where he thinks he has a competency, begins to wind up his enterprises, converts his possessions mainly into obligations due him by those who are still active in business, and retires to the position of a dependent investor. If he does not retire himself, his children are likely to do so. The existing generation of active capitalists gives way to a new generation, equally intent on large gains and large accumulations.

The fact of saving and postponed enjoyment thus leads to qualifications of our main conclusions chiefly in regard to the well-to-do classes, and, among those, most strikingly in regard to the successful business man. Those who save are *pro tanto* free from the conditions of present supply which, within greater or smaller limits, cause the available real income of all classes in society to be in some degree predetermined. The largest savers and the largest accumulators of capital are the successful men of affairs. These, then, may be said in a sense to have the most elastic, the least predetermined, real reward for their labor.

It need not be remarked that, in speaking of a predetermination of any sort, as to wages or any form of income, reference is made to wages in the mass, or other income in the mass. To say that the real wages of any

particular set of laborers are predetermined, would be an
entirely different proposition. The whole wages fund discussion,—the whole discussion of the relation of capital
to wages or other forms of income,—applies to the general phenomenon, not to the particular. But of this qualification or explanation more will be said in the next and
concluding chapter, whose object it will be to make clear,
in other respects also, the scope and significance of the
conclusions that have been reached.

CHAPTER V.

SOME CONCLUSIONS.

THE wages fund doctrine proper has now been done with, and, strictly, the end of our task has been reached. But there are some aspects of distribution at large so closely connected with the *pros* and *cons* of the wages fund controversy that they come within the scope even of an inquiry directed, as this is, to a very limited part of the general subject. There are some questions, also, as to the practical bearings of the discussion and its outcome, which call for careful consideration. These somewhat disconnected topics will serve also to make clear the significance and limitations of the conclusions reached, and the kind of aid which a discussion of the wages fund question can yield to economic theory in general.

It will be convenient to begin with the questions as to the practical bearing of the conclusions which have been reached in the preceding chapters. The general reader, and even the economist most intent on the larger generalizations of his subject, will not fail to ask himself, what light do these discussions throw on living subjects? What help do they give in reaching answers as to the right and wrong, the chances of success or failure, of strikes and lockouts? What basis do they give for settling disputes by arbitration or conciliation?

It may be said at once that the answer must be a disappointing one. The conclusions of the economist as to

the theoretical relations of wages and capital have little or no bearing on the disputes between laborers and
capitalists as they usually appear in the specific case.
Though students of economic principles may see, without
further discussion, the meaning and justification of this
apparently paradoxical answer, a more detailed explanation may not be unwelcome to one or another set of
readers.

Something was said, in the last chapter, as to the
elasticity of the sources whence wages come, and as to
the possibility of an immediate general rise at any given
moment. The conclusion, whether as to money wages or
real wages, was against any rigid predetermination of the
funds whence the total wages of a given period are derived. But, as was then noted, this result is of value rather
as illustrating the significance and the limitations of our
general reasoning, than as answering any questions likely
to arise in specific form. The attempt at a simultaneous
advance in wages all along the line never is made. An
all-inclusive combination of hired laborers (and to their
case, for obvious reasons, the discussion can be confined)
is not indeed inconceivable or impossible, but it is in the
highest degree improbable. What takes place in fact in
the dealings of workmen with their employers is a succession of isolated bargains and struggles. First one set of
laborers, then another, strives for an advance; the practical question is as to the limits and obstacles which may
be encountered by such separate endeavors.

It did indeed occur, in the older literature of our subject, that this sort of case was considered with reference
to the relations of wages and capital in general. It was
sometimes said that, while the laborers of a particular
trade might very possibly get an advance of wages in
consequence of a union and a strike, the advance would
take so much more out of the general wages fund, and

would thus be secured at the expense of the rest of the laborers. Such reasoning proceeded on the basis of a fixed fund, unalterable at the moment, whence alone laborers could be paid; it followed that if some got more, others must get less. It was not often made clear whether a money wages fund or a real wages fund was had in mind; nor was it explained how long the offsetting loss would continue, or what forces might tend to make it endure or disappear.*

Some degree of theoretic truth there may be in this reasoning. The reader will remember that while the source of wages, whether of money wages or of real wages, is elastic, it is elastic within limits. It is then true that a very great rise in the reward of a considerable set of laborers would take place, at least for a while, to the detriment of other laborers. As to money wages, the funds which the body of employers can turn to the hire of laborers are not indeed rigidly predetermined. They can be stretched to a certain extent, and can meet some new demands without curtailment in other directions; but any very great increase in the funds turned over to one group of laborers, carried far enough, must diminish those which go to the rest. The case with real wages, while presenting some variations, is in essentials the same. The flow of consumable goods whence all real income, whether wages or any other form of return, must come, is similarly elastic within limits. A rise in the money wages of a given group (taking place very possibly without a diminution in the money wages of others) would bring an increase in the total purchases of commodities by consumers. True, the new demand, if not very great, could be met by some hastening and stretching of the

---

* An unequivocal example of this sort of reasoning is in Mill's *Political Economy;* see the discussion of the passage *infra* at pp. 233–235.

existing supplies of goods nearly finished or half finished. On the other hand, if any large group of laborers suddenly had the means of buying much more than before,—so much more that no stretching of the commodities available would suffice to meet their added demands,—less would be left for the others. Only, in this case, the losers would not necessarily be other laborers; they might be any receivers of money income. Who would lose, would thus depend on the kind and amount of commodities which are bought with their new money means by the fortunate laborers, and on the response of prices and supplies to their new demand.

These conclusions are of the hopelessly inexact sort which exasperate the practical man, desirous of answers so precise as to admit of immediate concrete application. No one can say whether an advance of five, or ten, or twenty per cent in the wages of all the employees in textile industries, would cause a diminution either of money wages or of real wages for the rest of the laborers. To draw an exact line,—to say that so many millions of dollars and so many tons of goods, so much and no more, can be got without passing beyond the elastic limits of the general sources,—this is impossible. But it is safe to say that in concrete life it happens very rarely, probably never, that a specific rise in wages, secured by strike or trades-union pressure or simple agreement, can be shown to bring any offsetting loss in the wages of those not directly concerned. The sums involved in any particular case, though they may be absolutely large, are small in comparison with the total which must be considered if the general effects are to be examined. A rise of ten per cent in the wages of coal miners or of iron workers may mean a matter of millions, and yet is only a small fraction of total wages payments and of total purchases of real income by consumers at large. The chances are that such

an advance would bring real gain to the laborers involved, without loss to any of their fellows.   Doubtless,
if all the consequences of the change could be infallibly
traced, some justification for the misgivings of the writers
of the older school might be found.   It might appear that
the immediate employers were crippled by the added expenses, and had less to spend in hiring other sorts of workmen; or that the banks, which advanced them the funds
for this expense among others, had less to lend to other
employers.   These are possibilities of the sort which the
ultra-conservative would be disposed to make much of.
But it is out of the question in any concrete case to follow all the might-have-beens, or trace the have-beens in
their rapid interlacing with other forces and events.   The
chances, to repeat, are against any traceable loss which
would offset the visible gain.   Certainly an unbiased and
judicious adviser, having the interest of all laborers at
heart, would hesitate long before counselling any particular set of laborers against an endeavor to get better terms
from their employers, on the ground that as an ulterior
result of success, some of their fellows might suffer.   If
no other objection than this presented itself, he could safely
assert that economic science had nothing to say against
their endeavors, and much in favor of them.

The substantial obstacles which may prevent a rise in
wages are to be found in another direction.   The man of
affairs would say that the success of a move for higher
wages depended on the state of trade and prices.   The
economist would say the same thing in different language,
by laying it down that consumers' demand, or demand for
commodities, mainly determined the share of income which
could be got by any one group of laborers.   Let us follow
in brief review the chain of forces which would come into
play in such a case.

Proximately, the success or failure of an attempt to

get higher wages will depend much on the accidents of the particular situation. The extent to which the employers happen at the moment to be tied by contracts; the temper or pugnacity of one party or the other; the organization, the discipline, the available funds on either side, —such surface causes may decide the outcome in any given case. Forces of this sort are too often forgotten by the economists, intent as they are on the deeper currents of the industrial stream.

Even the forces next in order, likely to be referred to by the thoughtful man of affairs and the well-informed financial writer, are often neglected by the economists. The cautious everyday observer would describe these less accidental causes by saying that the success of the laborers' effort depended on the state of the market: whether sales and profits were such as to make the employer prefer the additional expense of a higher wages bill to the loss of a satisfactory season's trade. This, again, must depend largely on the expectations and previsions of the larger body of active capitalists of whom the direct employers are but one part. If the merchants, speculators, bankers, lenders, are all hopeful and eager, then trade will be good and the workmen may get a substantial slice of the profits of good times. Their share would probably be substantial, because not likely to go beyond the limits to which the real wages fund of available commodities could be stretched, and because they are likely to spend at once and so convert their money gains into immediate real enjoyment; whereas their employers, who habitually postpone the fruition of a large part of their income, may be overtaken by a financial revulsion before realizing and pocketing their profits.

Beyond such a stage as this in the play of social forces, the calculations and prophecies of those immediately concerned, whether workmen or employers, do not usually go. Only the most shrewd and thoughtful among them will go a step further, and point out that in the end the success of any particular group of workmen in permanently retaining a substantial advance in wages must depend on whether the consumers of the goods they make can and will pay more for them. The economist will say the same thing, though probably with a more distinct conception of who are consumers and what constitutes consumers' demand. The man of affairs thinks of almost any buyers as consumers: the woollen manufacturer is a consumer of wool, and the shivering individual who buys a coat is a consumer of woollens. The careful economist thinks of the latter alone,—of the person who has immediate wants to satisfy, who weighs one want against another, and is in truth the only real consumer. His purchases are made at the counter of the retail shopkeeper. Evidently he is separated by a long and complicated series of middlemen from the various workmen whose successive efforts have combined in producing the final enjoyable commodity. Whether his demand is such as to make possible a rise in the wages of some or all of the workmen who have so combined, is to be ascertained not by the ups and downs of a season or two, but by a stretch of experience which to the man of business seems of secular length. The economists who have insisted on consumers' demand as a determining cause or source of wages have not always set forth with sufficient emphasis the distance between the consumer and the chain of producers who combine to work for him. They have spoken of consumers' demand as a cause closely affecting wages,—misled perhaps by an unconscious confusion between proximate purchasers and ultimate consumers. But it remains true that, in the end, the wages which any particular group of workmen can get depend on what the consumers are able and willing to pay for the commodities produced, and that a real, steady, and permanent rise in wages can be got by such a group only if the permanent conditions of the market—that is, of ultimate demand—are favorable to them.

Something more will be said of consumers' demand in another place. This factor in the situation has played a curious and interesting part in the development of economic thought, elsewhere to be considered in detail.* Here it will suffice to point out, what follows clearly enough from the reasoning of the preceding chapters, that it bears only on the wages obtainable by a particular set of laborers. The older economists had a fashion of expounding with elaborate emphasis the theorem that demand for commodities was not demand for labor, but only determined the direction of the demand for labor. They were right, even though they put their theorem in terms and with applications that made the result seem paradoxical to the practical man. Consumers' demand, or demand for commodities, is the important force to be considered when we inquire whether and how a given set of workmen can get better wages,—whether more money wages, or their probable concomitant of more real wages. This is the last force involved in the specific struggles of the industrial world; for in practise we do not meet the attempt at a general advance in all wages. Yet the general advance alone would involve those wider questions as to the source of wages at large, and the relation of all wages to capital, which form the subject of the wages fund controversy. The form in which the concrete social question appears is in the efforts of this or that set of particular workmen, whose success will depend on the factors of closer or remoter operation which have just been described : on the accidents of the moment, on the state of trade, on consumers' demand.

---

* See Part II, Chapter XIII.

This analysis would need to be pushed still further if all the problems involved were to get their due share of attention. Back of consumers' demand there are other forces, or other phases of the same forces. Consumers' demand, or the play of supply and demand as to enjoyable commodities, can be translated into terms of final utility, and can lead to that psychological analysis which has played so large a part in recent economic discussion. On the other hand, the extent to which laborers or their children can transfer their exertions from one industrial group to another; the nature and permanence of the obstacles in the way of such transfer; the chances of an eventual equalizing tendency, if the conditions of consumers' demand have raised or lowered the returns of any one group,—here are other important aspects of the case. According as we do or do not conclude that an equalizing process exists, we get a different result as to the ultimate determining causes of the exchange values of commodities.* Every phase of the most intricate problems of value, as well as of production and distribution, would thus present itself before the final answer could be given to the questions raised by those successive isolated contests between laborers and employers which are carried on in the actual world.

---

* If there is effective movement from group to group among laborers, value is determined in the end primarily by the sacrifice involved in labor, that is, by real cost of production ; while relative wages depend on the intrinsic attractiveness of different sorts of work. If there is not effective movement from group to group, value and relative wages are both determined in the end by the final utility of the consumable commodities produced. In the recent discussions of the fundamental laws of value, the important bearing of the presence or absence of free choice of occupation by laborers has been strangely neglected. But, to repeat what is said in the text, questions of this sort,—perhaps the most difficult which the economist has to deal with,—carry us far from the immediate relation of capital and wages.

All this, however, would carry us further and further from the subject in hand, and the object of the digression into the field of particular wages and of value has perhaps been sufficiently attained. As the causes that affect the share of income and enjoyment accruing to particular classes of society are different from those that affect the income of society as a whole, so the causes that determine the share which a particular set of laborers shall have are different from those that determine the total that goes to laborers as a whole. It is only with the total that the wages fund or the discussion of wages and capital has to do. In the nature of the case, the practical questions and the concrete social problems which press for immediate attention are more likely to be of the particular sort. They are questions as to the wages of one trade, one group, one district ; struggles between the employers and workmen of a given time and place, affected by the accidents of temper, and the turns of trade often no less accidental, as well as by the remoter operation of consumers' demand and final utility. On such topics the economist is not helpless ; he may be able to give judicious advice, or at all events to bring a calm and farseeing mind to the consideration of the particular case. But the wages fund, and the theoretical relations of wages and capital, will not help him at all.

We may pass now to the other group of topics mentioned at the beginning of this chapter; namely, as to the connection between the wages fund controversy and some wider questions as to distribution. The relation of capital to wages has been much discussed, in recent years, in close association with another important subject,—the precise manner in which the machinery of distribution works, and more particularly the sense in which one or another share is to be regarded as residual. Here also the inquiry will lead to subjects far removed from that of the present essay : serving again to illustrate the limitations rather than the applications of its main conclusions.

A brief historical sketch will most conveniently introduce this part of the discussion. In the Ricardian analysis of distribution, profits were the residual element. Rent was fixed, very simply, by the differences between the natural sites in use. Wages, determined in the first instance by the ratio of capital to population, were fixed over any period but the shortest, by the standard of living or by what was "necessary" to maintain the laborers. Profits got the rest, and thus were the residual element in distribution; profits meaning what was got by capitalists actively engaged in the conduct of industry. In the long run profits would doubtless be affected by the rate of accumulation, and by the disposition of capitalists to accept a larger or smaller reward ; but this only by a slow-working process. Virtually, profits got what did not go to wages or to rent.

As time went on, as less abstract modes of investigation made their way, as the march of concrete events brought with it an unmistakable rise in general wages, a different mode of describing the working of distribution was gradually adopted. The return to capital was described as depending on the effective desire of accumulation, and was associated more closely with the inactive investor whose revenue comes solely and simply as a recompense for saving or waiting. Profits, in this sense, being fixed by the strength of the disposition to save, wages became more variable, and got the benefit of any general increase in the output of industry. This shift in the point of view was introduced insensibly, and at first without any change in the old doctrine as to the payment of wages from capital ; the change being simply in the assumption that the amount of capital turned over to la-

borers accommodated itself quickly and easily to variations in what the laborers produced.*

Next, when the wages fund doctrine had been effectively attacked and undermined, it was a natural step
to describe the laborers, already given a residual position in essentials, as the direct and immediate receivers of
so much of the product of industry as did not go elsewhere. The other sharers got parts sliced off in accord
with principles supposed to be settled. The receivers of
wages were then the residual holders in the distribution
of total income, with or without a further carving-out of
employers' profits from the general mass. Thus we have
the residual theory of wages, which during the last ten
years has been so much in vogue.

But if the description of the machinery of distribution
given in the preceding pages is accurate, this new version
of the industrial situation is not tenable; not tenable,
that is, as a description of the facts of modern industry.
More especially, it is not in accordance with the facts of
that case which is chiefly had in mind by every one who
discusses the economics of modern times,—the *régime* of
employing capitalists and hired workmen.

We have seen that, directly, the hired laborers, and
the inactive investors as well, get stipulated money shares.
They take no chances; they have been promised so much,
and so much they receive,—barring bankruptcy on the
part of the managing employer. Under the conditions
which prevail so preponderantly in the modern industrial
world, the true residual sharer, certainly in the first instance, is the active capitalist, the business man. He has
made his bargains for stipulated payments to investors
and to laborers. Usually he has interlacing obligations
with other business men which affect his operations, past

---

* Compare what is said below, Part II, Chapter XII, toward the end.

and future, so intricately that he can know where he stands only by elaborate and sometimes deceptive book-keeping. Indeed, he rarely knows where he really stands: for how much he is finally to secure, depends on the outcome of operations still in progress. But what proves to be left is his own. He wins or loses, according as the industrial venture turns out well or ill. Doubtless what he finally gets, or, in the phrase of the business world, what he makes, is not a simple income such as the economist of the present day would label with a single word. Ricardo would have called it profits, simply. A writer of the present generation would describe it, with a view to final classification and explanation, as consisting partly of interest on his own capital invested, partly of wages for work done; these wages, again, being susceptible of elaborate analysis, according to distinctions sometimes substantial and sometimes fanciful. But, however classified, and however susceptible or unsusceptible of accurate measurement at any given time, the income of the season appears as a net sum, the residual outcome of the operations of the season. The hired laborer gets his fixed wages, the investor his stipulated income: the managing business man takes the rest.

No doubt, as to independent laborers, the description of their situation as residual is accurate; but it fits the case, not because they are laborers, but because they are independent producers. They are owners of part of the gross output of society. They sell what they turn out, and so become holders in the first instance of part of the money income of society. They may have wages to pay, or interest or rent to meet: what is left is then their own. In their case, as in that of their fellow business managers on a larger scale, the gains received may be resolvable, when analyzed with regard to permanent causes, into wages and interest and rent. It may be a question, too,

how far the returns for labor, which are received by the
petty independent workmen, are in essentials similar to
the wages of the hired laborers, and how far they are
to be classed with the net returns for work which the
great employers earn. But their place in the direct process of distribution is the same as that of the business
man with whom business earnings or business profits are
usually associated.

If, then, setting aside the case of the independent workman carrying on operations in such small ways as to de-
prive him of the dignity of the capitalist's place, we attend
to that part of the community's industry which is conducted on a large scale by business managers, we have a
result bearing some surface resemblance to Ricardo's.
The net gains of this class, which he called profits, are the
direct residual element. The resemblance to Ricardo's
version of the case, however, is obviously more apparent
than real. He reached his conclusions by reasoning which
assumed wages to be fixed and unvarying: and the residual position of profits held good, if not as the definitive
outcome of distribution, at least for very considerable
periods. In the reasoning just set forth that residual
position is assigned to the business manager simply in the
first stage of distribution : in the division of that money
income which is the first step toward the concrete assign-
ment to one hand or to another of the real income of the
community.

So much is direct and unquestionable fact. If it be
maintained that the independent producer,—that is, under
typical modern conditions, the managing capitalist,—is not
the residual sharer of the social income, regard must be
had to some other than the first steps in distribution,—to
some later and more obscure steps. But in analyzing
such further steps, it is indispensable to keep close to the
facts of the living world, and to follow the concrete man-

ner in which income reaches the hands of those who are to enjoy it. The first actual step in the process by which the distribution of income takes place in the modern world is the payment of money sums by the business man to laborers and investors, and the retention in his own hands of the residual share.

Consider now the case as to real income. This reaches the member of an advanced society only by the expenditure of money income. Is there any ground for treating the real income of the community and of its various members in a different manner from their money income?

In the stage that immediately follows the distribution of money income, it would seem that no ground for a different statement of the case can be found. The finished and enjoyable commodities which are coming to market in a continuous stream constitute the real income which brings substantial satisfaction. The total volume of the stream is settled by the efficiency of a succession of productive efforts made in the past. The quality and quantity of the individual constituents have been adapted to satisfy the expected tastes and means of consumers. The money income which reaches various hands goes to the purchase of the inflowing commodities. Produced though these must have been with regard to the probable demand of purchasers, no precise determination of shares to one or another kind of income can appear; least of all can any part be said to be residual. None of the real income is settled in advance to be wages, or interest, or rent, or employers' profits. There is no residual share at all: there is a miscellaneous assortment of commodities which go to one person or another, according to the money means and the money expenditure of each one. In fact, the conception of a residual share would seem to be applicable only to the case of money income. There is nothing corresponding to it in the machinery by which real enjoyable income is secured.

There is still another sense in which a residual share may be spoken of. It might be maintained that one or another set of persons secure the main benefit of advances in the arts; not by any direct or quick-working process, but as the permanent outcome of the forces which eventually shape distribution. They would thus be in a position to receive what is left after other classes have received their settled shares. It may be contended that the laborers have the residual place in this sense; the incomes going to capitalists and rent-receivers being so determined by permanent forces that the progress of industry inures mainly to the laborers' benefit. Or it may be asserted, with the socialists, that the condition of the laborers tends to remain unimproved as the arts advance, and that the well-to-do classes,—investors, business men, and rent-receivers taken together,—monopolize the material gains of advancing civilization.

We are concerned here chiefly with the relation which these divergent views as to the permanent outcome of the march of progress bear to the wages fund discussion; and the answer is simply that the relation is *nil*. The residual position of laborers or of others, in this sense, has nothing to do with that direct and immediate relation of wages to capital which gave rise to the wages fund doctrine. Wages may be paid from capital or from product, may come from a rigid or an elastic fund of capital: whatever the answer, it will throw light only on the machinery by which their remuneration is secured, not on the nature and relative strength of the forces which move the machinery. If we would know whether the tendency in an advancing society is for the receivers of wages or interest or rent to become the chief beneficiaries of improvement, we must inquire as to the causes which in the long run determine the one or other sort of income. As to interest, for example, the inquiry must be mainly as to the promptness with which accumulation responds to a higher or lower rate of return. If capital is saved and invested rapidly when a certain rate of return is exceeded, and if its accumulation is promptly checked when that rate is not yielded, we may say that interest is fixed by a constant force at one point, and that the share of income going to the owners of capital is determined by a simple multiplication of the principal by the rate. Again, as to the earnings of managing business men (if these are to be regarded as a distinct class, as doubtless for many purposes they must be), we should need to consider, first, how great a degree of regularity and conformity to law exists in this special form of income; next, how far the qualities which mainly enable it to be earned are the result of education and training, how far of the traditions and the environment of the well-to-do classes, how far of varying degrees of inborn and unchangeable ability. On such lines we might reach a conclusion as to the extent to which this sort of return is likely to be kept at a fixed point. The examples need not be pushed further. What has been said suffices to indicate how the permanent causes which determine the distribution of income must be followed if we would know whether one class or another gets greater or less gain from the general progress of society. The cool and unbiased observer would probably find it equally difficult to accept either the optimistic view which makes the laborer, if only he be intelligent and alert, the chief beneficiary of the advance, or the pessimistic view which represents him as hopelessly excluded, under the *régime* of private property, from any real improvement in his·lot. However this might be, he would find no ground for one conclusion or the other from the analysis of capital and wages, or from the position of hired laborers and other laborers with relation to past product and inchoate wealth. The wages fund discussion, stripped of non-essentials, throws light simply on the process by which, in any advanced organization of the productive arts, the yield of an intricate succession of efforts finally reaches the consumer and becomes real income. What in the end determines real income and its apportionment to one class in society or another, is a very different question, or, rather, a mass of different questions, much less easy to answer, and at all events involving other and wider premises.

Nevertheless, by way of illustrating still further the relation between the permanent forces of distribution and the channels through which they work out their effects, we may follow in rapid review, on the lines of the reasoning presented in the last chapter, the mode in which a change in the permanent forces may bring about, proximately or remotely, a rise in general wages.

Money income, which, as the key to real income, must be followed in any such review, goes directly and in the first instance to the independent producers, and among these, in more or less complete preponderance in different communities, to the capitalist employers. Through their hands it passes to the others, hired workmen and investors, whose incomes have been classed as dependent. The most effective way in which any considerable and permanent change to the advantage of laborers can come about is by causes which increase this proximate source of their income; either through directly larger receipts accruing in the hands of active capitalists, or through the less direct process of larger money sums being turned over to the capitalists by investors. It may be admitted that, even in the absence of conditions swelling these sums, a general rise in wages is not impossible. The money means which employers can advance to laborers are not fixed or predetermined; the residual share which they are to retain is probably not at the absolute minimum, and certainly is not fixed by any rigid law; and well-directed pressure on them may squeeze out something which the laborers would not otherwise get. But it is still true that the money funds which the active employers can turn over to laborers are at any given time subject to a limit which, even though it be elastic, is not distant; and that a considerable and permanent gain in general money wages can come only when larger money means flow into the hands of the employing class.

This holds good, whatever the causes of the larger money means: even though it be only a greater plentifulness of money or of its substitutes. A general advance in prices, due to monetary causes, inures first to those who have products to sell. It reaches those who are in receipt of dependent incomes only by a secondary process, which usually works out its results after a longer or shorter interval. No phenomenon is more familiar in monetary history than the slow advance of money wages, as compared with the prices of goods, when a sudden increase of inconvertible money causes a depreciation of the circulating medium. This is not a necessity of the case; but it is a result which, obviously, is very likely to ensue from the position of the active manager of industry at the primary source of money income. When a general advance in total money income takes place by some more gradual process, it goes again first to the managing producers, and through their hands is again transferred, more or less slowly, to those whose incomes are derivatory.

An increase in the total money revenue of the community may bring also a substantial gain in its real revenue of consumable goods. Thus a more ample production of goods may sell for a larger total, even though prices are declining; the increase in quantity more than offsetting the decline in prices. Such has been the course of events during the last generation in almost all civilized countries. The larger gross money incomes of the active managers of industry, brought about in this way, have been the source of that unmistakable rise in money wages, as well as in other sorts of income, which has taken place concurrently with the fall in prices. Whether the position of the active capitalists at the starting point of the gain has enabled them to reap advantages similar to those which they almost invariably get from a sudden rise in prices, is not easily to be ascertained. The probabilities are that some substantial pickings have not failed, for a time at least, to remain in their hands. The optimist may assert, not without a good show of reason, that such gains are the justified reward of the initiative taken by the business man in those multiform improvements of the arts whose accumulated effect has been the general increase of well-being; while the philosophic observer may accept them as the outcome, inevitable even though not always agreeable, of the *régime* of private property, taking their place among the mixed results whose balance on the whole serves to justify the existing order of things. However this may be, the fact of the case is that the increase of the money receipts of the active managers of industry has been the proximate source and the main cause of the gain in secondary money incomes. The general and continued advance in money wages could not have taken place if the money inflow to the capitalist employers had not also enlarged.

No doubt, side by side with the general progress of the arts which has increased the total income of the community, other causes may have been at work to divert a larger part of that income to the laborers: causes which might have led to a result similar in kind, though less marked in degree, even if there had been no general prog-

ress.   The interest which from time to time has been paid
to investors may have been such as to move these latter
to save more, and put more money means into the hands
of the active business class.   The residual income which
has been retained by that class, again, may have been so
great and so tempting as to induce them directly or indirectly to enlarge their ventures.   From either source would
come larger money means for industrial operations, and
so the proximate causes of a rise in money wages : always
supposing the number of hired laborers remains the same,
or does not increase as much as the funds directed to
their hire.   How far the advance in money wages has in
fact been due simply to the general advance in production and in the community's total income; how far an
increasing disposition to accumulate and invest among
capitalists, active and idle, has had its share; how far
trades unions have been efficacious in securing for laborers a quicker and greater advance than unorganized workmen could have got,—these must be matters largely of
conjecture.   The facts of the situation, so far as they can
be made out, would seem to warrant no large generalizations as to the absorption of the whole gain by one class
in society or another, and so confirm neither an optimistic nor a pessimistic view as to any residual shares.   All
hands have gained, and the proximate cause of the gain
for all has been in the general and continued increase of
the gross revenues which flow first into the hands of capitalist employers.

Continuing such an investigation as to the mode in
which the condition of hired laborers may advance and
has advanced, we should have to consider real wages : the
flow of consumable goods to whose purchase money income is devoted.   That flow, so far as the production of
one or another sort of commodity is concerned, follows
the apportionment of money income; not indeed with

mechanical exactness, but, given time, with sufficiently accurate response. The traders buy, and the more distant producers turn out, such finished goods as are demanded by the purchasing consumers. For any one season the quantity and quality of consumable goods that may go to real wages are largely predetermined; but with the lapse of time, with the continual consumption of commodities now on hand, and the continual production of new commodities, we find the flow of real income responding to the apportionment of money income. The volume of real wages will then depend partly on the proportion of the productive efforts of the community which the laborer's share in money income will direct to the satisfaction of their wants, and partly on the efficiency of the productive efforts so directed. If one half of the revenue of society gets into the hands of laborers, probably one half of the work of society will be directed to making commodities for laborers' use.* How much of such commodities they will get will then depend further on the extent to which the arts make this part of society's work effective. If inventions and improvements happen to be applied with great effect to the commodities bought and consumed by laborers, their substantial real wages will be so much greater. The further possible developments of the situation, in case of a rise in money wages which brings also a rise of real wages, will readily suggest themselves. Population may or may not increase in such mode as eventually to neutralize the advance. The real

---

* Probably, but not necessarily. This would depend on the rate of pay earned by those who produced the commodities consumed by the laborers, as compared with the pay of those who produced the real income of other classes. Assuming all workers to be equally paid, or the different strata to be called on in the same proportion in the making of every sort of real income, the probability mentioned in the text becomes a certainty

happiness finally yielded to the laborers may or may not grow: the ethical philosopher and the psychologist, as well as the speculative economist, would have something to say at this point. No subject among the humanities involves a wider or more difficult set of questions: none needs to be approached with greater diffidence and caution.

The complication of causes and conditions which need to be considered for a full understanding of all that bears on the welfare of laborers, or indeed of any class in society, is thus almost infinite. To follow these causes and conditions would be to write a book not only on distribution, but on social philosophy at large. The present volume has a much more modest task, and this digression into the larger field has been meant chiefly to show, by comparison, the limitations of the subject now in hand. The fundamental questions as to wages and distribution; as to what makes wages high or low; as to the ultimate effects of the march of progress in bringing special benefit to one or another class in the community,—these can not be settled by any inquiry as to the wages fund or as to the proximate source of wages. Some aid in answering them must indeed be got by following the course of concrete industry. It is indispensable to any inquiry which shall bring solid results that not only the fundamental forces at work shall be discovered, but that the precise mode in which they work out their effects shall be traced step by step. It is here, and here only, that the analysis of the relation of wages to capital, as set forth in the preceding pages, may help us: pointing out the mode in which production and distribution take place in modern societies, and the machinery through which the abiding moral and material forces work out their effects.

This, then, is the conclusion of our inquiry. The old doctrine of the wages fund had a solid basis in its conception, incomplete yet in essentials just, of the payment of present labor from past product. The new theories which disregard this fundamental fact, and seek to explain distribution by considering labor as paid directly from its own present product, begin with a false premise and distort the facts of the actual world. But the analysis of the mode in which labor yields enjoyable products, of the grounds for considering the capital of the community as the source of real wages, of the relation of the money funds of employers to the wages of hired laborers,—all this is to take only the first step toward an understanding of the situation. To use a phrase which has already been applied, it describes the machinery of production and distribution, not the forces which move the machinery and cause its parts to shift and change. The wages fund theory—if that name can be given to the form in which it has here been set forth—shows the steps by which wages get into the laborer's hands, and so points to the nearest and most obvious causes which affect them. It shows what is the process by which goods are produced in the great and complicated organism of modern society, and what are the channels by which the enjoyable commodities reach the hands of its various members. To understand that process, to follow those channels, is indispensable to truth and accuracy of knowledge. But it does not tell the whole story.

PART II.

THE HISTORY OF THE WAGES FUND DOCTRINE.

CHAPTER VI.

BEFORE ADAM SMITH.

WE enter now on the second part of the investigation : the history of the wages fund doctrine, and of the mode in which the relation of wages to capital has been treated by writers of the past and present.

The history of some parts of economic thought goes far back into the past. But theoretic inquiry as to the causes which affect distribution under the conditions of modern industry is of very recent date. It does not reach back farther than the second half of the eighteenth century, and virtually begins with Adam Smith. With a single exception, presently to be mentioned, we find in the writers before Adam Smith hardly a trace of the sort of reasoning which has been applied during the last hundred years to wages and the return to capital, and to most of the modern phenomena of distribution.

No branch of knowledge, it is true, is without its link of connection with the past. Adam Smith was not an isolated growth. He began where his predecessors left off, and rested his new work solidly on what they had already accomplished. But in his case, as often happens, the fresh growth was in a different direction from the old, and in some respects was of an entirely novel sort. Of

the points of connection between the great Scotchman and
his predecessors something more will be said in the next
chapter. So far as the subject of this inquiry is concerned, the connection between earlier and later thought
happens to be singularly slight. The earlier writers had
virtually done no more than to clear some parts of the
field, and so make it easier for an acute and original
thinker to take a fresh start.

On the direct subject of wages, then, and on capital
in its relation to wages, we find practically nothing in the
earlier writers. Scattered through the literature of the
seventeenth and eighteenth centuries there are casual
allusions to wages, usually implying that they are determined by the price of food. Subjects connected with
money and international trade mainly occupied the attention of the writers of those times. On the problems of
distribution they gave no more than incidental expression to opinions half-consciously formed. Probably as
explicit a statement as can be found on the subject of
wages is that of Mildmay. " As plenty and scarcity will in
general determine the price of provisions, so the price of
provisions will, in general, determine the wages of labour,
and the price of labour will determine the price of all pro-
ductions and commodities whatsoever." * Some such opinion as this seems to have been entertained usually, though
not universally, by the writers of Mildmay's period. Petty
had indeed intimated a different view. " When corn is
extremely plentiful, the Labour of the poor is proportion-
ally dear : and scarce to be had at all (so licentious are
they who labour only to eat, or rather to drink)." † But as
great a mind as Locke's had accepted opinions like those

---

* Sir William Mildmay, *The Laws and Policy of England relating to
Trade*, London, 1765, p. 22.

† Petty, *Political Arithmetic*, London, 1691, p. 45.

of Mildmay,* and most of the mercantile writers did the same. They stated, or implied, that a low price of food made low wages,—a result desirable in that it brought low prices and ready exports. Such remarks, however, as a rule, were simply incidental to the discussion of money and the balance of trade. It is significant that writers like Child, Gee, and Steuart have not a word on the general causes that affect wages, or on capital as connected with wages. To all intents, the discussion of this phase of economics had not begun.

This blank among the earlier writers on the topic which in our own time has become the crucial one in economic theory, is to be explained in two ways. In part, it was due to their narrow point of view. They were concerned chiefly with the power of the sovereign, and the greatness and resources of the country in its dealings with foreign nations. As wars and international relations chiefly engrossed the attention of statesmen in the period from the Reformation to the French Revolution, so the nature and profit of dealings with foreign countries chiefly interested those who thought on economic subjects. The statesman of the nineteenth century is occupied with constitutional and social questions; the economist, similarly, with the problems of distribution.

Another cause of the silence of the earlier writers lies in the economic conditions of their time. The feudal *régime* and the industrial organization of the middle ages were gone. The modern conditions, while fast developing, had not yet emerged with distinctness. The phenomena which arose as employers and capitalists were unfettered and as labor became free, had not existed long enough to compel specific examination. Conse-

---

* Locke, *Some Considerations of the Consequences of the Lowering of Interest*, 1691, in his works, vol. v, pp. 23, 24.

quently even those writers whose point of view was wider and more humane than that of the typical mercantilists, did not strike the modern note.   Vauban and Boisguille-bert take the social point of view; they consider the causes of the condition of the masses; but of wages in the modern sense they have nothing to say.   Even the Physi-ocrats, important as is the place which they take in the development of modern economic thought, yield nothing on this topic.   Quesnay rarely touches on wages, never on the nature and functions of capital or on the relations between capital and wages.   English writers, like Hume, Cantillon, and Tucker, joined the Physiocrats in attacking the mercantile ideas on money and international trade, and in directing attention to abundance of commodities and productiveness of labor as the true sources of pros-perity.   But the problems of social happiness, as connect-ed with internal prosperity, which lead to a discussion of wages, did not attract their notice.

To this general silence on the subject of our inquiry before the time of Adam Smith, there is one noteworthy exception.   Turgot, great in everything that he touched, made his mark here also.   In the *Réflexions sur la For-mation et Distribution des Richesses*, published in 1767, we have a theory of capital which may justly be called the first modern discussion of the subject.*   It is true that Turgot's discussion begins from the old point of view.   He is led to a consideration of capital from his discussion of money; the whole treatment of capital is an episode in his examination of money, interest, and the "disposable" class.   But the treatment is a long step beyond anything reached before his time.   The function of capital is to make the advances which become necessary when a great

---

* See the *Works* of Turgot (edition of 1844), vol. i, sections 60–61, 69, 80, 90, of the *Réflexions.*

number of arts " exigent que la même matière soit ouvrée par une foule de mains différentes, et subisse très long-temps de préparations aussi difficiles que variées." The hall-mark of the Physiocrats appears in the curious doctrine that in agriculture there was, strictly speaking, no need of an advance; since land always produced a " revenu " or " superflu," which enabled its cultivators to dispense with advances. According to Turgot, it is only when a large part of society no longer cultivated the soil and " n'eut que ses bras pour vivre," that advances became necessary. Materials, implements, buildings, and subsistence must be provided,—say for making leather ; " et qui fera vivre jusqu'à la vente des cuirs ce grande nombre d'ouvriers " ? The constant advance or consumption of capital, its constant reproduction and return to the hands of the capitalist, the source of capital in " l'épargne," the distinction between money and capital, the absence of connection between the rate of interest and the quantity of money, the futility of attempts to regulate the rate of interest,—these varied subjects are presented with an insight far beyond that of any writer before the time of Turgot, and not less than that of many writers who have had the benefit of a century of further discussion.*

But while Turgot thus took an important step toward beginning the modern analysis of capital, he is silent on that aspect of the subject which has most prominence in the later discussions of distribution,—on the relations of capital to wages. It is true that he says more than once that capital provides subsistence for laborers, as well as materials, implements, and buildings. Some expressions which show that this function of capital was clearly in his mind have just been quoted. But that there might be

---

* See the *Works* of Turgot (edition of 1844), vol. i, sections 60–61, 69, 80, 90, *Réflexions*.

here a mode of approaching the problem as to what determined the wages of laborers, never seems to have occurred to him. Turgot's theory of wages is very briefly
stated in the first pages of the *Réflexions*; it is the same
as was held, so far as any was held, by all writers of this
earlier period. "En tout genre de travail il doit arriver
et il arrive en effet que le salaire de l'ouvrier se borne à
ce que lui est nécessaire pour lui procurer sa subsistence."
There is no hint of any Malthusian ground for the doctrine. It rests on the fact that the employer pays the
laborer as little as he can, and has "choix entre grand
nombre d'ouvriers." * Thus it serves chiefly to clear the
way for the discussion of net income, of the disposable
class, and of the physiocratic conclusions as to taxation
and economic reform. In all this the laborers are not
thought to need much attention. They get only what
serves to subsist them, and have no share in net revenue.
In short, they are simply eliminated from the problem.

Directly, therefore, Turgot left the subject of wages
and capital almost untouched, and so left a clear field for
Adam Smith. Doubtless it would be possible to find
scattered hints and pregnant sentences in other writers:
embryos which never developed, and never would attract
notice, had not the full-grown thought appeared elsewhere
from another beginning. Doubtless, too, the general speculations of the Physiocrats and of their contemporaries
on distribution at large had their share in directing
thought into new and better ways, and stimulated inquiry
into deeper and more substantial causes of prosperity
than had been commonly examined by earlier writers.
But, when all is said, it remains substantially true, as one
of the great Scotchman's immediate followers said, that

* See the *Works* of Turgot (edition of 1844), vol. i, section 6,
Réflexion.

"the theory of capital is new and entirely of Adam Smith's creation ": * and to the examination of his views we may now proceed.

---

* Ganilh, *Inquiry into the Various Systems of Political Economy.* I quote from the New York edition of 1812, page 162. Compare what is said of Ganilh below, at page 157.

CHAPTER VII.

ADAM SMITH.

DURING the first half of the present century, when Adam Smith's prestige was greatest, it was the custom to treat all earlier contributions to economic thought as of little account, and to begin the history of the subject with the *Wealth of Nations*. In the reaction of the second half of the century there has been a disposition to credit too much to Adam Smith's predecessors, and to belittle his own contributions. Before proceeding to the details of his discussion of capital and wages, we may consider for a moment his general position in the growth of economic theory : thereby supplementing what has just been said of the stage of earlier speculation as to wages.

On some subjects, and notably on those which most attracted the attention of his contemporaries, Adam Smith gained much and directly from his predecessors. The mercantile ideas, in their cruder forms, had been refuted by a long series of writers, by North and Hume among the English, by Boisguillebert, Cantillon, and the whole line of the Physiocrats. The functions of money in domestic and in international trade had been fully and adequately discussed by these writers ; and much had also been done toward clearing up the subject of money by writers who, like Locke and Steuart, were still befogged on international commerce and the balance of trade. On credit, paper money, and banking there had been active discussion since the close of the seventeenth century, when banks began to exercise their functions on a considerable scale, and paper-money experiments came to be tried in almost every form. Adam Smith was abundantly familiar with the literature of his subject, and accepted without hesitation what had been accomplished by his predecessors. The famous attack on the mercantile system bears, indeed, the unmistakable marks of his vigorous and independent mind, in the reasoning as to the limitation of industry by capital, and in the general discussion of foreign trade. But the ground had been prepared for it by a long line of writers; and the upper tier of the educated public was prepared to accept his views at once.

The subjects of production and distribution show Adam Smith, not perhaps at his best, but at his freshest. Here he broke new ground. On the division of labor and its causes and effects, the functions of capital, the partition of income into wages, profits, and rent, the causes determining the amount of each form of remuneration,—on all these topics he started economic thought on new lines, and on lines that have been substantially followed since his time. The very novelty of his investigation made it inevitable that his results here should be more crude than on the subjects which had been worked over by two or three generations of previous thinkers; a defect which, rightly considered, makes the debt of science to him so much the greater.

Even on these subjects, it would be a mistake to consider Adam Smith as an unaided pioneer. The division of labor, and its consequences in bringing exchange and necessitating a medium of exchange, had been noted by a long series of writers, from ancient times to modern. Further, some stimulus to his thought on capital doubtless came from the general reaction against the treatment of interest and money by the mercantile writers. The older and cruder notions as to the importance of an abundance of specie had been effectually exploded before he began. As these exaggerations in regard to the importance of plentiful specie crumbled away, it was inevitable that other ideas connected with them should be overhauled and reshaped. The function of money having become clear, interest could no longer be explained as affected simply by the abundance or scarcity of money. The better understanding of the medium of exchange, again, directed attention to the nature and qualities of the commodities whose barter was seen to be facilitated. All this paved the way to the consideration of real capital, and the real machinery of production. In such indirect ways Adam Smith probably got a stimulus to his speculations on capital and interest, and so, by a natural progression, on capital and wages.

The Physiocrats, moreover, had attacked the real problems of production and distribution. The place of land in production had been emphasized by them. The derivation of all net income from land, and the reasoning which led to the denial of net income in other directions, began the treatment of distribution on the lines of modern theory. The very emphasis on these deeper subjects, as compared with the almost exclusive attention of their predecessors to the more superficial phenomena of money, was an important advance. Turgot, as we have seen, had described the importance and functions of capital with great insight and ability. Adam Smith was familiar with the writings of his French contemporaries ; he used them freely, and certainly drew much from them.

But, when all is said, the essential novelty of Adam Smith's contributions remains unmistakable. The importance and consequences of the division of labor he followed into regions where his predecessors had left a blank. Any one who compares his discussion of the income from land with that of the Physiocratic writers must see that, both in the main lines and in the details with which they are illustrated, an essentially new turn had been given to the discussion. On capital and its functions, his treatment, in some respects no more profound than Turgot's, is yet fresher, more direct, and closer to the real phenomena which it is the object of the economist to explain. Distribution was practically created by him. The simple division under the three heads of wages, profits, and rent, in itself marks an epoch. Something of the sort may indeed be said to underlie the Physiocratic separation of the three classes,—the productive, the barren, the disposable; but the most cursory comparison shows how much closer to the actual phenomena was Adam Smith's classification of income and income-receivers. Under each head, again, he advanced far in the direction which subsequent thought has followed to our own time. This is especially the case with his treatment of the main subject of the present inquiry: wages and capital, and the relations of workmen and employers.

The point of departure in Adam Smith's reasoning on production and distribution is the division of labor. The first and second books of the *Wealth of Nations*, which contain chapters of most interest and importance to later generations, open with this topic. The emphasis was intentional, and is one of the marks of Adam Smith's insight. He rightly thought that the characteristic phenomena of advanced societies rest on the division of labor, developed under the conditions of free industry. And this he held to be true of distribution as well as of production. The account of the increase in the productiveness of labor from its division is one of the best-known, as it is one of the most interesting passages in the book.

" Observe the accommodation of the most common artificer or day labourer in a civilized and thriving country, and you will perceive that the number of people of whose industry a part, though but a small part, has been employed in procuring him this accommodation, exceeds all computation. The woollen coat, for example, which covers the day labourer, as coarse and rough as it may appear, is the produce of the joint labour of a great multitude of workmen. The shepherd, the sorter of the wool, the wool-comber or carder, the dyer, the scribbler, the spinner, the weaver, the fuller, the dresser, with many others, must all join their different arts in order to complete even this homely production. How many merchants and carriers, besides, must have been employed in transporting the materials from some of those workmen to others who often live in a very distant part of the country! How much commerce and navigation in particular, how many shipbuilders, sailors, sailmakers, ropemakers, must have been employed in order to bring together the different drugs made use of by the dyer, which often come from the remotest parts of the world! What a variety of labour, too, is necessary in order to produce the tools of the meanest of those workmen! To say nothing of such complicated machines as the ships of the sailor, the mill of the fuller, or even the loom of the weaver, let us consider only what a variety of labour is requisite in order to form that very simple machine, the shears with which the shepherd clips the wool. The miner, the builder of the furnace for smelting the ore, the feller of the timber, the burner of the charcoal to be made use of in the smelting house, the brickmaker, the bricklayer, the workmen who attend the furnace, the millwright, the forger, the smith, must all of them join their different arts in order to produce them." *

From this initial description, Adam Smith is led to the discussion of the exchange of commodities, the first effect of the division of labor ; then to that of money as the

* *Wealth of Nations*, Book I, chapter i, p. 6. The page numbers given here and elsewhere for the *Wealth of Nations*, refer to M'Culloch's edition. I have quoted only a part of this closing paragraph in the chapter : enough to indicate its character.

medium of exchange; then to price, and the component parts of price; and so to wages, profits, and rent, as the component parts of the price of commodities. His first Book, whose main subject is announced in the introduction to be "the causes of the improvement in the productive powers of labor," is thus occupied largely with the subject of distribution.

This is one of the many incongruities in the marshalling of the matter of the *Wealth of Nations*,—incongruities ascribable to the difficulty of presenting in systematic fashion so great a mass of new reasoning, new facts, new conclusions. Another of the consequences of the division of labor might have been advantageously taken up before entering on the discussion of distribution; but it does not appear until the first Book, with all its details and digressions, is done with, and the second Book, on capital, is introduced. The division of labor brings not only the cooperation of many thousands of laborers and the exchange of their products, but the succession, step by step, of different stages in the processes of production, and so the spreading of labor over a considerable time. With the element of time, capital appears. The best way of introducing the uninitiated reader to the fundamental truths of economics would be to bring close together at the outset the three topics between which Adam Smith has interposed his long account of distribution,—the division of labor, the use of money, and the nature and functions of capital. One consequence of their separation in the *Wealth of Nations* is that passages under each head, not professedly connected with each other, need to be put together in order to get a full understanding of the author's conclusions; while another consequence probably is that Adam Smith himself missed conclusions that would have suggested themselves from a more compact exposition of these related subjects.

When Adam Smith, after long digressions, gets to the third of the topics just mentioned,—the functions of capital,—he recurs to the first and fundamental thought. The second Book, whose subject is described as " the Nature, Accumulation, and Employment of Stock," begins thus, in the Introduction :

In that rude state of society in which there is no division of labour, in which exchanges are seldom made, and in which every man provides everything for himself, it is not necessary that any stock should be accumulated or stored up beforehand, in order to carry on the business of society. Every man endeavours to supply by his own industry his own occasional wants as they occur. When he is hungry, he goes to the forest to hunt ; when his coat is worn out, he clothes himself with the skin of the first large animal he kills ; and when his hut begins to go to ruin, he repairs it, as well as he can, with the trees and the turf that are nearest it.

But when the division of labour has once been thoroughly introduced, the produce of a man's own labour can supply but a very small part of his occasional wants. The far greater part of them are supplied by the produce of other men's labour, which he purchases with the produce of, or what is the same thing, with the price of the produce of his own. But this purchase can not be made till such time as the produce of his own labour has not only been completed, but sold. A stock of goods of different kinds, therefore, must be stored up somewhere sufficient to maintain him, and to supply him with the materials and tools of his work, till such time, at least, as both these events can be brought about. A weaver can not apply himself entirely to his peculiar business, unless there is beforehand stored up somewhere, either in his own possession or in that of some other person, a stock sufficient to maintain him, and to supply him with the materials and tools of his work, till he has not only completed, but sold his web. This accumulation must, evidently, be previous to his applying his industry for so long a time to such a peculiar business.*

---

* *Wealth of Nations*, Book II, Introduction, pp. 118, 119.
Thirty years later, a writer conversant with the writings of Adam

Here the essential function of capital is clearly explained. It enables labor to be spread over a long period, and so makes possible the division of labor and that development of the arts under the division of labor, which are the main causes of the efficiency of civilized industry. The analysis, it is true, is not complete. The process of production is regarded from the point of view of the individual producer. When the weaver has completed and sold his web, capital is supposed to be no longer needed. It has been shown, in the first part of the present volume, that capital performs its functions not by enabling the individual to carry on his operations until he gets a salable commodity, but by enabling society as a whole to carry on complicated operations involving a long interval between the beginning of production and the final enjoyable commodity. Though Adam Smith had himself given warning, often enough, against confounding the needs of the community with those of the individual, it is not surprising that he should himself have failed to observe the distinction in this, the most intricate part of the whole subject. As will appear more fully in the coming chap-

---

Smith and his immediate followers, expounded this matter as follows : " The accumulation of capital is necessary to that division of labour by which its productive powers are increased, and its total amount diminished. . . . The accumulation of stock enables one class of men to work in any line cheaper for the rest of the community, than if each class worked in every line for itself. The immediate saving of labour is here occasioned by its subdivision. It is a consequence of the same accumulation of stock, that one class of men collects the articles necessary for the others all at once, and thus saves each the necessity of collecting for itself, which would be a repetition of the same toil for every transaction. This saving, too, is occasioned by the division of labour ; and all writers have agreed in giving the same account of the connection between the division of labour and the accumulation of stock." *Edinburgh Review,* vol. iv, p. 370 ; the article being a severe review of Lord Lauderdale's *Inquiry into the Nature and Origin of Public Wealth.*

ters, most writers after him, to our own time, have stopped
short at the same point in analyzing the function of
capital.

It suffices for the present subject to consider very
briefly the further analysis by Adam Smith of the functions of capital. Not only is it essential to the division
of labor, but it increases the productive powers of labor;
it employs " productive " labor, and stimulates industry.
Its effects in getting raw produce from the land, in manufactures, in wholesale trade, in retail trade, are examined
and classified. Certain fundamental propositions, which
have made their influence felt in all the literature of economics, first appear in developed form in the *Wealth of
Nations*,—that capital is the result of saving; that it is
perpetually consumed and reproduced; that industry is
limited by capital. On some of these topics the reasoning
is carried only half way;—thus on the mode in which
capital limits industry, and, as has just been stated, on
the connection between capital and the division of labor.
On others, while the fundamental propositions laid down
by Adam Smith can not be shaken, he gave an undue
emphasis to some corollaries; as in the excessive eulogy
on parsimony which he attached to the solid truth that
capital had its origin in saving. In all this the order is
again confusing, and appears to be largely a matter of
accident: a defect which is due,—to repeat what was said
a moment ago,—to the fact that his analysis of the whole
subject was practically a new birth.*

We may turn now to that part of the discussion of

---

* Mr. Edwin Cannan, in his *History of the Theories of Production
and Distribution in English Political Economy from 1776 to 1848*, has
given an excellent critical account of Adam Smith's doctrines on production and distribution ; an account which comes short of justice, however,
in that Mr. Cannan could not warm himself to some cordial recognition
of the credit to which the great Scotchman is entitled.

capital which bears more directly on the question of wages. The eighth chapter of the first Book of the *Wealth of Nations* treats of the Wages of Labour : the first deliberate and extended treatment of that subject in the literature of economics. In Adam Smith's arrangement of his matter, it comes before the discussion of capital in the second Book ; but the doctrines set forth in the later passages were clearly in his mind when writing the earlier. The oft-quoted opening paragraphs of the chapter on wages are, in their essential parts, as follows :

In that original state of things which preceded both the appro priation of land and the accumulation of stock, the whole produce of labour belongs to the labourer. . . . But this original state of things . . . could not last beyond the first introduction of the appropriation of land and the accumulation of stock. It was at an end, therefore, long before the most considerable improvements were made in the productive powers of labour. . . .

It seldom happens that the person who tills the ground has wherewithal to maintain himself till he reaps the harvest. His maintenance is generally advanced to him from the stock of a master, the farmer who employs him. . . . In all arts and manufactures the greater part of the workmen stand in need of a master to advance them the materials of their work, and their wages and maintenance till it be completed. . . .

It sometimes happens, indeed, that a single independent workman has stock sufficient both to purchase the materials of his work, and to maintain himself till it be completed. He is both master and workman, and enjoys the whole produce of his own labour, or the whole value which it adds to the materials on which it is bestowed. . . . Such cases, however, are not very frequent, and in every part of Europe, twenty workmen serve under a master for one that is independent ; and the wages of labour are everywhere understood to be, what they usually are, when the labourer is one person, and the owner of the stock which employs him another.*

---

* *Wealth of Nations*, Book I, ch. viii, p. 29. In these excerpts, I have retained only the passages referring directly to wages, omitting

Here we have two fundamental propositions. First, that in civilized industry maintenance must be provided for some considerable time, until the product is completed. The division of labor is not referred to, in terms, as the essence of the "improvements in the productive powers of labor" which cause the need of such maintenance; but that Adam Smith had this in mind, is clear from the other passages, already quoted, in earlier and later parts of his treatise. As in the later account of capital, the time during which maintenance must be provided is not described with regard to the final attainment of enjoyable goods; it is that which elapses until the particular product in hand is ready for market. When the harvest is reaped, when the specific work in hand is "completed," the need of maintenance is supposed to cease. Secondly, we have the proposition that the needed supplies of food and materials are rarely owned by the workmen, and that hired laborers get their wages through a bargain with employers. How it happens that workmen hardly ever own "stock" sufficient for their materials and maintenance, Adam Smith does not stop to inquire; nor, for that matter, did any of the economists who came after him, until, in our own day, the assaults of the socialists compelled attention to the origin and justification of the unequal division of wealth. But Adam Smith was at least aware that the historical fact of unequal distribution was an essential premise to his reasoning on wages, and in that regard saw the situation more clearly than many of his immediate successors.

Wages, then, "depend everywhere upon the contract usually made between these two parties," the workmen and the masters. The conditions under which the bargain is made, and the extent and limit of the demand for

---

those which describe rent and profits as "deductions from the produce of labor."

labor by the masters, presently come up for consideration.

The demand for those who live by wages, it is evident, cannot increase but in proportion to the increase of the funds which are destined for the payment of wages. These funds are of two kinds: first, the revenue which is over and above what is necessary for the maintenance; and secondly, the stock which is over and above what is necessary for the employment of the masters.

When the landlord, annuitant, or moneyed man, has a greater revenue than what he judges sufficient to maintain his own family, he employs either the whole or a part of the surplus in maintaining one or more servants. Increase this surplus, and he will naturally increase the number of those servants.

When an independent workman, such as a weaver or shoemaker, has got more stock than what is sufficient to purchase the materials of his own work, and to maintain himself till he can dispose of it, he naturally employs one or more journeymen with the surplus, in order to make a profit by their work. Increase this surplus, and he will naturally increase the number of his journeymen.

The demand for those who live by wages, therefore, necessarily increases with the increase of the revenue and stock of every country, and cannot possibly increase without it. The increase of revenue and stock is the increase of national wealth. The demand for those who live by wages, therefore, naturally increases with the increase of national wealth, and cannot possibly increase without it.*

Here are mentioned two sources of demand for labor, "revenue" and "stock."

"Revenue" evidently means what is spent for servants and retainers, hired by the employer for the direct satisfaction of his own wants or whims. When Adam Smith gets to the elaborate treatment of stock and capital in his second Book, he has much more to say of laborers hired from revenue. They are "unproductive" laborers; and

---

* Book I, ch. viii, p. 31.

what is spent on them is "prodigality," and entails pure loss to the community.*

Without going into any extended consideration of the outlying topics which these distinctions suggest, we may note how the discussion of this part of the demand for labor, scattered as it is through various passages of the *Wealth of Nations*, illustrates both the strength and the weakness of Adam Smith's treatment of the course of production and distribution. His historical knowledge and practical bent led him to give more attention to the demand for "unproductive" labor than was given to it by his successors. He was living at a time when luxury still took in large part the form of a great retinue of servants; though it was beginning to take more and more the modern form of the purchase of commodities from capitalist middlemen, who have hired the laborers ministering to the wants and caprices of the rich. He reasoned as if the difference were of vital consequence to the community: the one course was the result of "prodigality" and led to

---

* Book II, ch. iii, p. 147. Some of the passages may be quoted in which Adam Smith mentions cases of "prodigality" such as he had in mind when describing the effects of this form of the demand for labor. " In those towns which are principally supported by the constant or occasional residence of a court, and in which the inferior ranks of people are chiefly maintained by the spending of revenue, they are in general idle, dissolute, and poor; as at Rome, Versailles, Compiegne, and Fontainebleau." (P. 148.) And again : "In a country which has neither foreign commerce, nor any of the finer manufactures, a great proprietor, having nothing for which he can exchange the greater part of the produce of his lands which is over and above the maintenance of the cultivators, consumes the whole in rustic hospitality at home. If this surplus produce is sufficient to maintain a hundred or a thousand men, he can make use of it in no other way than by maintaining a hundred or a thousand men. . . . The great Earl of Warwick is said to have entertained every day at his different manors, thirty thousand people ; and though the number may have been exaggerated, it must have been very great to admit of such exaggeration." Book III, ch. iv, p. 182.

waste, while the other entailed " parsimony " and brought progress.   There may be an important element of truth in the proposition that the workman hired by the capital-ist is likely to be more sober and industrious than the retainer of the nobleman ; * and there are important so-cial consequences from the rise of a class of capitalist *en-trepreneurs*.   But clearly the direction of production and consumption remains the same at bottom, whether the unequal distribution of wealth works itself out in one way or the other.   All laborers employed out of " revenue " are supposed to be unproductive ; a proposition which, in any larger consideration of wants and their satisfaction, is crude and untenable.   The further conclusions to which Adam Smith was thus led, in his consideration of " unpro-ductive " labor, while consistent in themselves, are unsat-isfactory enough.   They go with that undue emphasis which the classic economists, following his lead, put on the mere accumulation of capital as the one thing needful for public prosperity.   But he was certainly right on one point : in maintaining that the demand for "unproduc-tive " labor occurred under different conditions and with a different play of motives from those which appear in the case of " productive " labor.   In so far, he showed his in-sight into the complexities of real life, and set an example of close attention to varied facts which might have been usefully followed by the long series of his admirers and expositors.

On the second and more important part of the demand for labor,—that which comes from " stock,"—it is less easy to make the different parts of the *Wealth of Nations* hang

---

* On the probability of " the cultivation of the soil with the same kind of indolence and slackness as in the feudal times," under such a direction of luxurious expenditure, see an interesting passage, evidently reflecting Adam Smith's views, in Malthus's *Political Economy*, second edition. p. 235.

together. Sometimes, indeed most commonly, this "stock " is conceived in terms of money, or as consisting of funds in the hands of the immediate employer. Sometimes the money payments are described as of no essential importance, as only steps toward the distribution of real wages. The uncertainty and confusion which thus showed itself in Adam Smith continued to appear in almost all the discussions of wages for fully a century after his time.

The phrases "funds destined for the maintenance of labour," and " funds destined for the payment of wages," occur again and again : they are the undoubted parent of the word " wages-fund " as it is used in later literature. Sometimes, " capital " and " stock " are used to denote the source of wages. In the chapter on profits we find all these phrases used interchangeably : " The diminution of the capital stock of the society, or of the funds destined for the maintenance of labor, as it lowers the wages of labour, so it raises the profits of stock." * Whichever words were used, Adam Smith, when speaking directly of wages, seems to have conceived of their source simply as funds in the hands of the immediate employer. In the passage quoted a few moments ago,† again from the chapter on wages, the " stock " of the master is apparently thought of in terms of money. It is the amount over " what is sufficient to purchase the materials of his own work, and to maintain himself till he can dispose of it." In the later discussion of fixed and circulating capital, in the second Book, we read that " that part of the capital of the farmer . . . which is employed in the wages and maintenance of his labouring servants is a circulating capital." ‡ The funds controlled by the im-

---

* Book I, ch. ix, p. 43. † At p. 142.
‡ Book II, ch. i, p. 120.

mediate employer would seem to be referred to in all these passages.

On the other hand, when the independent discussion of capital is undertaken, in the second Book, a different view appears. Here Adam Smith comes so much nearer the truth,—indeed, states the essential truth so clearly,—that it is surprising he did not turn back to his chapter on wages in the first Book, and remodel its matter and its phrases. The same remark might be made, to be sure, of many passages in the *Wealth of Nations.* On a great range of topics,—rent, profits, value, international trade,—there are flashes of insight, pregnant statements, which yet fail to be carried to their last consequences.

The " stock " of society is divided, in the second Book, into two parts : the " stock," in a narrower sense, of finished commodities which is "reserved" for immediate consumption ; and the "capital," whether fixed or circulating, which is expected to afford a revenue. The distinction between fixed and circulating capital, (very different from that which became traditional with later writers) is largely fanciful ; but the confusion here does not affect the part of the reasoning that bears on our present subject. It is under the head of circulating capital, that we should expect a consideration of those forms of capital which make the demand for what Adam Smith called " productive " labor. Either the money funds in the hands of the immediate employer, or the finished consumable commodities on which the laborers spend their money wages, might here be given the chief emphasis. Both of them, in fact, receive their share of attention, and both are discussed in curious harmony with distinctions and definitions that have come to the front again in very recent times ; while yet, under either head, the reasoning is not carried to its logical conclusion as to the real and important source of wages.

Adam Smith rightly treats the commodities which in one sense are finished, but are not yet in consumers' hands, as capital. " The stock of provisions which are in the possession of the butcher, the grazier, the farmer, the corn merchant," and " the work which is made up and completed, but which is still in the hands of the merchant or manufacturer, and not yet disposed of or distributed to their proper consumers,"—these are parts of circulating capital.* Adam Smith did not indeed call them capital for the reason which would nowadays be given : that the butcher and merchant do a share of helpful work in production, and that goods in their hands are wealth not yet enjoyable. But the essence of the situation was grasped by him, even if all its connections and consequences were not perceived. Adam Smith had defined capital as that which yielded a revenue; whence it would have followed, that a dwelling house or a suit of clothes, if let for hire by the owner, became capital. Nevertheless he qualifies his general definition at this point : such revenue-yielding commodities belong not to the community's capital, but to its stock reserved for immediate consumption. " The stock of food, clothes, household furniture, etc., which have been purchased by their proper consumers, but which are not yet entirely consumed," are not capital : they are realized income. But " work which is made up and completed, but which is still in the hands of the manufacturer and merchant, and not yet disposed of or distributed to the proper consumers : such as the finished work which we frequently find ready-made in the shops of the smith, the cabinet-maker, the goldsmith, the jeweller, the china-merchant,"—all this *is* part of capital, being not yet in the hands of the " proper consumer." † At this point Adam Smith might be expected to look for the capital

---

which is the immediate real source of wages, as of all other income,—the consumable goods, in dealers' hands, ready for purchase by laborers. But he never did so. The illustration which he used for bringing out his meaning as to this form of circulating capital is " the finished work which we frequently find ready-made in the shops of the smith, the cabinet-maker, the goldsmith, the jeweller, the china-merchant, etc." The simpler goods which laborers will buy obviously belong in the same class ; they are capital in the same sense and for the same reason. But Adam Smith's thought seems turned to these only in dealing with other subjects, and never in connection with the payment of wages out of capital. The hints which he gave, the acute distinctions which he suggested, if followed to their consequences, might easily have led to the development of a theory of wages that would have kept close to the concrete facts, and avoided the vague generalizations of the wages fund doctrine of later days. Adam Smith himself never followed them out ; his successors did even less ; and thus the passages which have here been cited make the impression of curious but unfruitful anticipations of the essential truths.

So far as money and money wages, and the place of money in capital, are concerned, Adam Smith's direct discussion is admirable ; and the substantial ground for criticism can again be only that the truths here set forth were not brought to bear more fully on the question of real wages. While he classes money as part of circulating capital, he notes the peculiar place which it has in the capital of the community. It never wears out : hence " the fixed capital, and that part of circulating capital which consists in money, . . . bear a great resemblance to one another." * Money has a place of its own ; he de-

---

* Book II, ch. ii, p. 125.

scribes it, in language used with frequent emphasis, as simply "the great wheel of circulation," and as "altogether different from the goods which are circulated by means of it." The real revenue of society, and of each individual in society, is in "the quantity of consumable goods which they can all of them purchase with this money." * This simple and oft-neglected truth he dwells on at length, having an eye on the familiar fallacies of the mercantile writers, to which he was giving the finishing stroke. And yet, as we have seen, when capital is regarded as the source of demand for labor, he seems to think of the money funds with which the employer pays the hired laborer. It is true that a case to which he often refers, by way of illustrating the need of advances to the laborer, is that of the farmer, maintaining his laborers at his own table, and so owning *in natura* the capital which remunerates them: a case which emerges again and again in later literature. But Adam Smith usually has in mind the very different conditions which in fact prevail in the modern world. He describes a society with a developed money *régime*, in which all income appears first in the form of money payments and money rights. He does not fail to point out, with emphasis, the simple distinction between money wages and real wages; but he never goes into any further detail as to the connection between the two, or as to the nature and determination of the flow of consumable commodities whence real wages must come. Here, as on the question of the place of such commodities in " stock " or "capital," he advanced without error to a certain point, and then stopped short.

No doubt the reason why Adam Smith failed to carry further his reasoning both as to the relation between money wages and real capital, and as to the place of

---

* Book II, ch. ii, pp. 125, 126.

dealers' stocks in social capital, is to be found in his mistaken view as to the extension of the productive cycle. He thought of production piece by piece. The employer needed funds with which to pay laborers simply until the product was salable: the need of advances ceased when the particular article in hand was completed. This simple every-day operation is easily confounded with the larger and more intricate process by which the labor of the whole community is spread over a lengthened period. Many writers after Adam Smith have been guilty here of much worse confusion: the great master's fault was one of inattention rather than of express error.

To sum up the theory of capital and wages, as it stood with the appearance of the *Wealth of Nations*. Adam Smith had shown that, in a society having a developed division of labor, the process of production was spread over some length of time, and that for the laborers in such a society subsistence must be provided until their present labor should result in finished goods in the future. How great this provision must be, was not indeed considered with a full appreciation of the position of the whole community; but the fundamental fact had been clearly pointed out. Further, he had shown that, under the unequal distribution of wealth in modern societies, the supplies from which laborers must for the moment get their subsistence, are in the hands of others: hence laborers get them by a bargain with those others. Exactly what the employers have to offer in that bargain, he did not consistently and fully set forth. Some of them have "revenue," more of them have "capital" and "funds," with which they remunerate labor. All laborers hired by those who employ them for gain from the sale of the product, are dependent on advances from the capital of the employers. But what that capital consists of, is not clearly stated. The remarkable analysis of capital in the second Book might easily have led the way to a more explicit statement: but Adam Smith did not advance farther on the path which he here opened.

CHAPTER VIII.

THE IMMEDIATE FOLLOWERS OF ADAM SMITH.

In the ferment of economic discussion which followed the appearance of the *Wealth of Nations*, other subjects than those with which the present investigation is concerned, were uppermost. Attention was given chiefly to external and internal commerce, and so to the questions of free-trade without and of unshackled industry within. Adam Smith's was a catholic mind, and he had the interests both of the scientific thinker and the practical agitator. But his immediate followers laid stress mainly on those parts of the subject in which he had called for prompt legislative reforms. It was the drift of the time, too, to treat economics chiefly with reference to production. The path of progress was believed to be by the increase of the production of wealth. This was to be secured chiefly by freeing exchange from all restrictions. So much done, general prosperity must follow. Not until the middle of the present century, when the complaints of the socialists began to demand attention in louder and louder tones, did distribution become the central problem in economic reasoning.

The urgency of some immediate loosening of restrictive legislation, and the importance attached to problems of production, thus caused Adam Smith's treatment of wages and capital to receive comparatively little attention. What was said by his immediate successors on this topic, was chiefly in acceptance of his views. So far from carrying his reasoning further, the economists of the next thirty years rarely succeeded in getting as far as he did. What was the general situation, will appear from an examination of the more prominent writers, both among those who accepted the doctrines of the *Wealth of Nations* with unquestioning loyalty, and those who ventured to differ, on one point or another, with their acknowledged master.

In France, the leavening influence of the Physiocrats, and the upheaval of the Revolution, prepared the way for a more rapid advance in economic thinking than at first appeared in England. Among the writers who took up the cause of reform, none was more enthusiastic than the historian Sismondi ; none was more eager for the advance of freedom than he in the earlier stage of his remarkable intellectual career. In 1804, he published at Geneva two volumes, *De la Richesse Commerciale, ou Principes d'Économie Politique*, which are expressly stated in the preface to do no more than expound what Adam Smith had discovered. Much the larger part of the book is given to foreign trade and the subjects that go with it ; though the wide range of interest which Sismondi showed in later life, appeared at this stage in the attention given to the other topics. Following Adam Smith, he points out that the division of labor brings a departure from the simple conditions of primitive industry. Rich and poor emerge ; " comme tout homme est forcé de consommer avant de produire, l'ouvrier pauvre ce trouve dans la dependance des riches." And later :

Toutes les fois qu'on met à l'ouvrage un ouvrier productif, et qu'on lui paye un salaire, on échange le présent contre l'avenir, les choses qu'on a contre celles qu'on aura, l'aliment et le vêtement qu'on fournit à l'ouvrier contre le produit prochain de son travail. L'argent n'entre dans ce marché que comme signe: il représente toujours une richesse mobiliaire, applicable à l'usage et à la consommation de l'homme, c'est cette dernière qui est le vrai capital circulant. Le numéraire est comme une assignation, que le capitaliste donne à l'ouvrier, sur le boulanger, le boucher, et le tailleur, pour qu'ils lui livrent le denrée consommable qui appartenoit déja en quelque sorte au capitaliste, puisqu'il en possédoit le signe.*

The laborer and capitalist find it to their advantage to make the bargain, because the laborer has " rien enfin pour se nourrir ou se vêtir " ; while the capitalist wants a profit. Sismondi notices that the laborers almost always have " quelque petit fonds accumulé " with which to subsist for a day or a week, until their wages are paid. But this fund only suffices until " l'échange de l'objet qu'ils ont produit soit accompli " : and in any case it is capital, the laborers being in so far both laborers and capitalists.

This is a neat and compact statement of what Adam Smith had worked out ; in some respects it is perhaps an improvement on what Adam Smith had said. There is a touch of originality, perhaps even a presentiment of modern ways of stating the situation, in the description of the laborer as bargaining away the future for the present ; and the function of money in regard to wages could not be better put. On the other hand, Sismondi, like his master, evidently regards the period during which advances must be made to the laborers as that only which elapses until a salable product is made.

Thenceforth, in the brief attention he gives to wages in general, Sismondi speaks of them as determined in the first instance simply by the quantity of capital compared with the number of laborers : while other forces, again, are at work to determine them in the long run.

Quelque soit le nombre des ouvriers proportionellement au capital qui doit les nourrir, ils ne pourront se contenter longtems d'un salaire moindre que celui qui leur est absolument nécessaire

---

* *De la Richesse Commerciale*, vol. i, pp. 36, 53.

pour vivre : la misère seroit bientôt suivie de la mortalité, et l'équi-
libre seroit rétabli par ce contrepoids aussi redoutable qu'efficace.
Quelque soit d'autre part le nombre ou la valeur des capitaux
destinés à maintenir le travail, ils ne pourront jamais être réduits à
ne donner aucun profit net. . . . Le propriétaire préféreroient alors
de les dépenser en objets de luxe.*

This consideration of the permanent causes which determine wages still rests mainly on Adam Smith. There
is again an original turn in the mention of a minimum
and maximum of wages; which bears a curious similarity
to a mode of stating the theory of wages common among
German writers of our own time. But the treatment is
summary; the subject enlisted Sismondi's interest much
less than free-trade, internal and external, and the French
legislation restricting it.

In later years, Sismondi recanted many of the doctrines of his first book. In the *Nouveaux Principes d'Économie Politique*, published in 1819, he joined the reaction
against the optimist advocacy of the wonder-working
effects of unfettered industry, and set forth the doctrine
of over-production and "engorgement des marchées."
His anxiety as to the excess to which free competition
could lead colored his conclusions on international trade,
corporations, population, poor-laws, and other subjects.
But on wages he did not find occasion to modify what he
had said. Indeed, the subject is treated even more briefly
than in the earlier book. Capital is analyzed as resolvable ultimately into food : it is rather implied than explicitly stated that laborers must be supported out of capital.
When the independent treatment of wages is taken in
hand, the relation of capital to wages is not mentioned.
Sismondi there discusses chiefly the need of high wages as
a means of putting larger purchasing power into the hands

* Ibid., vol. i, p. 63.

of the masses and so supplying a market for the threatened over-supply of goods.* Indeed, it was hardly to be expected that he should find occasion for revising what he had said in the earlier book on the relation of wages and capital; for the course of discussion in the interval, while it had elicited differences of opinion on other subjects, had tended to strengthen the hold of Adam Smith's views on this one. Practically nothing had here been done to advance or develop the results reached in the *Wealth of Nations*.

The same remark may be made of the treatment of economic theory at large by two other Frenchmen,—Say and Ganilh. Say's famous and popular *Traité d'Économie Politique*, published in 1803, was in the main an exposition of the doctrines of Adam Smith. Capital, according to Say, consists of tools, materials, and subsistence. Subsistence must be advanced to the laborers, and must be replaced in the product: "he [the employer] is obliged continually to make the advances." † The husbandman's capital must include, besides buildings, tools, and cattle, "seed, ground, provisions, fodder for cattle, and food as well as money for his laborers' wages, etc." ‡ Here we find Adam Smith's farmer, and the subsistence for the laborers as part of the farmer's capital, without further analysis of the character and functions of this form of capital. When Say, in a later part of his treatise, discusses wages independently, the subject of capital, notwithstanding the earlier analysis of it, does not reappear.# Wages are said to depend on the laborer's subsistence as modified by his habits. They are adjusted by bargain between master

---

* *Nouveaux Principes*, Book II, ch. iv, on the return from capital, and Book IV, ch. v, on wages.

† *Traité*, Book I, ch. iii.

‡ Ibid., Book I, ch. x.   # Ibid., Book II, ch. vii, § iv.

and man; and Adam Smith is followed in the statement that the bargain usually works to the advantage of the master. But the part which the master's capital plays in the bargain is not considered: Say does not attend to the lead, uncertain as it was, which his chief had given. In truth, Say's books, wide as was their circulation and influence, were thin in intellectual quality, and could hardly be expected to reflect more than the current ideas of the time.

Ganilh's *Inquiry into the Various Systems of Political Economy* is in many ways not unlike Say's *Traité*; it is neat and lively, and shows the skill of the French in exposition. An eclectic performance, it yet follows in the main Adam Smith, differing with him only on a few topics, like the distinction between productive and unproductive labor and the doctrine of labor as a measure of value, on which Say and Lauderdale had undertaken to correct their acknowledged leader. On capital, Ganilh paraphrases Adam Smith without effort at independence. Capital is an accumulation of the produce of labor, including not only machines and instruments, but "the advances and raw materials necessary to all kinds of labor . . . and produce kept in store for present, future, and distant consumption." But of capital in its relation to wages Ganilh has nothing to say. In the chapter on Wages,* the fluctuation of wages with the price of provisions receive attention: but the proximate source of the demand for labor is not treated as it was by Adam Smith. The demand for labor varies with the progressive, stationary, or retrograde state of national wealth. This is an echo of the doctrine of the *Wealth of Nations* that wages are high only in advancing communities: it does not touch the detailed analysis of the demand for labor with which Adam Smith had begun. Neither Ganilh nor

---

* Book II, ch. vii.

Say touched the really intricate and difficult parts of their subject.

Among English writers of this period, there was even less of direct discussion than among the Frenchmen of the relation of capital to wages. In England, as elsewhere, Adam Smith's attacks on the mercantile system chiefly attracted attention. What he said of capital in general, abstruse as it was, and far removed from the pressing problems of the day, aroused little discussion: what he said of capital and wages, apparently none at all.

Lord Lauderdale, to mention one of the ablest and most independent of Adam Smith's immediate successors, in his *Inquiry*, protested against several of Adam Smith's doctrines, notably those on labor as a measure of value, and " parsimony " as the mainspring of public prosperity. Lauderdale was a keen and able thinker, and his corrections of some of Adam Smith's doctrines deserved more attention than the later classic school gave them. But on the subject of capital and wages he made no advance, and indeed did not fairly attend to what Adam Smith had said. Capital he regarded as consisting only of tools and machinery, and (perhaps) materials ; and these were treated as simply " supplanting " labor. Lauderdale failed to see that tools do not supplant labor, and that they are simply a different mode of applying labor. But this view of capital had no bearing on the relations of labor and capital ; in fact, it tended to prevent a consideration of that relation. Commodities advanced to laborers were apparently not considered to be capital by Lauderdale. This is certainly a tenable view ; but it does not obviate the need of considering the problem how the finished or nearly finished commodities, which are not dubbed capital, get into laborers' hands. To that problem Lauderdale gave no attention. His *Inquiry*, indeed, makes no pretence at covering the whole ground. It is a series of detached essays on certain points on which the author had thought for himself and had reached conclusions different from Adam Smith's. Like others of his time, he was concerned with questions of production rather than with those of distribu- tion. His writings are of interest to the present subject because of the evidence they give that Adam Smith's dis- cussion of it, when not followed in express terms, aroused no adverse comment.

Malthus is the most important figure in the interval between Adam Smith and Ricardo. The *Essay on Popula- tion* far surpasses any other economic publication of that time, both in the attention which it aroused with the gen- eral public, and in the influence it exercised on the subse- quent course of economic speculation. Directly, it said little or nothing on capital, or the relations of capital and wages; indirectly, it had a very marked effect on the dis- cussion of this part of economic theory.

Directly, Malthus in the *Essay on Population* touched very lightly on general economic questions. Indeed, he was then very slenderly equipped for doing so. He had drifted, as it were, into the discussion of economic topics, publishing the first edition of the *Essay* (1798) as a pam- phlet against Godwin and Condorcet; and the pamphlet- eering spirit did not entirely disappear even when he enlarged it, with the second edition (1803), into the for- midable volume which established his fame. Malthus had read Adam Smith, and even in the first edition of the *Essay* made reference to Adam Smith's discussion of wages; but it was not until a later period that the questions of wages and profits, and the theory of distribution proper, engaged his attention. Of his contribution to these ques- tions in his later years, when he had become a professor of political economy, and had begun to write more on eco- nomic subjects at large, something will be said when the development of thought after the time of Ricardo comes to be taken up. For the present, it will suffice to note what Malthus had to say when his thinking still turned almost exclusively on the question of population. The only passage on the general theory of wages is in the sixteenth chapter of the first edition of the *Essay*,—a chapter which, though revised and rewritten in later editions, remained unchanged so far as the gist of the reasoning went.* Here Malthus attacked, with a diffidence that was quite unaffected,† the doctrine which he attributed to Adam Smith, that the demand for labor increases *pari passu* with the growth of the total wealth, or the combined stock and revenue of society. Malthus maintained that the demand for labor came from " the real funds destined for the maintenance of labor,"—a phrase evidently derived from Adam Smith, and often repeated by Malthus. These real funds, in Malthus's opinion, must be mainly food; and so he brings the emphasis to the point about which the whole *Essay* centres,—the possibilities and probabilities of the relative growth of population and of food.‡

---

* This chapter became chapter VII of Book III in the second edition of 1803, and is chapter XIII of Book III in the last edition. Its caption is: " Of Increasing Wealth as it affects the Condition of the Poor."

† " I can not avoid venturing a few remarks on a part of Dr. Adam Smith's *Wealth of Nations ;* speaking at the same time with that diffidence, which I ought certainly to feel, in differing from a person so justly celebrated in the political world." *Essay on Population*, first edition, p. 302. The diffidence seems to have been no longer felt when Malthus reached his second edition ; for these apologetic sentences do not appear in the volume of 1803.

‡ " Little or no doubt can exist that the comforts of the labouring poor depend upon the increase of the funds destined for the maintenance of labour ; and will be very exactly in proportion to the rapidity of this increase. The demand for labour which such increase would occasion, by creating a competition in the market, must necessarily increase the value of labour ; and, till the additional number of hands required was secured, the increased funds would be distributed to the same number of persons

Malthus was on the right track, as Adam Smith had been before him, in saying that the real funds which constituted the demand for labor were the consumable commodities which constituted real wages. But he hardly got as far as Adam Smith in analyzing these funds. He simply told the world that mankind, physiologically considered, had the potentiality of multiplying much faster than the most important element in real wages—food—could probably increase. Other constituent parts of real wages, as manufactured goods, might be increased in quantity with comparative ease, and wealth in this form might advance rapidly ; but such an increase would not mean a greater supply of food, and would not enlarge the real funds for supporting and maintaining labor. This was the only point of view from which Malthus approached his predecessor's doctrine of wages. Evidently it does not touch in any way the theory of capital, or of capital in relation to wages, or of the connection between the acts of the capi-

---

as before the increase, and therefore every labourer would live comparatively at his ease. But perhaps Dr. Smith errs in representing every increase of the revenue or stock of a society as an increase of these funds. Such surplus stock or revenue will, indeed, always be considered by the individual possessing it, as an additional fund from which he may maintain more labour ; but it will not be a real and effectual fund for the maintenance of an additional number of labourers, unless the whole, or at least a great part of this increase of the stock or revenue of the society, be convertible into a proportional quantity of provisions ; and it will not be so convertible, where the case has arisen merely from the produce of labour, and not from the produce of land. A distinction will in this case occur, between the number of hands which the stock of the society could employ, and the number which its territory can maintain." *Essay on Population*, first edition, pp. 305, 306.

In the second edition, this passage is retained with no substantial change ; but Malthus now was more sure of his ground, and stated roundly that "the error of Dr. Smith lies in representing" and so on. *Essay*, second edition, p. 421.

talist employer in hiring laborers and the mode in which the laborers' real income is determined. As we shall presently see, Malthus hardly got any further than this even in his later writings, directed though these were to a wider field than the *Essay on Population*. At all events, nothing that he said in this earlier period made any direct advance in the discussion.

Indirectly, however, the *Essay on Population* had a very great influence on that discussion. Malthus fastened attention on the standard of living as the determining cause of wages. Population tended, within the limits set by the standard of living, to press on subsistence; changes in wages, unless the result of a changed standard, were unimportant. However explicitly Malthus admitted the possible effect of moral restraint in checking the pressure of population, and however eloquently he preached the virtue of such restraint, he retained throughout a conviction of the strong probability that every increase in food would bring a corresponding increase in numbers, and that wages, in terms of the habitual food of the laborers, would remain at one dead level. When, twenty years later, Senior, in his correspondence with Malthus, maintained that as an historical fact food had increased faster than population, Malthus, admitting that this might be true, pointed out that his theory would not thereby be impugned.* He was thus ready to say, when squarely brought to the issue, that the simple *tendency* to pressure was the essence of his teaching. Yet the very need of such a question as Senior's showed how firmly he had impressed on his contemporaries the belief that the tendency to pressure was strong, and so little likely to be mitigated or counteracted as to leave it practically true that wages

---

* See the correspondence between Senior and Malthus, appended to Senior's *Two Lectures on Population* (London, 1829).

depended on a fixed low standard of living, and that an increase in subsistence meant simply an increase in numbers. The consequence was that the inquiry which Adam Smith had begun, as to the immediate causes determining wages, seemed superfluous. It was sufficient that wages were regulated by the "principle of population." The effect of Malthus's teaching in the *Essay* was to fix attention on the ultimate causes which determined wages, and to divert attention from the proximate causes and the exact mode of their operation.

The result of this chapter is thus mainly negative. No writer of the period between Adam Smith and Ricardo got beyond the point reached by the former in his analysis of capital at large, and of the place of capital in the payment of wages. Anything new that may appear on this topic in the period that begins with Ricardo, may therefore be treated as a direct advance from the *Wealth of Nations ;* anything old and familiar as derived from that source. It will be seen that the additions were, for a long series of years, slight in substance, and not even considerable in the mode of statement. The influence of Adam Smith, on his later followers as well as on those closer to his own time, was here greater and more lasting than on the treatment of almost any other parts of the theory of distribution.

CHAPTER IX.

RICARDO.

NEXT in order, for the development of the wages fund doctrine, as for economic theory at large, comes Ricardo. In regard to the direct relation of capital to wages, he reflected faithfully the views of his own generation; while the mode in which he stated that relation, and connected it with other parts of economic theory, served to impress these views strongly on the generation that followed.

Ricardo was a brief writer, and sometimes an awkward one. Moreover, he was concerned, especially in his writings on value and distribution, with permanent causes and permanent results. He was convinced of the fundamental validity of certain premises, such as the effective working of competition, the equality of profits, the adjustment of money wages to the price of food, the law of diminishing returns from land; and the bent of his mind was to follow out these premises to their conclusions by quasi-mathematical reasoning. Ricardo was perfectly conscious—when he stopped to think about it—that his conclusions could be true only in the rough, in the long run, "hypothetically"; but he was so intent on working them out that he usually spoke and reasoned as if they were absolutely and unqualifiedly true. In any case, it was the conclusions reached in this manner as to eventual results, that he habitually looked to; saying little or nothing of the phenomena which, rightly or wrongly, he regarded as temporary and comparatively unimportant.

Another cause served to add to Ricardo's habitual brevity of statement, so far as the immediate relations of capital to wages were concerned. Neither Ricardo nor his contemporaries were much concerned with the questions of distribution as they appeal to us. Wages, profits, rent, did not interest them from the social point of view, or because great inequalities in the means of enjoyment might be explained, and either justified or not justified, by analyzing them. They were interested mainly in the ways and means of increasing the production of wealth. Ricardo himself, as he went further in economic study, gave more and more attention to questions of distribution, which gradually assumed greater theoretical and practical importance in his mind.* But in the main, they did not strongly appeal to him ; they were attractive largely because they presented complex problems for logical solution. It was natural, therefore, that he should concern himself little with the causes which might directly determine the welfare of the laborers.

Hence we find in Ricardo's writings no such detailed discussion of the relation of capital to wages, as we find of value, rent, changes in wages with the price of food, the causes and effects of international trade. The questions involved in the wages fund doctrine, bearing as they do on the phenomena of the moment, are precisely such as Ricardo was in the habit of passing by. We must make out his views partly from brief statements and incidental remarks, still more from suppositions and premises which, though tacitly assumed rather than expressly stated, are

---

* See the instructive essay on *The Interpretation of Ricardo*, by Professor S. N. Patten, in the *Quarterly Journal of Economics*, April, 1893 (vol. vii, p. 322).

yet of the essence of his reasoning. While his opinions were thus briefly stated, they were none the less clear and explicit. Precision and accuracy of thought are in everything that he wrote; and his chief contribution to the wages fund doctrine was in the precision with which he stated it, and in the example of unqualified statement which he set for his successors.

The first thing to be noticed in Ricardo's treatment of our subject is the simple assumption that wages as a matter of course are paid from capital. Why this should be, he never thought it necessary to explain. Nothing more clearly shows the hold which Adam Smith had on the economists who followed him, than their unquestioning acceptance of this cardinal proposition. A writer having the wider historical interests of Sismondi might indeed stop to explain why wages must come from capital; but most of Adam Smith's successors simply accepted his doctrine.* Ricardo treated it as he did many other conclusions of Adam Smith's: accepted it as a thing settled, and needing no further discussion. All his reasoning shows that he perceived clearly the fundamental fact on which it rested,—the fact that the operations of production are spread over a considerable period of time. Much of his reasoning, indeed, rests squarely on this fact. But its importance as the foundation of the doctrine of the payment of wages from capital, he never mentioned, and probably did not fairly realize.

Next it may be noticed how the problem is simplified at Ricardo's hands. The laborers whom Adam Smith had described as paid out of "revenue," drop entirely out of his ken. Only laborers who are hired by capitalists aim-

---

* No doubt the great growth of the capitalist system between 1776 and 1815 had much to do with the exclusive attention which the later writers give to laborers hired by capitalists.

ing to make a profit are considered. This simplification of the problem may be due in part to changing conditions in society,—the more complete disappearance of the feudal practice of large arrays of retainers, and the increase in more modern forms of luxury. Chiefly it is due to Ricardo's mental habits: his tendency to cull out the central problem, and consider that only, and in its fundamental aspects only. The laborer producing commodities under the guidance of a capitalist middleman is the typical figure; the one, too, whose case gives opportunity for the intricate figuring and reasoning in which Ricardo was in his element. Hence not only retainers, but independent workmen producing commodities for direct sale, disappear. Adam Smith had noted that laborers are not necessarily hired by masters, but may sometimes work independently; Sismondi too had remarked that such a situation would present peculiarities. Ricardo never mentions the case. He considers only the laborers hired by capitalists.

The industrial conditions under which he wrote undoubtedly contributed very greatly to this limitation of Ricardo's treatment. In England, during his time and since his time, the bulk of the laboring population has been divorced from the capital and the land. Perhaps a writer of academic training and of larger historical attainments might have been led to consider that this was not a necessary or universal state of things; though the procedure of Ricardo's successors hardly encourages the belief that a wide academic culture would have prevented the narrow point of view. But certainly in a country where many laborers had some land and some capital, it would not have been so easy to treat the agricultural laborer, who was the type of all labor in so many of Ricardo's illustrations, as necessarily hired by a capitalist employer. The unfortunate position of Hodge caused

English economists with hardly an exception to do as Ricardo did: accept as a matter of course the dependence of all laborers on capital owned by others.

The problem, thus simplified and reduced to its barest elements, was naturally answered in more precise and unqualified terms. Not only, as Adam Smith put it, are wages paid out of capital, and determined by a bargain in which the demand for labor comes from employers' capital: but the amount of that capital, compared with the number of the laborers, fixes wages definitely. It is one thing to say that wages are paid out of capital; another thing, to say that the amount of capital determines wages once for all. Ricardo's habit of close calculation and unflinching reasoning might be expected to bring forth a more sharply defined statement than Adam Smith's. In fact, he made wages dependent directly on the amount of capital, and put forth a wages fund doctrine as unqualifiedly as any of the later writers with whom that doctrine is usually associated.

We may proceed now to consider more in detail Ricardo's conception of capital, and of the manner in which wages depend on capital. "Capital," he says in the chapter on Wages in the *Principles of Political Economy*, "is that part of the wealth of a country which is employed in production, and consists of food, clothing, tools, raw material, machinery, etc., necessary to give effect to labor." The last clause was the important one in Ricardo's mind. Capital was needed to give effect to labor: and the essential form in which it gave effect to labor was by supporting it. Capital was ultimately resolvable into food, or into advances to labor.

This proposition became, consciously and unconsciously, a corner stone of the Ricardian structure; it underlies all the reasoning of Ricardo and of his followers on distribution. It can be applied, however, in very different ways. It can be easily translated into the statement that wages at any time depend simply on the proportion of the total capital of the community to the total number of laborers of the community. This simple proposition we shall find commonly laid down by the later writers of the classic school; having its roots partly in Adam Smith's first discussion of the subject, but quite as much in Ricardo's identification of capital with advances to laborers. Ricardo himself, however, used it chiefly in other ways and for other purposes.

The mode in which he drew conclusions directly from the analysis of all capital into advances to labor, appears most clearly in the third, fourth, and fifth sections of the opening chapter of the *Principles*. The chapter deals with value; and in the sections mentioned he considers how far the employment of capital affects his fundamental doctrine that value depends solely on the quantity of labor necessary to obtain a commodity. Under the simplest conditions, or, as Adam Smith and Ricardo put it, "in that early and rude state of society, which precedes both the accumulation of stock and the appropriation of land" it is clear that, if "competition operates without restraint," * commodities will exchange in proportion to the labor necessary for producing them. The accumulation and employment of capital do not change the situation; because they simply bring a different mode of applying labor to production.

If we look to a state of society in which greater improvements have been made, and in which arts and commerce flourish, we shall still find that commodities vary in value conformably with this principle: in estimating the exchangeable value of stockings, for example, we shall find that their value, comparatively with other things, depends on the total quantity of labour necessary to manu-

* This supposition Ricardo made in terms. *Works*, p. 10.

facture them and to bring them to market. First, there is the labour necessary to cultivate the land on which the raw cotton is grown ; secondly, the labour of conveying the cotton to the country where it is to be manufactured, which includes a portion of the labour bestowed in building the ship in which it is conveyed, and which is charged in the freight of the goods ; thirdly, the labour of the spinner and weaver ; fourthly, a portion of the labour of the engineer, smith, and carpenter, who erected the buildings, by the help of which they were made ; fifthly, the labour of the retail dealer, and of many others, whom it is unnecessary further to particularize.*

The modern reader would expect to find this description of the successive division of labor, in a discussion of the sequence of production or of the functions of capital. But Ricardo mentions it and uses it for a different purpose. He proceeds to point out how his principle that value depends on quantity of labor bestowed, is modified according to the mode in which capital is advanced to laborers ; applying the reasoning to a consideration of value in a community where all laborers are employed by capitalists. We are not concerned with the details of the proof that value, in such a community, will not depend on quantity of labor alone, and that a general rise or fall in wages will affect the value of commodities made with the aid of much fixed capital, compared with commodities made by the more direct application of labor,—a proposition which both Ricardo and his followers set forth at wearisome length. The point essential for the present subject is that the reasoning rests simply on the assumption that capital means nothing more than advances to labor. In general, if more labor of one sort or another is needed to make a given commodity, more capital needs to be advanced in the same proportion ; the profit to capital

---

* Ricardo, *Works*, p. 17.

is in proportion to the advances to labor, or to the quantity of labor ; hence the fact of production under the lead of capitalists, and the appearance of profit, do not *per se* modify the principle that value depends on labor bestowed. " Fixed capital," in fact, is only " accumulated labour." *

We have only another phase of the same line of thought when, in the familiar and much-abused proposition, profits are said to depend on wages. Profits are high when wages are low, and are low when wages are high, simply because the investment of capital is ultimately resolvable into advances to laborers. All the advances of the capitalists as a body consist at bottom of payments to laborers ; what capitalists get back in return for their advances, is what the laborers produce ; profits at large depend on the relation between what is turned over to laborers and what is produced by them. Perhaps Ricardo's meaning is best expressed (Ricardo himself did not so put it, but Senior and other writers of later date did so for him) by saying that profits depend on the *proportion* between wages and product ; profits being high or low, according as the proportion of general wages to general output was small or large. However stated, there is a solid and unquestionable basis to the proposition : it brings into bold relief the essential fact in capitalist operations and the essential cause of profits and of interest. In so far, economic science owes a permanent debt to Ricardo, however his own deductions may need correction, and however much his theorem may have been twisted by later interpreters. Ricardo deduced conclusions from it on the assumption that wages fluctuated closely with the price of food, and that the price of food rose regularly, under the law of diminishing returns, with every addition to the sup-

---

* *Works*, p. 23, where these two phrases are used as equivalents.

ply ; assumptions to which the historical facts correspond so little that many of his conclusions have, even in the long run, but a very limited application.   On the other hand, the proposition that all capital stands for advances to laborers, when stated in the questionable phrase that capital is " accumulated labor," has been twisted by the optimists into a defence of profit, and so has been, not unfairly, the occasion for plentiful ridicule by the socialists. But the essential truth in it remains incontestable.   Without it the phenomena of capital and interest can not be understood.

This, however, is not the wages fund doctrine, nor is it of service in answering the question which that doctrine tried to answer: namely, what are the proximate causes determining wages at any one time.   Its bearing is on profits, not on wages.   The total advances to labor, represented by the total capital of any one time, have been spread over a long period.   Some advances were made years ago, and are represented by tools and machinery still in use.   Some were made within the year, and are represented chiefly by wheat on the fields.   When all the tools are gone, and all the wheat has become bread, it will appear how much the laborers have produced during the whole prolonged period, in comparison with the total which has been turned over to them.   But the demand for labor, in any given season, comes only from the fresh advances then made.   For the question of " market " wages, it is necessary to cull out from total capital that part which is effective at the moment in rewarding laborers.

To this special part of the subject, Ricardo never stopped to give much attention.   His phraseology is loose and uncertain.   Frequently, he used language which would imply that market wages depended simply on the proportion of laborers to capital at large, so giving color to the opinion, not seldom maintained since his time, that the

wages fund doctrine is but another version of the doctrine
that wages and profits vary inversely. Thus,—to cite but
one passage from many of the same tenor,—he says, in so
many words, that "profits might increase, because, the
population increasing at a more rapid rate than capital,
wages might fall." Yet the remainder of the same sentence shows that he conceived of the demand for labor at
the moment as identical not with total capital, but with a
part of capital : "instead of the value of 100 quarters of
wheat being necessary for the circulating capital, 90 only
[out of a total capital of 190] might be required."* Here
we have the phrase "circulating capital," used to designate that part of capital which serves directly to yield
wages. Ricardo rightly declared the distinction between
fixed and circulating capital to be "not essential, and in
which the line of demarcation can not be accurately
drawn."† Nevertheless he accepted the convenient use
of circulating capital as meaning wages-capital. He so
used it in the passage just cited ; and in another, on the
very page which in a note criticises the distinction between
circulating capital and other capital, the text says that in
in some trades "very little capital may be employed as
circulating capital, that is to say, in the employment of
labour." Ricardo was not trained to great nicety in
phraseology. Sometimes he used circulating capital to
stand for the part of capital which constitutes demand for
labor ; quite as often, as has just been noted, he used
capital alone. He speaks roughly of "the impulse which
an increased capital gives to a new demand for labour";
"in proportion to the increase of capital will be the increase in the demand for labour ";‡ "experience teaches

* *Essay on the Influence of a Low Price of Corn, Works*, pp. 371, 372.
† *Works*, p. 21, note.
‡ *Works*, p. 51 ; *Principles*, ch. v. Both of the passages first quoted
are on the same page.

that capital and population alternately take the lead, and wages in consequence are liberal and scanty."* The demand for labor is frequently mentioned rather as proportioned to the total amount of capital than as equal to that amount; and such a mode of stating the relation, it may be observed, is more common in the *Principles* than in the earlier writings. We have thus a considerable variety of phrases, strictly consistent only in that the immediate source of wages was regarded as some part of capital.

That Ricardo was thus careless in his language, arose in part perhaps from lack of literary training,† but more largely from the fact that his attention was fastened mainly on permanent profits and permanent wages. As to permanent profits it was immaterial whether capital at any one time consisted in large or in small part of "circulating" capital or wages fund. The essential thing was that the whole of capital represented advances to laborers. Whether the advances were made earlier or later, and whether spread over a longer or shorter period, profits depended in the end solely on what the laborers produced over and above what had been turned over to them. Permanent or "natural" wages, on the other hand, depended simply on the price of food. The immediate advance of "capital" or "circulating capital" to laborers determined only market wages, which adjusted themselves to "natural" wages by the process, believed by Ricardo to be comparatively rapid, of a variation in the number of labor-

---

* *Works*, p. 379 ; *Essay on the Influence of a Low Price of Corn.* This was an idea of Malthus's, by whom Ricardo thought the proof from experience had been supplied.

† "Like most people who have not had the advantage of a literary education, Ricardo was apt to think that a word ought to have whatever sense he found convenient to put upon it." Cannan, *History of the Theories of Production and Distribution*, p. 195. There is a good degree of truth in this remark, however ungraciously it is put.

ers. It thus made no difference, either as to permanent profits or permanent wages, how much of total capital happened to take in any one season the form of fresh advances to laborers.

Up to this point, the conclusions of the present chapter are not of any precise sort; showing indeed that Ricardo emphasized, in one way and another, the proposition that wages are paid from capital, but not showing that he held to the doctrine of an inelastic and predetermined wages fund. It was intimated at the outset of the chapter, however, that he had laid down, even though in brief terms, a doctrine of a more specific and rigid sort. It remains to be seen what further and more detailed views on this part of the subject he can be shown to have entertained.

Ricardo follows Adam Smith in speaking of " the funds destined for the maintenance of labour "; using this phrase quite as often as " capital " or " circulating capital," when he is speaking of the proximate causes determining market wages. What he conceives these funds to be, he says most explicitly, not in his chapter on Wages, where we might expect to find the statement, but in the later chapter which treats of taxes on raw produce and food. Incidentally to the discussion of the incidence of such taxes, we have a deliberate and detailed explanation of the nature and the limitation of the funds for the maintenance of labor.*

A tax on food will not permanently affect real wages. One of the simplest applications of Ricardo's doctrine on " natural " wages was that such a tax would raise the price of food; that " wages would inevitably and necessarily rise "; and profits would have to shoulder the tax. The dependence of profits on the price of food, *via* wages,

---

* Chapter ix of the *Principles*, " Taxes on Raw Produce."

is the cornerstone of Ricardo's theory of distribution,— and, at the same time, it may be admitted, its weakest part. But it might be objected "that there would be a considerable interval between the rise in the price of corn and the rise of wages, during which much distress would be experienced by the labourer." The objection leads Ricardo to consider how close is the connection between the price of food and money wages, and so to consider the causes which at any one time determine real wages.

"The wages of labour are really regulated by the proportion between the supply and demand of necessaries, and the supply and demand of labour; and money is merely the medium, or measure, in which wages are expressed." This is the sound view, which Adam Smith had stated so emphatically; but Ricardo carries it to consequences which Adam Smith never dreamed of. Anything which decreases the supply of necessaries (the real "funds for maintaining labourers") lowers wages, so long as population is the same; anything which leaves that supply fixed, can not affect them. A bad harvest reduces the quantity of necessaries; and however money wages may be made to rise "through misapplication of the poor laws," real wages must fall. Any attempt to regulate wages in such time by the money price of food "affords no real relief to the labourer, because its effect is to raise still higher the price of food, and at last he must be obliged to limit his consumption in proportion to the limited supply."

The situation is different if a tax is imposed on food. Then the quantity remains unchanged; real wages are not affected even for the moment.

"A tax on corn does not necessarily diminish the quantity of corn, it only raises its money price; it does not necessarily diminish the demand compared with the supply of labour; why then should it diminish the portion paid to the labourer? Suppose it true that it did diminish the quantity given to the labourer, in other words, that it did not raise his money wages in the same proportion as the tax raised the price of the corn which he consumed; would not the supply of corn exceed the demand?—would it not fall in price? and would not the labourer thus obtain his usual portion?" *

The result is the same in any other case in which the price of food is raised, but the quantity of it constituting the demand for labor remains unchanged. Thus, there

---

* The rest of the passage may be given, though it does not bear directly on the present subject:

" In such case, indeed, capital would be withdrawn from agriculture; for if the price were not increased by the whole amount of the tax, agricultural profits would be lower than the general level of profits, and capital would seek a more advantageous employment. In regard, then, to a tax on raw produce, which is the point under discussion, it appears to me that no interval which could bear oppressively on the labourer, would elapse between the rise in the price of raw produce, and the rise in the wages of the labourer; and that therefore no other inconvenience would be suffered by this class, than that which they would suffer from any other mode of taxation, namely, the risk that the tax might infringe on the funds destined for the maintenance of labour, and might therefore check or abate the demand for it."

It is not easy to make out by what process Ricardo thought the tax on food would raise its price. His language in this chapter usually implies that the effect would be immediate; and certainly he thinks that, if this happened, money wages also would rise immediately. But it is more in accord with his general mode of reasoning, and with the drift of this passage, to interpret him as concluding that the price of food would not rise at once. The first incidence of the tax is on agricultural profits; then comes a withdrawal of agricultural capital, a diminution of the supply of food; and so a rise in price. How, after this, " no interval which could bear oppressively on the labourer, would elapse between the rise in the price of raw produce, and the rise in the wages of the labourer," it is difficult to see. Apparently money wages can then rise only in consequence of a decline in population: a process which in fact must bear very oppressively.

may be a general rise of prices, and so a rise in the price of food,

"in consequence of an influx of the precious metals from the mines or from the abuse of the privileges of banking. It leaves undisturbed too the number of labourers, as well as the demand for them; for there will be neither an increase nor a diminution of capital. The quantity of necessaries to be allotted to the labourer, depends on the comparative demand and supply of necessaries, with the comparative demand and supply of labour: money being only the medium in which the quantity is expressed; and as neither of these is altered, the real reward of the labourer is not altered." *

It would be difficult to find in the writings of the classic economists a more direct statement of a predetermined fund, all of which must go to the laborers. The demand for labor is here treated as that part of capital which exists in the form of necessaries or food. No doubt Ricardo is discussing primarily the effects of a tax on food, not of capital and market wages. But he habitually spoke of wages as consisting of food which the laborers can not dispense with, and, in the very passages cited, identifies the food with their real reward. At any moment, there is just so much food on hand, and all of that the laborers will certainly get. No tax on food, no artificial rise in prices, can prevent them from getting, during the season, what is on hand for the season.

Another question would naturally be asked by one who followed Ricardo so far. If the laborers must get at least so much, does it follow that they can not get more? Ricardo never was led to give a clear intimation of his opinions on this further point. In the course of the same discussion of taxes on food, he remarks that "an accumu-

---

* *Works*, pp. 93–97. I have not followed Ricardo's arrangement of the matter in this summary; but the changes in no way affect the substance of his reasoning.

lation of capital naturally produces an increased competition among the employers of labour, and a consequent
rise in its price. The increased wages are not always immediately expended on food, but are first made to con-
tribute to the other enjoyments of the labourer." * This
might perhaps be interpreted to imply an elastic supply of
commodities which, though not food, yet constituted part
of "the real funds for maintaining labourers." But it is
more in accord with Ricardo's general reasoning to interpret him as speaking here of the results of several seasons
of higher wages. At first, higher money wages could not
bring higher real wages; but after a season or two, the
increased money demand for "other enjoyments" by laborers and the consequent higher prices of these "other enjoyments" would lead to a greater production of them.
Eventually, the laborers would increase in numbers, and
demand more food. The other enjoyments would disappear, food would be more costly from the resort to poorer
land, money wages would permanently rise, real wages (in
the sense important for the laborers) would return to the
point from which they started. Such are the details by
which, if this interpretation of his views is sound, Ricardo
would have described the changes in wages resulting from
a greater demand for labor.†

---

* *Works*, p. 95.

† One other passage from Ricardo's writings may be cited at this
point. In one of his letters to Malthus, written in 1815, he expresses
himself thus:

"If, instead of 4, 10 measures could be produced by a day's labour,
no rise would take place in wages, no greater portion of corn, cloth, or
cotton, would be given to the labourer, unless a portion of the increased
produce were employed as capital, and then the rise in wages would be in
proportion to the new demand for labour, and not at all in proportion to
the increase in the quantity of commodities produced. . . . In the case
of great improvements in machinery . . . no demand for additional
labour will take place unless the increased production in consequence of

It would be a mistake to infer too much from these passages. They intimate, undoubtedly, a rigid sort of wages fund,—an inflexible predetermination of the wages of the moment. But they are incidental to another topic, and Ricardo probably was not reflecting at all on the question of market wages except in its connection with the price of food. They are important, not so much in the specific content, as because they bring into vivid relief the unflinching manner in which Ricardo carried his reasoning to its last consequences. His habit of mind, and his general doctrines, would have led him easily to maintain the existence of such a fund; but, except in such incidental discussion as has just been noticed, Ricardo never made any careful statement of his views as to a clear-cut and predetermined wages fund.

At all events, it is in the example which he set of rigid reasoning and unqualified statement, that Ricardo exercised greatest influence on the presentation of the wages fund doctrine by later hands. The particular passages just discussed were not referred to, in their bearing on wages, by any of the writers of the next generation. But his modes of reasoning and of statement affected his successors powerfully, and gave economic theory a method and a direction which were retained, in England at least, for half a century. The prominent place which the analysis of capital into advances for laborers held in his writings at large, probably affected the wages fund discussion more than did the comparatively brief passages in which the question of market wages is specifically considered.

---

the improvements should lead to further accumulation of capital."— *Letters of Ricardo to Malthus*, edited by Bonar, pp. 98, 99.

This does not throw any further light on the details of Ricardo's thinking as to the wages fund; but it is interesting, because expressing in terms a conclusion which would certainly flow from his general reasoning, and which touches the gist of much recent controversy on the wages fund.

The operations of capitalists consist in making advances to laborers; market wages depend on the ratio between population and capital,—these two general propositions, combined with the example of rigid deductive reasoning, had most effect on the treatment of the theory of wages by Ricardo's successors and followers.

To summarize. Ricardo developed the theory of capital and wages in two directions. He put forth the doctrine that all capital is resolvable into advances to laborers, and that therefore wages and profits are inverse to each other. Faint germs of the doctrine are to be found in Adam Smith; the conclusion as to the inverse relation of wages and profits is explicitly stated by him; but the ground on which Ricardo reached it was never really touched by the earlier writer. Ricardo himself stated it rather by implication than explicitly; but it runs so plainly under all his reasoning on distribution that no one thereafter could fail to consider it. Next, Ricardo laid it down that "market" wages depended on the demand and supply of labor, and that the demand for labor came from the capital of those who hired laborers for production. Here Adam Smith had done more than to furnish the germs of the doctrine: the doctrine itself is prominent in the *Wealth of Nations*. But Ricardo gave it sharper outline, and a more universal application. He brushed aside all laborers except those hired by capitalists. If asked whether other laborers existed, he must have replied in the affirmative; and if asked whether their remuneration presented problems to which his theories on wages gave no sufficient answers, he must at least have hesitated, and considered the case further,—with what result every student of Ricardo will make his own guess. But the questions were rarely asked and, if asked, got no attention. The insular horizon of almost all the English economists of that period prevented them from touching other phenomena than those presented in their own country. Ricardo's simple formula as to the proportion of capital to population, reinforced as it was by what Adam Smith and his immediate successors had said, seemed to answer all questions worth the asking about the proximate forces determining wages. And, finally, there is evidence of a distinct opinion on Ricardo's part as to the rigidity of the part of the capital which could go to laborers in any one season; but this bears rather on Ricardo's own conclusions than on the influence which he exerted on the generation of economists who followed him.

CHAPTER X.

WE come now to the period of active discussion which begins with Ricardo and ends with John Stuart Mill; the period in which the doctrines of the classic economists gradually secured their strongest hold on students and thinkers, and in which the wages fund doctrine is often supposed to have arisen and flourished. All of the writers of the period were contemporaries of Ricardo; most of them knew him, or might have known him, in person. Their writings, however, were published after his, and with hardly an exception were profoundly affected by his compact array of clear-cut and consistent doctrines. On wages, as on other subjects, they showed the unmistakable traces of his influence; and it is very doubtful if all their discussion on this topic added anything substantial to what had been built up by Adam Smith and Ricardo.

In following the discussion by these later writers, it will be convenient to neglect the chronological sequence of their publications, and to group them according to the temper in which they approached economic questions. We may consider first those writers who, like the elder Mill and M'Culloch, followed Ricardo and Adam Smith with loyal fidelity, and made little profession of differing with their masters or of improving on them. Thereafter, the writers of earlier or later date may be taken up, whose attitude was more independent and critical; whether, like

Senior, they were in general accord with the dominant views, or, like Richard Jones, protested vigorously against them.

First in the list of the *Epigonen*, as the Germans, not without a good show of reason, dub this group of writers, comes James Mill, the intimate friend of Ricardo and Bentham. James Mill probably exerted a more enduring influence on the course of economic thought through the remarkable training in Ricardian economics which he gave his son, than through his own writings ; * yet these have an independent value, and are significant of the stage which the theory of wages now had reached.

In the opening chapter of his *Elements of Political Economy*,† James Mill starts in a fresh and promising fashion. He distinguishes sharply between capital and wages. Instruments and materials are "all that can be correctly included in the idea of capital. It is true that wages are in general included in that idea"; but this is an error, "the idea of the subsistence or consumption of the labourer, for which wages is but another name, is included in the idea of the labour." ‡ Here we have a distinction which anticipates some very modern discussion. Mill presently adds that the laborer's subsistence or wages, "being advanced by the capitalist out of those funds which would otherwise have constituted capital in the distinctive sense of the word, and being considered as yielding the same advantages, it is uniformly spoken of under the name of capital, and a confusion of ideas is the consequence."

If this first step had been followed up, we might have

---

* See the younger Mill's *Autobiography*, pp. 27–29.

† First published in 1821 ; a second edition appeared in 1824, a third in 1826. I quote from the second edition, the only one I have seen.

‡ *Elements*, pp. 17, 18.

had with James Mill a new and important stage in the
development of the theory of capital and wages. But he
never got beyond this first step, and seems to have forgotten that he ever took it. When he has completed the
introductory chapter on capital and labor, from which the
passages just quoted are taken, and proceeds to the
separate treatment of distribution and wages, he has nothing more to say of the confusion of ideas in regard to
capital and labor. He slides easily and quickly into the
familiar statement that wages depend on capital. It is true
that he begins by saying that both laborers and capitalists
get their reward from the commodity they produce, "or
the value of it"; and that "to suit the convenience of the
labourers," they receive their share of the commodity in
advance, in the shape of wages. But he passes at once to
the proof that "the rate of wages depends on the proportion between Population and Employment, in other words,
Capital,"—this being the italicized summary of the section in which the rate of wages is examined. Apparently
"capital" here means not only tools and materials, but
subsistence also. For the supposition is made that the
number of laborers increases, while the amount of "food,
tools, and materials" remains the same: then wages must
fall. The point of view is shifted within a page, within a
paragraph, from a treatment which contemplates a sharing of product between laborers and capitalists, to a consideration of the ratio between the number of laborers
and the total "means of employment" or "requisites of
production,"—both phrases being used. Thereafter we
hear simply of a ratio between capital and population: the
familiar formula emerges. "Universally, then, we may
affirm, other things remaining the same, that if the ratio
which capital and population bear to one another remains
the same, wages will remain the same; if the ratio which
capital bears to population increases, wages will rise; if

the ratio which population bears to capital increases, wages will fall."*

The use made of this formula is characteristic of the drift of the discussion of wages among English economists for the next half-century. Mill proceeds at once, after giving but a page or two to the universal proposition, to the corollary which, to his mind and that of his contemporaries, made it mainly important. Population had a "natural tendency" to increase faster than capital: hence are wages low, and the condition of the great body of the people poor and miserable. Their condition can improve only if the tendency of population to increase is checked by prudence. This was the point, however speciously it was concealed at the outset, at which the whole reasoning was aimed. And for this, it was not material whether the thing to which population bore a ratio was entitled "capital" or "subsistence" or "commodity" or "wealth," so long as it was made to appear that population had the "natural tendency" to increase at the more rapid rate. James Mill accepted the familiar phrase "capital" to describe the resources which could not be expected to grow as fast as population, even though he had expressly defined capital in a manner which might have led him to consider afresh the precise grounds on which his predecessors had laid it down that laborers were paid or supported from capital. But he had no great interest in such an inquiry, absorbed as he was, in common with his brother economists, in questions of production and exchange. So far as wages were concerned, the Malthusian doctrine and the pressure of population were the main things to be considered: the details by which wages might be shown to depend on capital at any given time, called for no special attention.

---

* *Elements*, p. 44.

A much less important personage than James Mill, and a much less familiar name to economic students, is Mrs. Jane H. Marcet, who seems to have been the pioneer in the many endeavors made in this eager century to popularize political economy. Mrs. Marcet published in 1816 her *Conversations on Political Economy*, a series of imaginary conversations between "Caroline," an ingenuous maiden, and "Mrs. B.," a wise old lady, who naturally does most of the talking. The book had no little vogue in its day, going through four editions between 1816 and 1821; and it gives interesting indications of the shape in which economic doctrines then were interpreted by a person of good intelligence who did not affect to have any theories of her own making.

In the conversation on capital, the difference between rich and poor is first referred to; then the circumstance that the rich, to maintain and employ their capital, must advance it to the poor; the perpetual consumption and reproduction of capital; profit arising from the fact that laborers produce more than is advanced to them,—all this is neatly expounded, with a characteristic comment that it is "one of the most beneficent ordinations of Providence that the employment of the poor should be a necessary step to the increase of the wealth of the rich." * Those who are disposed to judge the classic writers by their fruits may not unnaturally be roused to wrath by such a teleology. When it comes to wages, the inquiring Caroline is informed first that they depend on the habits of the poor and the degree of prudence they practice in multiplying,—the exposition resting faithfully on Malthus. Shortly after, it is laid down in terms that wages depend on the ratio of capital to laborers. Plenty of capital may indeed coexist with low wages, if the laborers

---

* *Conversations*, p. 98.

also are numerous,—thus in China; while capital, though absolutely scarce, may yet be plentiful relatively to the number of laborers,—thus in America. The primary proposition that wages depend on capital is proved, after the fashion of the time, by analyzing a simple case: a ship-wrecked crew is supposed to land, stripped and forlorn, on an island where, obviously enough, they must depend on the original settlers " for maintenance and employment." *

The reader conversant with the economic literature of England during the first half of the present century, need not be told how familiar a ring all this has, or how faithfully it reflects the expositions long current of the theory of wages. The reason for singling out for mention this particular bit of popularizing literature is the early date at which it appeared, and the evidence it supplies of the source whence the whole train of thought was derived. Mrs. Marcet first published her *Conversations* in 1816, at a time when Ricardo was known almost exclusively by his pamphlets on monetary subjects, and when the writers to whom the maker of a tract would look for guidance were mainly Adam Smith and his immediate successors.† Ricardo is mentioned in the preface, and evidently is followed by Mrs. Marcet in the exposition of money, coinage, and prices. But on value, Adam Smith's analysis of cost of production into its constituent parts,—wages, profits, and rent,—is faithfully followed. On foreign trade there is similarly no trace of Ricardo's unmistakable doctrines; indeed, Adam Smith is followed in a doctrine which no

---

* *Conversations*, pp. 122, 124, 136, 143. The illustrations from China and America are obviously taken from the *Wealth of Nations*, Book I, ch. viii, p. 32.

† Ricardo's *Essay on the Influence of a Low Price of Corn* was published in 1815, and the essence of all his characteristic doctrines can be found in this compact tract ; but they are presented in a manner to reach the understanding of only a very small circle of readers.

follower of Ricardo would fail to reject,—his eulogy on the home trade as yielding more " encouragement to industry " than the foreign trade.   Clearly, the wages fund, essentially in the form in which it was retained for the next generation, is here found in a writer who derived her knowledge and inspiration from economic literature as it stood before Ricardo's peculiar doctrines had been incorporated into it.   The dependence of wages on capital, the ratio of capital to population, the standard of living and the " habits " of the population as the important determining factors,—these are the doctrines which the popularizer gathered from the political economy of the day. They are evidently derived, in the main, from Adam Smith and Malthus.   Ricardo soon put his stamp on them ; but before his day the essentials could easily be put together.

Next among those who represent the views current in their day, comes a writer who would have been highly indignant at finding himself ranked in any way with so modest a personage as Mrs. Marcet,—John Ramsay M'Culloch, member of the Institute of France, editor of the works of Adam Smith and Ricardo, author of a widely-accepted exposition of the *Principles of Political Economy* and of many other works of repute, ever a welcome contributor to the reviews and the cyclopædias, honored witness before Parliamentary commissions,—in fact, the most prominent figure in the economic world in the period from 1820 to 1850.   The fate of M'Culloch is a warning to those who bask in the sunshine of general favor.   Once the authoritative expounder of the economic gospel, he is now, in the minds of those who would be in the van of thought, the representative of all that is bad in classic political economy.   In fact, M'Culloch has been made somewhat of a scapegoat.   He was an honest and an able man, who did good service in his day in spreading knowledge and in contributing helpfully to the understanding

of many concrete questions.   Having a great faith in the
completeness and accuracy of his own knowledge, and a
great willingness to apply the formulas of the day to any
and every problem that might appear, he naturally stated
the doctrines current in his time in their most unqualified
form, and became a ready butt for those of a later day who
had shaken loose from them.   However great his preten-
sions as a man of science, M'Culloch was but a popularizer of the doctrines of Adam Smith, Malthus, and Ricardo, and stood for no views that were his own except by a
process of absorption from others.

M'Culloch has been sometimes spoken of as the author
of the wages fund doctrine; * but there is an *a priori* im-
probability that he really originated any independent doctrine whatever, and no indication that he did more in this
case than to restate and put into more definite form what
had been worked out by others.   M'Culloch first set forth
his views on distribution and on wages in the article on
Political Economy which he contributed to the supplement
to the *Encyclopædia Britannica*, and which he expanded into
his *Principles of Political Economy* in 1825.   That book
went through five editions in his lifetime, the last being
published in 1864.   Meanwhile he printed in 1826 an *Essay
on Wages*, which in 1854 was revised and enlarged as a

---

* Thus Mr. John Rae remarks (*Contemporary Socialism*, 2d edition,
p. 360) that M'Culloch was "more than merely the expositor of that
['orthodox'] system ; he is really one of its founders, the author of one
of its famous dogmas, at least in its current form, the now exploded doctrine of the wages fund."   And Mr. James Bonar (*Malthus and his
Work*, p. 155, American edition) tells us that "the theory of a wages
fund was formed from the facts of a perfectly exceptional time, and on
the strength of two truths misapplied, the doctrine of Malthus (on Population) in its most unripe form, and of Ricardo (on Value) in its most
abstract.   J. R. M'Culloch seems to have been the first who put the two
together."

Treatise on Wages.   In all these writings, not to mention others, the conclusions and the form of statement, even the very words, are repeated with exemplary and monot-onous consistency.

To quote the words of the first edition of the *Political Economy* :

" The capacity of a country to support and employ labourers is in no degree dependent on advantageousness of situation, richness of soil, or extent of territory. . . . It is obviously not on these cir-cumstances, but on the actual amount of the accumulated produce of previous labour, or of capital, devoted to the payment of wages, in the possession of a country, at a given period, that its power of supporting or employing labour must wholly depend.   A fertile soil affords the means of rapidly accumulating capital : but that is all. Before this soil can be cultivated, capital must be provided for the support of the labourers employed upon it, just as it must be pro-vided for the support of those engaged in manufactures, or in any other department of industry." *

This is all that M'Culloch has to say as to the basis of the doctrine that wages depend on the capital available for paying them.   The same language, substantially, is used in all the editions of the *Political Economy*, and in the two versions of the *Essay on Wages*.   Elsewhere, in discussing capital as a means of increasing the produc-tiveness of labor, he follows Adam Smith in saying that the accumulation of capital must precede the division of labor ; † beyond this, there is no further consideration of the why and how of the dependence of wages on capital. M'Culloch was an ardent and faithful follower of Adam Smith and Ricardo, and his writing has the easy flow of the former with yet the angular and unqualified doc-trines of the latter.   His exposition differs from theirs

---

* M'Culloch's *Political Economy*, 1st edition, p. 327.

† *Ibid.*, p. 95.

mainly in emphasis. In the note on wages which he appended to his edition of the *Wealth of Nations* (1828), he put the doctrine of wages and capital, as it stood with Ricardo's stamp on it, with characteristic vehemence: "No other fund [than capital] is in existence from which the labourers, as such, can draw a single shilling." *

This much seemed to M'Culloch, as to a long series of writers of his generation, so simple and self-evident that, to be proved, it needed but to be stated. He passed at once to the phase of the wages question which did seem to need all possible proof and illustration: to the relative growth of population and capital, and the pressure of population on subsistence. Thus he reached, in the phrase which forms the caption of a section in the *Essay on Wages*, the topic of "natural or necessary wages, different in different countries and periods; dependent on the quantity and species of the articles required for the subsistence of the labourer." When he thus proceeded to the discussion of the relative growth of population and capital, he evidently meant by "capital" simply food, and used the proposition that market wages depended on the ratio of population to capital, chiefly as an easy introduction to the Malthusian doctrine. It was with more or less conscious thought of the ratio of food to population that he laid it down in sweeping terms that "the rate of wages *in all countries and at all periods* depends on the ratio between the portion of their capital allotted to paying wages, and the number of their labourers." †

---

* *Wealth of Nations*, M'Culloch's edition, p. 470.

† *Treatise on Wages* (1854), p. 7.—In this tract the reader will find also some remarks (at pp. 49, 50) about the advantages of high wages to the capitalists, because they bring "security and tranquillity" and are "incomparably the best defence of the estates and mansions of the rich." That M'Culloch could insert such remarks in a tract designed primarily

There is little indication that M'Culloch ever got beyond this stage in the wages fund doctrine. It remains, in all his many disquisitions, simply an introduction to the Malthusian discussion. It is true that in the *Political Economy*, he inserted, in later editions, a paragraph or two which went a trifle farther. He drew the corollary that the interests of laborers and capitalists are identical, because " a capitalist can not increase his own stock without at the same time, and to the same extent, increasing the wealth, or the means of subsistence of the working classes,"—a comforting doctrine very like that of Mrs. Marcet, just referred to. He insisted, too, on the practical certainty that " all the capital, through the higgling of the market, will be equitably distributed among all the labourers "; hence " it is idle to suppose that the efforts of capitalists to cheapen labour can have the smallest influence on its medium price." * This has something of the ring of a wages fund doctrine with rigid lines, sufficient for the explanation of any and all questions concerning wages. M'Culloch, in another passage inserted in his later editions, mentioned the possibility of an inquiry whether " an increase of capital is synonymous with an increase of the means of employing labour." † He disposes of the inquiry summarily by referring to his previous discussion of the effects of machinery on wages, where he conceived that he had shown that "the introduction of machinery uniformly increases the aggregate demand of society for labour and wages." These additions to his

for laborers' reading, shows how hopelessly he lacked any saving sense of humor.

* These passages are quoted from the fourth edition of the *Political Economy* (1849), pp. 399–400. I have not seen the second or third editions, but suspect that this new matter may have been inserted as early as the second edition (1830)

† Fourth edition, p. 401.

first statements show that M'Culloch did come to have some glimpse of the fact that there were some questions on the relations of capital to wages which did not connect themselves once for all with the theory of population. But he never followed them out, or discussed them: briefly touched on them, still retaining his exposition in essentials as he had first given it to the public when a young man barely in his majority. It is significant that when he touched on combinations of laborers and the concrete questions of wages which arise regarding them, he said not a word of a limitation of wages by capital, or of any light thrown from this point of view on the possible effects of trade unions. We shall have occasion presently to consider his attitude, as well as that of other writers, on combinations and trade unions. For the present it suffices to note that he virtually did not cite the wages fund at all on this aspect of the problem: a further bit of evidence as to the use of the doctrine, by the writers of this period, as a means primarily of proving the need of restraint in the growth of population.

One or two other writers who illustrate still further the manner in which wages were usually set forth by the group to which M'Culloch belonged, may receive brief mention. Like M'Culloch, they assume once for all the determination of wages in the first instance by the ratio between capital and population, and then proceed without further ado to the consideration of other less simple matters. Torrens, in his *Essay on the Production of Wealth* (1821), tried to take a middle ground between Ricardo and Malthus in regard to the mooted questions of value; but on wages he assumed as a matter of course that they depend on the advance of subsistence by capitalists to laborers, and then pushes this line of thought no farther. On one point only does he even stop to consider the relation be-

tween wages and capital; influenced perhaps by a suggestion of James Mill's, referred to a moment ago. It occurs to him to inquire whether subsistence should after
all be classed as capital; but he concludes that this is not
"a forced or unwarrantable extension of the meaning of
the term, capital," since the capitalist advances wages, as
he provides materials and tools, "for the express purpose
of obtaining a reproductive return." * Thirteen years
later, when the doctrines of the classic school had been
much more frequently worked over, and had gained much
wider acceptance, Torrens wrote on *Wages and Combinations* (1834). Here we have a discussion at large of the
theory of wages, by an able hand, and might expect some
detailed inquiry into the meaning and grounds of the
proposition that wages are determined by the amount of
capital. But no such inquiry is undertaken. It is assumed without question or argument that wages are paid
from capital; capital is conceived in terms of food,—so
many quarters of wheat; and the upshot of the whole
book is that wages can be little influenced by combinations, but can be effectively raised through a check to the
growth of numbers and through free trade in grain. It is
significant that Torrens, while reasoning that wages are
paid from capital, evidently does not see herein any ground
for alleging that combinations of laborers can not affect
wages. On the contrary, he argues that a universal combination might conceivably raise all wages, until they
reached the point where the curtailment of profits would
check accumulation and reinvestment. All this goes to
show that the payment of wages from capital did not present itself to Torrens as a hard-and-fast barrier to efforts
on the part of the laborers to better their lot; while, on
the other hand, it did not appear to him to be of crucial

* See the *Essay*, pp. 26, 27, 88.

importance, as compared with the other forces that affected wages.*

A similar brevity in the treatment of the doctrine appears in De Quincey's *Logic of Political Economy* (1844),
which is confessedly no more than an exposition of Ricardo's doctrines.   It is chiefly concerned with value, and
juggles with the subtleties of that subject in De Quincey's
most elaborately polished style.   In the chapter on wages,
he proceeds to mention four determining factors: (1) the
rate of movement of population, (2) the rate of movement
of capital, (3) changes in the price of necessaries, (4) the
standard of living.   Little is said of capital, and it is simply assumed, in direct acceptance of the usual compact
statement, that the ratio of capital to population determines wages.   De Quincey's reasoning rather than reasonable mind brought him to the curious conclusion that a
rapid and immediate effect on wages could be exercised
only by the third of his four factors,—changes in the price
of food.   The other factors could vary but slowly ; hence,
by a residual process, he was led to the conclusion that
"the daily cost of necessaries alters sometimes largely in
a single day, and upon this, therefore, must be charged
the main solution of those vicissitudes in wages which are
likely to occur within one man's life."   For the present
subject, De Quincey's discussion deserves notice only as
yielding one further piece of evidence as to the general

---

* Torrens laid it down that there was a minimum of wages, determined by the laborers' necessaries ; and a maximum of wages, determined
by the product.   Between these limits, combinations of masters and of
men might affect wages.   This reminds one of the mode of expounding
the theory of wages which in later times became current among the German economists, and is still much in vogue among them.   See the *Quarterly Journal of Economics*, vol. ix, p. 16 (October, 1894).

As to the position of Torrens on trades-unions and the wages fund,
see also what is said at the close of the present chapter.

acceptance of the doctrine as to the payment of wages from capital, and the slightness of the emphasis placed on it.

We come now to a writer who at least saw that there was a question here, and stopped to think about it,—Nassau W. Senior.   Professor Böhm-Bawerk,* in his admirable history of the theories of capital, has pointed out the merit of Senior in appreciating the need of some independent explanation of interest as a share in distribution ; and an equally able and certainly no less critical historian, Mr. Cannan, has similarly given him credit for perceiving the inadequacy of what his predecessors had said on interest and profit. †   Praise of the same sort can be given to Senior's treatment of wages also.   He did not on the whole advance the discussion of wages as much as that of interest ; but he faced it squarely, and showed himself awake to the inadequacy of the simple phrases and generalizations which had been current since the days of Adam Smith and Ricardo.   Senior, in fact, was the most acute critic of his day.   Intellectual indolence prevented him from pushing his work beyond the stage of criticism. He began his contributions to economic literature with a burst of promising activity : lecturing at Oxford on value, on wages, on population, on international trade.   Ricardo's peculiar doctrines and phraseology were subjected to criticism which was severe, but in the main just ; and Malthus's excessive emphasis on the pressure of population led to a correspondence in which Malthus virtually accepted Senior's version of his own views.   Perhaps the most successful constructive part of his work was in the lectures on interna-

---

* Böhm-Bawerk, *Capital and Interest*, p. 272.

† Cannan, *History of the Theories of Production and Distribution*, p. 214.

tional trade and the movement of the precious metals, where Ricardo's general reasoning on those subjects was carried to new and important corollaries. On wages he published in 1830 *Three Lectures on the Rate of Wages*, which contain almost everything that he ever said on that subject. The matter of these lectures, as well as that of the lectures on other topics, was later incorporated in the general essay on political economy, amounting to a small book, which Senior prepared in 1836, in the form of an article for the *Encyclopædia Metropolitana*. With this article,—written presumably to order and with no great deliberation,—his contributions to economic theory unfortunately came to an end. Other matters of public and private interest engrossed his attention, and he published nothing more on economic theory. His work was thus never carried beyond its first stage of promise, and his results were never maturely developed.

For our purposes, it will suffice to consider the presentation of the theory of wages in the encyclopædia article on *Political Economy*, in which, as was just remarked, Senior incorporated substantially everything he said on this subject in the earlier essays. He begins by laying it down that wages depend proximately on the commodities appropriated to laborers as compared with the number of laborers ; "or, to speak more concisely, on the extent of the fund for the maintenance of labourers, compared with the number of labourers to be maintained." So much is "nearly self-evident." But various current opinions are inconsistent with it, and Senior proceeds to examine at length seven propositions which are thus inconsistent and therefore unsound. Among the doctrines dissected in this prolonged introduction are some that do not touch the present subject, and others that have no longer a living interest ; such as the effects of absentee-landlordism, of the importation of foreign commodities, of the luxurious expenditure of the rich. But two of the rejected propositions were those most widely accepted of the time. One, the most familiar of all, was that wages depended on the ratio between capital and the number of laborers : which Senior rejects because " we know of no definition of that term [capital] which would not include many things that are not used by the labouring classes, and, if our proposition be correct, no increase or diminution of *these* things can *directly* affect wages." The other important doctrine set aside by Senior was probably mentioned by him because it was attributable, with some show of reason, to Adam Smith, and (as will presently be seen) to Malthus. It was that wages depended on the proportion between the number of laborers and the whole revenue of society. Neither Adam Smith nor Malthus, so far as they held any such opinion, seem to have had anything more in mind than that wages tended to go up or down in sympathy with the general movement of the whole income of the community. In any case, Senior has no difficulty in showing that this is no precise statement of the specific causes determining wages at any one time.

It is clear that Senior set out with the intention of examining in detail the causes determining the real "fund for the maintenance of labourers," and with a strong sense of the vagueness and inadequacy of the current generalizations about the proportion of capital to population. Doubtless he was led thus to inquire more searchingly how wages at any time were exactly fixed, by his comparative freedom from the Malthusian tinge of his contemporaries. But, as he digressed needlessly in his introductory examination of the opinions he rejects, so he wandered from his subject when he came to the statement of his own views ; and before he came to the end, was so weary of the task, or uncertain of his ground, that he ended with little more than that simple statement of the problem with which he had begun.

After the introduction, Senior returns to his main subject, and points out that the fund for maintaining laborers depends on two things : the general productiveness of the laborers of the community on the one hand, and the proportion of those laborers, on the other hand, who are engaged in producing goods for the use of laborers. This is simple, but none the less good because it is simple. While only another statement of the problem, it is a statement and a beginning from a promising point of view. It brings out the fundamental fact that all production comes from labor, and brushes away any notion of an independent "productiveness" of land or capital. It brings out another important side of the same fundamental fact,— namely, that income from capital and land means simply that some laborers are working to satisfy the wants or caprices of the owners of these instruments, and that the share of the laborers in distribution depends primarily on how many of them are working for the satisfaction of the wants of their whole number. The right statement of a problem is a good step toward its solution ; and a modern writer could do worse than to follow Senior in this mode of approaching the subject.

Fairly started, Senior digresses again. He stops to discuss the first of the two factors he has mentioned,—the general productiveness of labor. The intelligence and skill of the laborers ; the quality of the natural agents ; the aid given "by abstinence, or to use a more familiar expression, by the use of capital"; the interference or non-interference of government,—are successively examined. These are clearly questions of production, and not of distribution ; they distract the reader's attention from the main inquiry, and one may suspect that Senior lingered over these comparatively simple matters because of an instinctive hesitation in grappling with the more involved problem of distribution proper. When at last he reaches this, he sets aside at once, as presenting no difficulties, rent and taxes. Rent means that some laborers produce commodities for the use of landlords, and "such labourers may be considered as existing only in consequence of the existence of natural agents of extraordinary productiveness." * Taxes mean that some laborers work "for the supply of the consumption of the government": and here again Senior digresses to discuss some evils of taxation, holding off for a while longer from the crucial question. At last, rent and taxes are left behind, somewhat after the residual method which has come so much into vogue in our own time. He reaches profits, and "the extent to which wages may be affected by the employment of labour to produce, instead of wages, things for the use of capitalists."

Unfortunately, at this important stage, the exposition becomes obscure, and difficult to follow or to state. What the capitalists get,—*i. e.*, how many laborers work to supply their wants,—is said to depend on the rate of profits and the length of time over which the advance of capital is spread. But the rate of profits is surely the consequence

---

* Senior considered rent no deduction from wages, and no burden on the laborers, because rent was the consequence of the unusual productiveness of certain land. "The labourers who are employed for the benefit of the owners of natural agents may be in general considered a separate class, not withdrawn from the general body, but added to it by the existence of those natural agents." It is a natural corollary from the classic theory of rent to say, as Senior here does, that the laborers who work for the landowners do not diminish real wages ; but might not they add to real wages, by working to supply the needs of other laborers, instead of working to supply the landlords? Both as to rent and taxes, Senior failed to follow the line of reasoning which he had marked out at the beginning.

rather than the cause of the share of the capitalist in the
result of production; or rather it is the same phenomenon
defined in different terms. Senior seems to fall into a
vicious circle, and to get no farther than to state his problem in another way. He illustrates his principle by sup-
posititious figures, in which the shares of the capitalists
and the laborers are stated in terms of the product of so
many days' labor. But, in fine, we get nothing that clears
away the real difficulties. " The rate of profit depends on
the previous conduct of the labourers and capitalists of
the country,"—which probably expresses an intuition that
at any given time distribution, and especially wages, must
be predetermined by forces that have operated mainly in
the past. But exactly how the previous conduct either of
laborers or of capitalists affects the situation, is not lucidly
set forth. We might expect to find here some reference
to the mode in which capitalists have been induced to
" abstain," and to the manner in which their reward for
" abstinence,"—so much discussed by Senior in earlier
passages of this same essay,—is worked out; but we
hear nothing of it. Almost imperceptibly, Senior drifts
back into the familiar mode of approaching the question.
Capital is stated in terms of so much food; and the income of the laborers is made to depend at any given time
on the quantity of food as compared with the number of
the laborers. He forgets, apparently, what he said at the
outset, of wages *not* depending on the ratio between capital and population. It is true that he professes to examine only the simplest state of society, in which all capital may be food; but he examines no other; and he does
not introduce at the close those qualifications which appear in a complicated society and which he clearly had in
mind when he began.

It may be suspected that if Senior, after writing this
statement of the theory of distribution, had laid it aside,

and re-examined it after the lapse of two or three years, he would not have given it to the public in its present form.   How far a riper consideration would have affected his views, it is idle to speculate.   Senior had good sense, a clear and independent head, the easy style of a man of letters : a more mature and deliberate piece of work from his hand might have profoundly affected the subsequent course of thought.   As it was, his discussion of wages served on the whole to keep the traditional statement where it was.   When he came at close quarters with the subject, he followed Ricardo in analyzing capital into advances to laborers, or food ; he laid stress on the proximate dependence of wages on the " fund for the maintenance of labourers " as compared with the number of laborers ; and, while he criticised Malthus, he did little to distract the attention of economists from the standard of living as the one great factor to be insisted on in the presentation of the wages question.

We may turn now to some of the writers who dissented more or less from the general theories of the reigning school.   On the wages fund doctrine, in the form in which it was then commonly stated, we shall find their dissent neither important in substance nor strong in emphasis.

Malthus's attitude in the *Essay on Population* has been already described : he had shown some disposition to differ with Adam Smith, and had attempted to give his own analysis of " the funds for the maintenance of labour."   In the books and pamphlets which he published in later years, after Ricardo had turned economic thought so largely into new channels, he attempted a modification of the doctrine that the demand for labor came from capital, which followed substantially the lines of his first modest difference with Adam Smith.

Malthus's opposition to Ricardo and his followers cen-

tered about his insistence on demand and supply as the
primary forces determining exchange and distribution.
Hence, in regard to wages, he laid stress on the importance of the proximate demand for labor, and protested
against the emphasis on a "natural" rate of wages determined by the habitual subsistence of the laborer.   Malthus himself was mainly responsible for the almost exclusive
attention which the Ricardian school gave to "natural"
wages; and it is part of the irony of fate that he found it
necessary to protest against doctrines which were largely
of his own making.   He insisted on the importance of
supply and demand, as they worked at any given time, in
the determination of profits, protesting against Ricardo's
teaching that profits depended on the price of food; and
similarly he insisted on the importance of the proximate
demand for labor in determining wages.

As to the nature of this direct demand, however, and
the causes which made it large or small at any given time,
Malthus after all had not much to say.   In the first edition of the *Principles of Political Economy* (1820) he begins
by saying that wages depend primarily on demand and
supply, and that "what may be called cost of production
of labour only influences wages as it regulates the supply
of labour."*   Demand, thereafter, he speaks of in terms
that vary much: sometimes as coming from the "capital"
of the community, sometimes from the "capital and revenue," sometimes from the "resources," sometimes from
the "general value of the produce."   Apparently he did
not at this time think it of much moment to consider
and define the demand for labor with any painstaking accuracy.   In the second edition (1836), he changed his general introductory statement in a manner indicating that he
had given more specific attention to this part of the theory

---

* *Political Economy*, ch. iv, section i.

of distribution. It may be guessed that Senior's discussion led him to stop to think more carefully about it; beyond question, the steady controversy which he had carried on, since the appearance of the first edition, with Ricardo and his followers, led him to define his views more sharply in this second edition. The most important passage in the later edition may be quoted in full:

"It has been generally considered that the demand for labour is proportioned only to the circulating, not to the fixed capital of a country. But in reality the demand for labour is not *proportioned* to the increase of capital in any shape; nor even, as I once thought, to the increase of the exchangeable value of the whole annual produce. It is proportioned only, as above stated, to the increase in the quantity and value of the funds which are actually employed in the maintenance of labour.

"These funds consist in the necessaries of life, or the means of commanding the food, clothing, lodging, and firing of the labouring classes of society,"—*

and then Malthus goes on to point out that a large expenditure of "neat surplus" in hiring "menial servants, soldiers, and sailors" will add to the demand for labor without an increase of capital. Evidently he was here on very much the same ground that he had taken in the *Essay on Population:* we must consider "the increase in the funds specifically destined for the maintenance of labor, instead either of the increase of wealth, or the increase of capital, or the increase of the exchangeable value of the whole produce." †

Yet Malthus never got even as far as Senior did in the inquiry what precise relation these funds bore to the capital, or the wealth, or the exchangeable produce of the

---

* *Political Economy*, 2d edition, p. 234.

† This is the summary given at p. 260 of the second edition of the *Political Economy*, at the close of the chapter on Wages.

country.   More than this: when discussing other related subjects, and more particularly the closely related one of profits, he fell into the traditional way of speaking of capital simply as constituting the demand for labor, and of the relative advance of capital and population as determining profits.*   His insistence on the "funds" rather than "capital" as making and measuring the demand for labor arose, in fact, from a desire to influence other parts of economic theory than those connected with the wages fund doctrine proper.   He meant to protest against the notion that "natural" wages, determined by cost of production, told virtually the whole story.   Further, he had in mind the question how far a market for an increasing supply of commodities could be found among laborers, as capital accumulated and profits tended to decline.   All of Malthus's speculations in later years were colored by his adherence to the theory of gluts, or general over-investment and over-production.   His views on gluts never gained acceptance, and on the whole did not deserve to; and this aided to prevent his attempt at a re-statement of the immediate demand for labor from making much impression.   In any case, Malthus never questioned that commodities turned over to laborers by employers engaged in production were capital; on the contrary, one of the many points on which he quarrelled with M'Culloch was in in-

---

* In the discussion of profits in the first edition occurs this passage, which indicates sufficiently how far his reflections had carried him in 1820: "I have stated in a former chapter that the demand for labour does not depend on capital alone, but on revenue and capital taken together, or the value of the whole produce ; but to illustrate the present *supposition* [the italics are Malthus's: the supposition is that capital is abundant] it is only necessary to consider capital and labour."—Ch. v, section ii (p. 234, note, in the American reprint of 1821). So in the second edition (p. 277): "As capital and produce increased faster than labour, the profits of capital would fall"; and so on.

sisting that food became capital simply by virtue of being in fact turned over to laborers.* This fundamental part of the current doctrine being accepted, it was natural that corrections in the precise statement of the total demand for wages, applied as they were chiefly in connection with unpopular doctrines like that on gluts, should have failed to affect in any visible way writers of that day or of later days.

Another writer may here be briefly mentioned : Thomas Chalmers, who joined with Malthus in asserting that something like a general glut was possible, and so dissented from the dominant school on at least one fundamental doctrine. Unlike Malthus, Chalmers, in his *Political Economy* (1832), always speaks of "capital" simply as the source whence wages are paid. Capital, in Ricardo's fashion, is treated as resolvable ultimately into a succession of advances to laborers : the point on which Chalmers dissented being the possibility of indefinitely increasing those advances without annihilating profits. In his reasoning on the ultimate consequence of investment, and the ultimate source whence capitalists were recouped, Chalmers suggested, though very briefly, a doctrine which later was made much of by German economists,—that ultimately wages were derived from what was paid for the product by consumers and so from the "replacing power in the hands of consumers." † Of this turn in the development of the theory of wages more will be said in a later chapter. In the main Chalmers, even more than Malthus, retained and even reinforced the current doctrines as to the immediate determination of wages by capital, and made no impression on the course of thought on wages and the wages fund.

---

* See Malthus's *Definitions in Political Economy* (1827), p. 85.
† *Political Economy*, vol. i, p. 98.

A much more vigorous protest than came from either Senior or Malthus or Chalmers, against the general doctrines in vogue, was made by Richard Jones. Jones was an able and scholarly thinker, with views broadened by a wide knowledge of history and an appreciation of the lessons of history. His attitude on the wages fund doctrine, as the doctrine stood at that date, is significant. He admitted that it was true *hic et nunc*, but insisted that in the sweep of history it had but very limited application. His views on our subject appear in the *Literary Remains, consisting of Lectures and Tracts on Political Economy*, published in 1859, after his death. At what date these fragments were composed does not appear; but from passages in his *Essay on Rent*, published in 1831, it is clear that he had matured his opinions in all essentials as early as that date.*

Jones laid stress on the fact that, taking the world over, only a small proportion of laborers were paid out of capital. He divided laborers into three classes: (1) unhired laborers tilling the ground as peasant proprietors or serfs; (2) laborers paid directly out of "revenue" by those employing them, such as servants in modern times and retainers in the Middle Ages; (3) laborers hired by capitalists and paid by advances from them. He maintained that the great bulk of laborers in the world belonged to the first class, and were not paid out of capital. The commodities on which they lived were a fund for "immediate consumption, constituting part of the revenue of the country." The second class were also paid out of "revenue," and not out of capital. In a society like that

---

* See p. xxvi of the Preface to the *Essay on Rent*, where there is a clear intimation of the distinctions amplified in the later volume. See also his *Introductory Lecture on Political Economy, and Syllabus of a Course of Lectures on Wages* (1833), where the same distinctions are summarily stated, pp. 45–52.

of the Middle Ages, this class would include not only the great numbers of feudal retainers, but many artificers engaged directly by those wanting their services.   As to the third class, England was the only country in which the bulk of the laborers belonged to it ; and even in the England of the author's day, the members of the second class were " a body not unimportant."

Here we have on the one hand an echo of Adam Smith's distinction between capital and revenue, on the other hand a large-minded view of the great variations in the machinery of production and distribution among different communities and in different times.   The differences which he pointed out between modern advanced communities, and older communities having a fundamentally different organization of industry, deserved much more attention than they received.   The English economists of that time had a singularly insular horizon.   They regarded only the phenomena that were before their eyes in their own country, and generalized from them with a strange disregard of the absence elsewhere of the conditions on which their generalizations rested.   Jones's protests against the undiscriminating rashness with which they applied their doctrines were not heeded ; yet they deserve, as they have received, high praise for the historic sense which they evince.*

Nevertheless, as to the third class of laborers, and so as to the conditions of modern societies, Jones does not question the doctrines of the day.   Such laborers are paid out of capital, and their wages depend on the amount of capital.   " The whole fund from which they are paid is a

---

* Dr. Ingram, in his *History of Political Economy*, pp. 142–145, has justly pointed out Jones's merit, and the important place he should have among the early thinkers who used a really historical and comparative method.

fund which has to be saved, which goes through a process
of accumulation with a view to profit." As their numbers
increase, "it is necessary for their continuous prosperity
that the community should save and accumulate capital
at least as fast as they are multiplying their numbers." *
The wages of such laborers depend on the relative growth
of capital and population. This is laid down in unquestioning acceptance, as to modern advanced societies, of
the doctrine then current.

Jones gave little space to his third class of laborers,
hired by capital. In the fragments, attention is given
chiefly to the other two classes, which his contemporaries
had so completely left out of sight. He thus questions
rather the scope of the classic doctrine, than its validity
where the assumed conditions are to be found. He maintains, indeed, that the organization of industry by which
laborers are hired by capitalists, represents an advance in
the methods of production. The laborers work more continuously and efficiently : the capitalists plan and develop
inventions and improvements. In fact, there is a tinge
of optimism, unexpected in a writer of his stamp, in the
reasoning as to the advantages of the capitalist system
for the laborer. It brings greater competition for his
services, and "nothing can prevent the whole sum paid as
wages being dictated by the wants and demands of the
whole body of capitalists made more pressing and eager
by each successive accumulation of capital. This competition is the workman's real safeguard,—he interferes with
it, ordinarily, much to his disadvantage." †

---

* *Literary Remains*, p. 173.   Cf. also p. 460.

† *Ibid.*, p. 459.—In another passage (p. 453), Jones touched on the
doctrine, which Chalmers had also suggested, that the "real source of the
workmen's subsistence " was in the " revenues of the surrounding customers." We have here another hint (no more than a hint) of that teaching

In all the discussions of this period, the mode in which capital served to reward labor was treated in general terms and with a loose touch. Hence it is not often that we find any intimation on a point which in a later period became of prime importance,—the rigidity of the funds "destined" for the maintenance of labor. The point, in fact, was hardly ever raised in terms. Such opinions as were entertained in regard to it are to be gathered from what was said on other aspects of the question, and more particularly on the possible effects of combinations and strikes among laborers. No aspect of the proposition that wages are paid from capital has caused it to be treated with greater contumely than the corollary, supposed to flow from it, that trades-unions and combinations can not secure any rise in wages. What was said on this topic by the writers of the generation here considered is in itself of interest, and at the same time gives some clue to their views on the fixity or elasticity of the wages fund.

It has already been seen * that one of the prominent members of the Ricardian school, Colonel Torrens, writing specifically *On Wages and Combinations*, gives no intimation of any rigid barrier mocking the efforts of laborers to secure better terms. In that essay, the soldier-scholar admits that a universal combination of laborers might secure an immediate general rise of wages, provided that profits were not at the minimum ; and he does not conceive profits as necessarily at the minimum, even though he agrees that high profits will stimulate accumulation, and so raise wages eventually at the expense of profits. In reasoning of this sort, wages are assumed as a matter of course to depend on capital : but capital does not ap-

---

as to the bearing of consumers' income on wages and capital which the German economists later developed so fully.

* See above pp. 194–195.

pear as a fund unalterable at any given time, predetermining wages once for all.   Similarly, the reviewer of Torrens in the journal in which the classic writers had full sway, the *Edinburgh Review*,* evinces indeed a spirit sufficiently out of sympathy with workmen and their unions; but at all events does not fling the wages fund at their heads. The familiar remarks about the certain failure of strikes, the committees who spend the union funds on liquor, the slack trade and diminished employment which must neutralize any temporary success,—these appear in characteristic form.   But no law of political economy in the way of an unalterable wages fund is propounded for the confusion of the unionists.

Much the same may be said of M'Culloch.   That arch-sinner among the classic writers has something to say of trade-unions and combinations in the two editions of his *Essay on Wages*; and the spirit of it is by no means of that intolerant sort which the traditions as to the tenets of his school would lead us to expect.   In the first edition, of 1825, he defends unhesitatingly the repeal, in the year preceding, of the act prohibiting combinations. While scolding laborers freely for every individual strike he mentions, he yet admits that combinations may sometimes raise the wages of some workmen to their " proper " rate.   Of any difficulties in the way of a general rise in wages he has nothing to say.†   That question is taken up more specifically in the second edition of the essay (1854), —an edition given to the public immediately after the great strikes of 1853, and largely with the purpose of spreading among workmen themselves the economic views

---

* Vol. lix (July, 1834), pp. 341, 342, 348.

† *Essay on Wages*, 1st edition, pp. 186, 188.—There is virtually nothing on combinations and strikes in the various editions of M'Culloch's *Political Economy*.

which the author thought pertinent to the events of the day. Here the case of a general combination and strike is considered. M'Culloch predicts the failure of any such move; not, however, because it is inherently doomed by economic law, but because the masters are likely to out-last the men. He concludes that strikes to force up wages are likely to result in the emigration of capital to foreign parts: an effect which presupposes that there was at least a temporary success in bringing wages up.* All this, to repeat, suggests nothing rigid or inflexible in the capital from which alone M'Culloch and his fellows maintained that wages could be paid, and shows once more how vague were their views as to the precise meaning and limits of the wages fund.

The explanation of this general vagueness of state-ment and unexpected silence on crucial points in the ap-plication of the doctrine, has already been indicated. The main interest of the writers of the period was in other sub-jects. They believed that the chief means of bettering the condition of mankind was on the one hand by the mainte-nance of a high standard of living, on the other hand by improvements in the machinery of production, more espe-cially by the relaxation of all restrictions on domestic trade, still more of those on foreign trade. Given unfet-tered play to self-interest and competition (the mainsprings of individual and national prosperity) and economic diffi-culties would disappear. The only serious danger under such conditions lay in the possibility,—in the minds of many of these men a probability,—that population would increase so fast as to swallow up all gain from increased production. Hence the ready statement of the causes on which wages depended in a form which made it easy to pass at once to the all-important aspect of the question:

---

* *Essay on Wages*, 2d edition, pp. 84, 86.

the necessity of restraint on the advance of population.

The main results of this account of the stage which the wages fund doctrine reached between 1815 and 1848 may now be summarized. The writers of the period have been considered at length, perhaps at wearisome length, because it is the period during which the doctrine was most widely accepted and might be expected to be most explicitly stated. In fact, however, we find it to be stated usually in the vaguest terms, and with little emphasis. Wages are paid from capital, and depend on the amount of capital compared with the number of laborers: so much is laid down in general terms, and then, as a rule, the writers pass at once to other subjects. The reasons which Adam Smith and his immediate successors gave, to explain and prove the dependence of laborers on capital, are not thought to need attention. Ricardo had set the example of assuming, as one of the things settled by Adam Smith, that wages of "productive" laborers are paid from capital. The same tacit assumption was made by most of his successors. Some writers, indeed, like Senior and Malthus, paused to analyze more in detail the nature of the demand for labor; but neither they, nor other writers who might dissent from the current doctrines, denied that capital constituted a demand for labor; and not only a demand, but the most important, even if not the sole, constituent part of the total demand. Jones, the most radical among the critics of the reigning school, denied that wages depended on capital universally; but that the dependence existed in modern advanced communities, he assumed as unhesitatingly as M'Culloch.

While the general doctrine was thus accepted almost without qualification, it was also stated in terms not likely to provoke opposition. The sting of the doctrine, as it was attacked and reprobated in later days, was in the

supposed predetermination and rigidity of the wages
fund : in the obstacles which it was supposed to present
against efforts at immediate improvement in the condition
of laborers. Whatever may have been the case in later
years, there is no evidence that fixity or rigidity in the
wages fund was prominent in the minds of the writers of
the period considered in the present chapter. Such evidence as we get on this point, derived mainly from their
discussion of combinations and strikes, is in the negative.
The wages fund is there certainly not described as rigid,
and by inference is treated as elastic.

CHAPTER XI.

JOHN STUART MILL.

WITH the younger Mill's *Principles of Political Economy* we may advantageously begin a fresh chapter. Not that the book can be said by itself to have made any substantial change in the discussion of the wages fund. On this topic, as on most others of economic theory in its narrower sense, Mill hardly did more than to set forth and codify the accepted views of his time. But his exposition dominated economic thought for near a generation, and, moreover, gave the impetus both to the first bold attack on the wages fund doctrine and to the first deliberate attempt at its rehabilitation. As an indication of the stage at which the doctrine stood for many years, and as the point of departure for the later movement, Mill's position then deserves an attentive examination. For the present, it will be convenient to limit the examination to Mill's views as they were formed at the time when he published the *Principles of Political Economy*; leaving for later consideration, in connection with the next stage in the discussion, his recantation of the doctrine.

What Mill's views were, and how he reached them and presented them, is to be gathered from various passages in the *Political Economy :* not only from the chapters dealing directly with wages, but from those on the place of labor in production, on capital, on changes in distribution under the influence of progress, and on other related topics.

These passages are not always consistent.   They give un-mistakable evidence of Mill's failure to revise his book in cool blood, and so to give coherence to the scattered dis-cussions of the same subject as it was approached from different points of view.   The two large volumes were composed in a surprisingly short space of time,—less than two years.*   In that regard they constitute a remarkable intellectual feat; but they suffered from the hasty compo-sition.   It is true that Mill's mind had been busy with economic topics almost from childhood, and that on some subjects he had written out in early manhood much that he incorporated in the *Principles.*   Yet he had never at-tempted an exposition of the subject at large; and when he came to dash it off in the evenings of two busy years, he could not bring the whole into consistent unity.

It might be expected that the dependence of wages on capital would be set forth by a writer like Mill, deliber-ately engaged on an exposition of economic doctrine at large, in connection with the element of time in produc-tion.   The fact that the operations of production are spread over a long stretch of time, though it underlies the whole classic theory of the relation of wages to capi-tal, had rarely received, since the days of Adam Smith, more than passing attention.   Mill is not much more ex-plicit than his predecessors.   In one place and another, he

---

* "The Political Economy was commenced in the autumn of 1845, and was ready for the press before the end of 1847.   In this period of little more than two years there was an interval of six months, during which the work was laid aside, while I was writing articles in the Morn-ing Chronicle urging the formation of peasant properties on the waste lands of Ireland."—Mill's *Autobiography,* p. 235.

Dr. Ingram remarks with justice in his *History of Political Economy* (p. 150) that Mill never succeeded in fusing his economic theories with his social and philosophic views.   It is equally true that he never suc-ceeded in entirely welding together his strictly economic views.

presents the fundamental point with sufficient clearness;
but usually as an incident to the discussion of other matters. At the very outset, in describing labor as an agent
in production, he remarks that the labor "employed in
producing subsistence, to maintain the labourers while they
are engaged in production, requires particular notice.
This previous employment of labour is an indispensable
condition to every productive operation, on any other than
the very smallest scale. . . . Productive operations require to be continued a certain time, before their fruits
are obtained."* Here Mill takes the first important step
in the analysis of the functions of capital in production;
but almost at once he moves off in another direction, by
proceeding to consider the nature of the return secured
by the persons possessing that subsistence, produced by
previous labor, which is needful for present labor. By
thus passing at once to the "remuneration for abstinence,"
he anticipates, probably to the confusion of readers fresh
to the subject, the discussion of profits and interest; while
he fails to describe with clearness the mode in which different steps in production, of necessity succeeding each
other and so spread over some length of time, result finally in the finished and enjoyable commodity. The simple
and fundamental fact is but obscurely presented; the
more complicated corollary, though its discussion occupies some pages, is yet insufficiently explained.

This failure to develop simple and fundamental truths,
while emphasizing abstruse doctrines of uncertain sound,
appears throughout the treatment, in the earlier chapters,
of capital in relation to wages. "What capital does for
production," says Mill at the outset, "is to afford the
shelter, protection, tools and materials which the work
requires, and to feed and otherwise maintain the labourers

---

* Book i, ch. ii, § 2.

during the process." * Thence he proceeds at once to another and much more complicated proposition,—that the distinction between wealth which is capital and wealth which is not, depends solely on the intention of the owner. Little space is given to that function of capital which is all-important for Mill's later reasoning on wages,—the furnishing of food and maintenance for laborers. Only as an afterthought, at the close of another section of the same chapter, does Mill bethink himself to touch again on this simple but essential matter. " It will be observed," he says, " that I have assumed that the labourers are always subsisted from capital; and this is obviously the fact, though the capital need not necessarily be furnished by a person called a capitalist," †—after which there is no further reference to a fact so obvious.

It may serve still further to show in what manner Mill handled this part of his subject, if we follow some of the reasoning which rested on it. The deduction on which most stress is laid in the earlier part of his book, and which he probably had most at heart in the earlier part of his career, was that the luxurious expenditure of the rich did not benefit the poor. It was to dispose of this notion that he endeavored at such length to show that capital could find indefinite employment in advances to labor, or in his own words, that " the portion [of capital] which is destined to the maintenance of labourers may be indefinitely increased without creating an impossibility of finding the employment." The same motive led him to the elaborate proof that demand for commodities is not demand for labor.‡ This much-maligned proposition is a simple corollary from the axiom (such to Mill's mind it seemed) that laborers are supported by the product of

---

* Book I, ch. iv, § 1.   † *Ibid.*, § 2, at the end.
‡ In § 9 of chapter iv, Book I.

previous labor, dubbed capital. There is much more to say than is found in Mill's pages of the part which luxurious expenditure and demand for commodities play in the working machinery of modern society. The economist of our own day would be likely to connect the discussion of demand for commodities with the general law of demand, with final utility, with non-competing groups among laborers, and with the general interaction of exchange and distribution. And, so far as expenditure by the rich is concerned, he would not think it necessary to linger long, in the earlier stages of his exposition, on the notion that luxurious expenditure, which is the concrete result of unequal distribution, can be of essential advantage to those whose share in distribution is small. But Mill not only lingered over this topic: he pushed the reasoning in another direction, and to topics of the greatest difficulty and complexity. From the statement that the real demand for labor was to be found once for all in the commodities turned over to the laborers for their use, he proceeded to the doctrine that capitalists could turn over an indefinitely large quantity of commodities to laborers, without encountering any obstacle or embarrassment. This was the point at which the whole discussion was aimed. What he meant was that "a market" for such goods could be found without difficulty in supplying all possible wants and whims of the laborers. He failed to consider,—failed at least in this discussion,—that a stage might be reached where it no longer was profitable to increase the advances.

We have here one illustration,—a multitude such might be found,—of Mill's tendency, partly the result of early training, in part doubtless inborn, to follow to its last conclusion one single line of reasoning, regardless of the mode in which other considerations must be taken into account, if we would have, not merely an irrefragable train of argument, but a sufficient explanation of real phenomena. In this particular case, the steady advance of an increasing quantity of commodities to laborers would not continue unless they produced something over and above what was handed to them; and in the end the possibility of steadily enlarging the advances, must depend on a steady increase in productive powers among the laborers, either by an increase in numbers or a gain in efficiency. This ultimate regulation of wages (*i. e.*, of advances from capitalists to laborers) by what the laborers produce, is touched by Mill in later chapters; but it is hardly more than touched. At all events, in his first presentation of the relation of wages to capital, he never hinted at any bearing of product on wages or profits. He confined himself to the axiom that saving means the making of advances to laborers, and to the deduction that laborers would consume any quantity of goods if they had the chance. Thus the discussion, like so much of the deductive reasoning of the classic school, has an unreal tone and a paradoxical end; and even taken at its best, is but a half treatment of a subject which particularly needs full and complete treatment.

This digression from our main subject may serve to make clear how Mill, in his first grappling with the relation of capital to wages, gave much more prominence to other questions than the immediate forces at work. He simply took it for granted that wages were paid from capital. We may proceed now to consider in what way he used this proposition when he came to the specific treatment of wages; and more especially whether he gave it more precise and definite form than his predecessors and contemporaries.

Mill's brief statement of the causes on which wages depend, familiar as it is, may be quoted once again: not only because it is significant in itself, but because we shall

have occasion to refer to it when considering the writers
who came after Mill. After a preliminary statement that
competition, not custom, must be regarded in the present
state of society as the principal regulator of wages, he
proceeds thus:

> "Wages, then, depend mainly upon the demand and supply of
> labour; or, as it is often expressed, on the proportion between
> population and capital. By population is here meant the number
> only of the labouring class, or rather of those who work for hire; and
> by capital, only circulating capital, and not even the whole of that,
> but the part which is expended in the direct purchase of labour.
> To this, however, must be added all funds which, without forming
> a part of capital, are paid in exchange for labour, such as the wages
> of soldiers, domestic servants, and all other unproductive labourers.
> There is unfortunately no mode of expressing by one familiar term,
> the aggregate of what may be called the wages fund of a country;
> and as the wages of productive labour form nearly the whole of that
> fund, it is usual to overlook the smaller and less important part,
> and to say that wages depend on population and capital. It will be
> convenient to employ this expression, remembering, however, to
> consider it as elliptical, and not as a literal statement of the whole
> truth.

> "With these limitations of the terms, wages not only depend on
> the relative amount of capital and population, but cannot, under the
> rule of competition, be affected by anything else. Wages (mean-
> ing, of course, the general rate) cannot rise, but by an increase of
> the aggregate funds employed in hiring labourers, or a diminution
> in the number of competitors for hire; nor fall, except either by a
> diminution of the funds devoted to paying labour, or by an increase
> in the number of labourers to be paid." *

Here we have some promise of an analysis, more detailed than was common among previous writers, of the
"funds" which make up the demand for labor. Only a
part of circulating capital is to be considered; and all

---

* *Political Economy*, Book II, ch. xi, § 1.

funds with which " unproductive " laborers are paid are also to be taken into account. Both of these qualifications of the usual statement had been mentioned by other writers. Ricardo had spoken of " circulating" capital as alone belonging to the demand for wages; Adam Smith, Malthus, Senior still more, had referred, in one way or another, to the unproductive laborers. So far Mill was on much-trodden ground.

Mill did not go beyond this familiar stage. The sentences just quoted contain all that he ever said directly and explicitly on the theory of the wages fund. He passes at once from this simple statement, of which no part evidently seemed to him to need proof or explanation, to the dissection of certain notions inconsistent with it. This was Senior's method; in fact, the whole *modus operandi* appears so far to be copied from Senior. After brushing aside the inconsistent doctrines, which are again disposed of with reasoning unimpeachable as far as it goes and inconclusive because not going far enough, he proceeds to the point which he conceived really to need proof and emphasis and all possible illustration,—the principle of population and the standard of living. For three long chapters every phase of this topic is discussed and re-discussed. The persistence with which it is hammered at, compared with the light and rapid touch on the constitution of the wages fund, indicates that Mill thought the fund a matter of little moment for the really important problems of wages. For most of his reasoning, as for that of almost all writers after the time of Malthus and Ricardo, the details of the process by which an increase in numbers lowered wages were not of much moment. It made little difference whether wages were said to depend proximately on capital, or subsistence, or wealth, or product. The main moral deduced from the dependence of wages on the funds for paying them was that the growth of population must be restrained and the standard of living raised.*

Thereafter, through the greater part of the *Principles*, the simple and familiar formula is applied. As Mill summarizes it in the first chapter of the series in which wages are treated: "Wages depend, then, on the proportion between the number of the labouring population, and the capital or other funds devoted to the purchase of labour; we will say, for shortness, the capital." † Like Ricardo, Malthus, and Senior, not to mention lesser lights, Mill began by using " capital " consciously as an " elliptical expression." Before long, he used it, more or less unconsciously, as a complete and sufficient statement of what constituted the demand for labor.

When Mill came to use and apply, in other directions, the proposition that capital was, once for all, the source of immediate demand for labor, he followed, in the main, the lines on which Ricardo had reasoned. In the third chapter of the fourth Book, on the " Influence of the Progress of Industry and Population on Rents, Profits, and Wages," the proximate cause determining wages is conceived to be simply the relative growth of capital and population. " Let us first suppose that population increases, capital and the arts of production remaining stationary. One of the effects of this change of circumstances is sufficiently obvious: wages will fall." This chapter is an

---

* Professor Nicholson remarks (in his *Principles of Political Economy*, vol. i, p. 341): " It follows, then, according to this view [the wages fund doctrine] that wages can only rise either owing to an increase of capital or a diminution of population, and this accounts for the exaggerated importance attached by Mill to the Malthusian theory of population." The converse seems to me nearer the truth: it was the exaggerated importance attached to the Malthusian theory which accounts for the stress laid on the wages fund doctrine.

† Book II, ch. xi, § 3.

elaboration, with no essential additions, of Ricardo's *Essay on the Influence of a Low Price of Corn ;* and Mill, in following up Ricardo's conclusions, accepted the practice which his master had adopted even in this early essay, of dismissing "market" wages summarily as determined by capital and population. Unlike Ricardo, Mill had keen social interests and sympathies. But he had been inured from boyhood to Ricardo's rigid and quasi-mathematical reasoning; and his own intellectual bent was in the same direction. In his discussion of distribution, he was absorbed, as his exemplar had been, in deducing certain consequences as to profits and rent which rested on the assumption that real wages were fixed at a stationary point by ingrained habits of the laborers. The wider views to which he was led by his social sympathies were never brought into direct connection with this comparatively narrow reasoning. At all events, they did not serve to bring his attention more closely to the problem of the immediate and direct determination of wages.

There is, however, another aspect of Mill's teaching on capital, which deserves notice : his conception of the relation between the general advance of capital to all laborers on the one hand, and the payment of wages by individual employers on the other ; and, in connection with this, his conception of the rigidity or predetermination of the funds for hiring laborers.

Reference has already been made to Mill's distinction between capital and non-capital, as resting solely on the intention of the owner. This mode of defining capital he inherited, like other doctrines, chiefly from Ricardo, who had defined capital briefly as "that part of the wealth of a country which is employed in production." M'Culloch had tried an independent flight by propounding the doctrine that anything which *might* conceivably be used for further production was capital ; Malthus had brought him to earth by answering that only that wealth was capital which was in fact used for production. Whatever these varieties in the tradition of the day, Mill followed its main trend in insisting on the intention of the owner as the decisive element in determining whether a particular quantum of wealth was or was not capital.

It has already been explained, in the first part of this volume,* how far Mill and his contemporaries were right, how far wrong. They were wrong in supposing that, at any given moment, the intention of the owner settles whether a particular item of wealth is or is not capital. Under any possible definition, plant and materials can be nothing but capital. It has indeed been sometimes suggested that the owner of a machine may sell it, and squander the proceeds: thus it would cease to be capital simply by his change of intention. Obviously, however, such a process would be a mere shifting of the ownership of the capital from one hand to another: the machine still remains inchoate wealth and capital. The real and important truth which underlies this part of the classic doctrine appears only when it is brought into connection with another part,—the proposition that all wealth is perpetually produced and consumed. That proposition, originating with the Physiocrats and Adam Smith, † was set forth by Mill in lucid terms; yet, curiously enough, he failed to apply it to that other proposition, on the determination of capital by intention, which, standing by itself, could be so misleading. In the long run only, and in view of the steady waste and steady reproduction of all wealth, is it true that the intention settles what shall be capital and

---

* See Part I, Chapter III, pp. 61–62, 67–68.

† See Cannan, *History of Theories of Production and Distribution*, p. 15, and *Wealth of Nations*, Book II, ch. iii, p. 149. Compare Mill's *Principles*, Book I, ch. v, § 6.

what shall not be. On this topic, as on others, Mill followed Ricardo's example of sliding rapidly over the concrete details by which the truth of his propositions appeared in real life: with results sometimes confusing to himself, and certainly confusing to later students of his writings.

The cause of confusion in this case was that Mill's vague doctrine as to capital and intention prevented him from making any clear distinction between the advance of money wages by employers, and the advance of real wages from the flow of the community's consumable goods. We have seen that he did not linger long on those causes which, in the nature of complex production, make necessary the support of laborers from past product. It was natural, therefore, that he should fail to separate sharply the real provision of consumable goods which maintains laborers during the prolonged period of production, from the immediate advance of funds by the individual employer to the laborer directly hired by him. Usually he simplifies the matter after Ricardo's method, by getting far away from the facts of concrete industry, and supposing the capitalist to possess so many quarters of wheat which he advances to laborers. This is the plan which he followes in the discussion of the effects of the conversion of circulating capital into fixed,—"circulating" capital there meaning wages fund. But in presenting and illustrating the doctrine that intention determines whether wealth shall or shall not be capital, he considers the case in more realistic fashion.

"A manufacturer, for example, has one part of his capital in the form of buildings. Another part he has in the form of machinery. A third consists, if he be a spinner, of raw cotton, flax, or wool ; if a weaver, of flaxen, woollen, silk, or cotton, thread; and the like, according to the nature of the manufacture. Food and clothing for his operatives, it is not the custom of the present age that he should directly provide. . . . Instead of this, each capitalist has money, which he pays to his work people, and so enables them to supply themselves : he has also finished goods in his warehouse, by the sale of which he obtains more money, to employ in the same manner, as well as to replenish his stock of materials, to keep his buildings and machinery in repair, and to replace them when worn out. His money and finished goods, however, are not wholly capital, for he does not wholly devote them to these purposes : he employs a part of the one, and of the proceeds of the other, in supplying his personal consumption and that of his family, or in hiring grooms and valets, or maintaining hunters and hounds, or in educating his children, or in paying taxes, or in charity. What then is his capital ? Precisely that part of his possessions, whatever it be, which he designs to employ in carrying on fresh production. It is of no consequence that a part, or even the whole of it, is in a form in which it cannot directly supply the wants of labourers." *

Here the capital of the community is analyzed in a manner that implies that it is all in the hands of the employers who directly hire laborers, or under their control : the money and the proceeds of the finished goods being the sources from which wages are paid. In the next paragraph Mill illustrates his reasoning by supposing the case of a hardware manufacturer whose

" stock in trade, over and above his machinery, consists at present wholly in iron goods. Iron goods cannot feed labourers. Nevertheless, by a mere change of the destination of the iron goods, he can cause labourers to be fed."

The attentive reader of the passages that follow this statement will see that Mill did not fall into the error of supposing that laborers could be fed without the wherewithal to feed them. If there is no additional food in the country,

" it must be imported, if possible ; if not possible, the labourers will remain for a season on their short allowance ; but the consequence

---

* Book I, ch. iv, § 1.

of this change in the demand for commodities, occasioned by the change in the expenditure for capitalists from unproductive to productive, is that next year more food will be produced, and less plate and jewels."

Here we have a sufficiently explicit hint that it may take *time* for the intention of the capitalists to work out its effects on the form which the community's possession shall have; and it is surprising that Mill did not come back to this point when in the next chapter he dilated on the perpetual consumption and reproduction of capital. As it was, his language might be easily interpreted to mean that the sources from which wages came were the funds or proceeds in the hands of the immediate employer: an interpretation freely made by later writers, and, as we shall see, the source of a long and unprofitable controversy.*

---

* In the earlier *Essays on Some Unsettled Questions of Political Economy*, written in 1829 and 1830, though not published till 1844, there is a passage which deserves to be read in connection with those quoted in the text. In the second of the essays, the question of gluts is taken up, and, as part of it, the effect of a "brisk demand" on production. Mill presented, in the main, the orthodox view, but conceded something to Malthus, by admitting that a brisk demand might serve virtually to increase the community's capital. Capital he defines, as he did later in the *Political Economy*, by intention: it is "all wealth which the individual or nation has in possession for the purpose of reproduction. . . . All unsold goods, therefore, constitute a part of the national capital, and of the capital of the producer or dealer to whom they belong. . . . If, after having sold the goods, I hire labourers with the money, and set them to work, I am surely employing capital, though the corn, which in the form of bread those labourers may buy with the money may be now in the warehouse at Dantzig, or perhaps not yet above the ground." This is dubious doctrine; and the consequences which Mill draws from it show how he confounded the advantages from a rapid succession of the different stages in production, with a real increase in the community's productive apparatus. "An additional customer, to most dealers, is equivalent to an increase of their productive capital. He enables them to convert a portion of their capital which was lying idle (and which never could have become produc-

The same lack of precise statement as to the way in which capital performs its function of supporting laborers, appears in other parts of these earlier chapters on capital. Such terms as "funds," "sums," "capital paid out," are used, in a manner that, not unfairly construed, connotes money ; and the reader is led to think of money available for paying wages as the important thing for the welfare of laborers. When a great loan is raised for war purposes, "it must have been wholly drawn from the portion employed in paying labourers "; and "if they produce as much as usual, having been paid less by so many millions sterling, these millions are gained by their employers." *   The attentive reader will here again read between the lines,—and indeed in places within the lines,—that Mill was really intent on the consumption for military purposes of food and other consumable goods that would otherwise have gone to productive laborers; the breach in the capital of the country coming from the "unproductive" consumption of these commodities.   Even from this point of view, it would need

---

tive in their hands until a customer was found) into wages and instruments of production ; and if we suppose that the commodity, unless bought by him, would not have found a purchaser for a year after, then all which a capital of that value [note this phrase] can enable men to produce during a year is clear gain,—gain to the dealer or producer, and to the labourers whom he will employ, and thus (if no one sustains corresponding loss) gain to the nation."—*Essays*, p. 54.

From this sort of reasoning as to capital, it would clearly follow that the circulating capital whence wages are paid, so far from being a rigid quantity, is a very flexible and expansible one.   Although Mill published the essay in 1844, he did not incorporate the matter of it, as he did that of others, in the *Political Economy*, printed in 1849.   Indeed, the chapter on excess of supply (Bk. III, ch. xiv) does not mention the effects of brisk demand among the things that might palliate Malthus's errors. Perhaps, on maturer consideration, the reasoning of the essay struck him as unsatisfactory.

* Book I, ch. v, § 8.

to be explained that the unproductive consumption is a matter of no consequence to the mass of the laborers at the outset; during the first year, or the first cycle of production, it makes no difference to them whether they get their food in exchange for the work of tilling the ground or of destroying human life. Only in the next stage, when no food has been created in place of that destroyed, will the final effects of the wastefulness of war be felt. But Mill's language is of capital in millions sterling, and of funds borrowed and spent. Whether his own thought was confused, or—as is more likely—he was so intent on other parts of the reasoning that he half-unconsciously adopted a convenient short cut at this stage, he certainly bred confusion in the minds of his later expounders and critics.

So, in discussing the conversion of circulating capital into fixed, Mill does indeed often describe this circulating capital in terms of so many quarters of corn ; but he refers to the possibility that the fixed capital may be created, "not by withdrawing capital from actual circulation, but by the employment of the annual increase." * As a matter of fact, the mode in which the steady growth of savings supplies the resources for increasing real capital without entailing even a temporary diminution of the commodities constituting " circulating capital," is very complicated, and can be understood only by analyzing the operations of production over a considerable period. But Mill here again made a short cut for himself and his readers by considering both the circulating capital and the fresh accumulations in terms of money. The same thing is implied in the passage in which Mill refutes those who maintained that an income tax, while apparently falling on the rich alone, really takes from them what they would

* Book I, ch. vi, § 3.

otherwise have spent among the poor.* Mill makes a distinction : "So far, indeed, as what is taken from the rich in taxes, would, if not so taken, have been saved and converted into capital, . . . to that extent the demand for labour is no doubt diminished. . . . But even here the question arises, whether the government, after receiving the amount, will not lay out as great a portion of it in the direct purchase of labour, as the tax-payers would have done." This looks again to the money in the hands of one or another set of spenders as the thing whose volume and movement should be considered, if we would ascertain whether the laborers' wages will be raised or lowered.

In a paragraph immediately succeeding that last quoted, Mill remarks that "error is produced by not looking directly at the realities of the phenomena, and attending only to the outward mechanism of paying and spending." Unfortunately, that outward mechanism was all too prominent in his own exposition ; especially in discussions of the effects of any specific measure which involved an incidental consideration of the mechanism of payment, as to laborers and their welfare. On the relation between the money funds or proceeds held by the immediate employer, and the food, clothes, and enjoyments, constituting the community's real "circulating capital," he gave ambiguous and unsatisfactory statements, from which only a sympathetic interpreter could patch up a consistent and tenable doctrine.†

---

* Book I, ch. v, § 10.

† A characteristic passage, illustrative of the uncertain tone with which Mill spoke, is the following, taken from the chapter on the Consequences of the Tendency of Profits to a Minimum. I have italicized some significant words. "What is laid out in the bona fide construction of the railway itself is lost and gone ; when once expended, it is incapable of ever being paid in wages or applied to the maintenance of labourers again ; as a matter of account, the result is that so much *food and cloth-*

Some further light on the form which the wages fund doctrine assumed in Mill's hands, may be had, finally, by considering one question more,—his views on that rigidity or predetermination of the fund which was so hotly discussed by later writers.

In the chapter specifically devoted to wages, the passages quoted above show no stress on the rigidity of the fund, and indeed hardly give an indication one way or the other as to Mill's opinion. Like his contemporaries, he did not stop to consider the point. He passed so quickly from "market" wages to normal or "natural" wages, that he was not led to ask deliberately whether market wages at a given period were or were not predetermined. We have just seen how often, in other passages than those which were expressly concerned with wages, he discussed the relations between capitalists and laborers as if the essential thing were the advance of money funds or proceeds by the individual employers. On this basis, he could hardly have entertained the notion of any rigid source of wages; for he had set forth that these funds would shrink or swell with the capitalist's change of intention, and had implied that they varied with his control over immediate money funds. In the main there is thus little direct indication in the body of the *Political Economy* of any iron-clad doctrine, and certain proof that such a doctrine, if entertained at all, was far from prominent in Mill's own thinking.

There do not lack intimations, however, that underneath, and without much emphasis on the matter in his own mind, Mill held to a doctrine of the iron-clad sort.

---

ing and tools have been consumed, and the country has got a railway instead. But what I would urge is that *sums* so applied are mostly a mere appropriation of the annual overflowing which would otherwise have gone abroad," and so on.—*Political Economy*, Book IV, chapter v, § 2.

In the very discussion of the effect of the owner's intention on the increase or decrease of capital, he suggests that it will take time to alter the existing supply of food; the food being treated, in Ricardian fashion, as the one essential constituent of real wages. The implication is that in any one season, this "circulating capital" is so much and can be no more. The same uncompromising view appears more explicitly in the chapter in the fifth Book which treats of combinations among laborers. There it is reasoned that even if a general combination of all laborers could be effected,

" they might doubtless succeed in diminishing the hours of labour, and obtaining the same wages for less work. But if they aimed at obtaining actually higher wages than the rate fixed by demand and supply—the rate which distributed the whole circulating capital of the country among the entire working population—this could only be accomplished by keeping a part of their number permanently out of employment. As support from public charity would of course be refused to those who could get work and would not accept it, they would be thrown for support upon the trades union of which they were members ; and the work-people collectively would be no better off than before, having to support the same numbers out of the same aggregate wages. In this way, however, the class would have its attention forcibly drawn to the fact of a superfluity of numbers, and to the necessity, if they would have higher wages, of proportioning the supply of labour to the demand." *

Here we have something like the stern and ominous wages fund which rouses the ire of the friend of the working-man. The succeeding paragraphs of the same section show with equal plainness that, sometimes at least, Mill had clearly in mind the doctrine that for the time being the total demand for labor was fixed unalterably. He argues that a partial rise in wages—*i. e.*, a rise in the

---

* Book V, ch. x, § 5.

wages of a particular group of laborers—may indeed be
secured without corresponding loss to other laborers; but
only in the end, not for the moment. It is only after the
lapse of some time that this happy result can be secured.

" It may appear, indeed, at first sight, that the high wages of
type-founders (for example) are obtained at the general cost of the
labouring class. This high remuneration either causes fewer persons
to find employment in the trade, or, if not, must lead to the investment of more capital in it, at the expense of other trades : in the
first case, it throws an additional number of labourers on the general market ; in the second, it withdraws from that market a portion
of the demand ; effects, both of which are injurious to the working
classes. Such, indeed, would really be the result of a successful
combination in a particular trade or trades, for some time after its
formation ; but when it is a permanent thing, the principles so often
insisted on in this treatise, show that it can have no such effect.
The habitual earnings of the working classes at large can be affected by nothing but the habitual requirements of the labouring
people : these, indeed, may be altered, but while they remain the
same, wages never fall permanently below the standard of these requirements, and do not long remain above that standard."

In other words, general wages are fixed definitively
at any one period by the wages fund. Only after a lapse
of time can any other factor enter ; and then the factor
which is important is that which all the thinkers of this
generation held to be promptly decisive : the standard of
living.

In Mill's case, as in Ricardo's, it would be unfair to lay
too much stress on brief passages of this sort, interjected
into a discussion of the policy which the legislature ought
to pursue in regard to labor unions. But they show
clearly how natural to Mill was the Ricardian way of unrelenting reasoning from an assumed premise : and one
premise was that in any given season there was so much
" circulating capital " in the community, and could be no

more. They show, too, how Mill, like Ricardo, lingered but for a moment on this phase of the wages question, touching it so briefly that we can not be sure how rigorously he would have maintained his doctrines if pressed to a more explicit and emphatic statement. Like Ricardo again, he passed at once to that other phase of the wages question which seemed to him of pressing importance: the "habitual requirements of the labouring people," which constituted the one force to be made prominent in the statement of the laws governing general wages.

So much for the theory as Mill left it. The wages fund doctrine is stated briefly and boldly; its foundation in the nature of civilized production is hardly noticed; its teaching is aimed chiefly at the need of repressing numbers. Its application in other directions is cumbered and confused by references to funds and capital in terms of money, which obscure the essential truths of the doctrine, and became the source of the memorable but fruitless controversy which resulted in Mill's recantation.

Before proceeding to the next chapter, in which that controversy is to be taken up, we may glance for a moment at Mill's more immediate followers. Little is to be learned for our purposes from an examination of the popularizers who belong to this period of placid content with the perfect completeness of economic teaching. In the main, they repeated what Mill had said, with slight individual variations. A very few words as to one or two typical expounders of what was then supposed to be established truth, will suffice to indicate the stage at which the wages fund doctrine stood in England for near twenty years.

Charles Morrison published in 1856 *An Essay on the Relations between Labour and Capital* which reflects faithfully the attitude likely to be taken by one trained in the economics of the day and not possessed of the will or capacity to follow the current doctrines to their roots. Wages are regulated by the ratio between capital and labor. The fund for paying wages is "that part of the active or productive capital of the nation which is not required for some other employment necessary to the business of production" [*i. e.*, not for plant and materials]. The division is determined by "the nature of things"; hence the wages fund is "a definite proportion of the entire active capital." So much the employers, it is implied, must pay away to laborers. Even if they were "universally misers," and were trying to get "the greatest possible profit," this would "not diminish the sum expended in labour; and consequently would not lower the rate of wages." *

As to combinations and strikes, Morrison argues that they are only harmful. True, some employers might be forced to pay higher than "competitive" wages; but "according to the laws which govern wages," such a result could not be permanent. Yet it is noted that "the existing generation of manufacturers might be ruined before the last results of the process were worked out": which seems to admit that for a while at least, and perhaps a good while, the conditions determining wages might not be so absolutely rigid after all.† There is an admission of a similar sort, again made without any glimpse of the consequences to which it might lead, in a curious bit of reasoning as to the possible effects of confidence and credit in swelling the wages fund. During a period of universal confidence a given fund would be turned over quickly by each capitalist. Thus a wages capital of £10,-000 would be turned over perhaps five times in an active year, three times in a dull one; the virtual wages fund would be £50,000 in the first case, £30,000 in the second.

---

* *Essay*, pp. 19, 20. † *Ibid.*, p. 99.

Hence the source of wages is defined, in a later summary, as "the funds available for their [the laborers'] payment, multiplied by the average rapidity with which those funds are turned over." Morrison considered this an important addition to the laws regulating wages: its innuendo as to the evil effects of strikes and disturbances is obvious enough.* Clearly it conceives the wages fund in terms of money or funds in the hands of the capitalist. But from this point of view, it is also clear that the wages fund might be flexible, not merely because of variations in confidence and commercial activity, but from pressure from the trades-union or any one of a dozen imaginable causes. That no turn of this sort in the reasoning occurred to Morrison, a man of candid intelligence and real public spirit, shows how rare after all is the capacity for even comparatively simple steps in independent thinking.

Of a different type, and worth noting because of the prominent place which he long held as an authoritative text-book writer, is Henry Fawcett. His *Manual of Political Economy*, first published in 1863,† was for near a generation an accepted text-book for those not able to undertake Mill's larger and more abstruse volumes; and its dilution of the strength of the original has caused it to be described, not unfairly, as "Mill and water." Here capital is defined as the fund from which labor is remunerated; it follows at once that "wages in the aggregate depend on a ratio between capital and population." This is not qualified or explained, as it was by Mill, as an "elliptical expression": it simply serves to introduce, with-

---

* See chapters xvii and xviii of Morrison's *Essay*. His doctrine here is virtually the same as that which Mill set forth in his *Essays in Political Economy*, but did not see fit to retain in the *Political Economy*. See the note to p. 229, above.

† I have used the third edition, published in 1867. The passages referred to are in Book II, chapters iv, v, ix.

out delay, the Malthusian proposition. On the other hand, practically nothing is made of the wages fund when Fawcett comes to the question of trade-unions and their effect on wages,—questions which absorbed public attention when he wrote, and led him to more pointed writing than was possible in the simple process of condensing Mill. In the discussion of these living questions, Fawcett's views, so far as they bear on the wages fund, are certainly not excessively orthodox. The slow and imperfect working of competition is explained, and the greater tactical strength which laborers get from combination is fully set forth. On the other hand, as to strikes and their success, the wages fund simply does not appear at all.

Much the same is the case in Fawcett's volume on the *Economic Position of the British Labourer*, published in 1865. Here again we find at the outset the old and wearisome phrase as to the ratio between population and circulating capital; and with it an equally wearisome phrase to the effect that "the laws regulating wages are as certain in their effects as those which control physical nature." But in the chapter on Trade-Unions, the wages fund and the natural laws fade away into nothingness. "Natural" wages, it is explained, do not result at once or even quickly from mere competition. Combinations have their effects, among masters as well as among men. The tendency of profits to a minimum, and the check to accumulation from a fall in profits,—these, rather than the wages fund, are the obstacles in the way of deep-reaching effects from combinations and strikes. Of profits and their minimum and the accumulation of capital we shall hear more in due time: what the classic writers and their expounders had to say on this topic was stated better and more fully by Cairnes, whose position we shall consider in the next chapter. It is significant, as to Fawcett, that we find in him little of the disposition to fling the wages fund at the head of the laborers which is so much associated with the orthodox doctrines. We have seen that writers of the previous generation,—Torrens, M'Culloçh, and their fellows, —made little use of it in this direction. Like them, and like his master, Mill, Fawcett thought of it but little in connection with disputes about wages, and used it chiefly as a means of inculcating the need of that prudence in multiplication which seemed to all of these men the main instrument of social salvation.

CHAPTER XII.

WE come now to the most dramatic episode in the history of the wages fund doctrine,—the attacks on it by Longe and Thornton, and Mill's surrender to the latter. Immediately after, came Cairnes's endeavor to reshape and rehabilitate the doctrine; the first attempt, since Adam Smith's day, at a deliberate and careful statement of its meaning. All this stir was due, as is usually the case with such a burst of active discussion, to the pressure of practical problems. The trade union question had entered on a new phase: the great commission of 1867 was both a result and a further cause of the concentration of public opinion on disputes about wages. Naturally the theory of wages in general received a larger share of attention.

Francis D. Longe, a London barrister, not known before or much noted after as a writer on economic subjects, published in 1866 an eighty-page pamphlet under the title, *A Refutation of the Wages Fund Theory of Modern Political Economy, as enunciated by Mr. Mill and Mr. Fawcett.* As the title indicates, Longe made no pretence of examining the history of the theory, or its presentation by any long series of writers. He took the two books then most in vogue, and examined the current doctrine as there expounded. To that doctrine, he found three objections to make: (1) that there is no definite fund, distinct from the general possessions of the community, devoted to the pay-

ment of wages; (2) that the laborers do not constitute a
body among whom the aggregate fund could be divided
by competition; (3) that the wages fund doctrine "involves an erroneous notion of the demand and supply
principle." Of these objections, we may consider for the
present the first only. The second, as to the distribution
of the wages fund among different classes of laborers,
does not deal with the essence of the old doctrine, whose
expositors had always referred, more or less clearly, to
the multiform causes that might influence the particular
share of the general fund which might go to one set of
laborers or another. In any case, this part of the controversy was not handled by Longe in a manner to attract,
or indeed to deserve, much attention. The third objection, as to the general law of supply and demand in relation to wages, was put more effectively, and had a wider
hearing; but its consideration may be postponed until we
reach, in a later part of the present chapter, the same
line of reasoning in the pages of Thornton and Mill. It
is the denial of a definite wages fund which marks most
signally the new phase on which the discussion now entered. This first objection is the beginning of a long
series of similar attacks on the old doctrine; and at the
same time it hinges directly on what Mill and other of
Longe's immediate predecessors had said.

Longe denies that there is "a definite fund, distinct
from the general wealth, destined for the purchase of labour." He has a brief word of criticism on Mill's two funds,
of "capital" for productive laborers, and "unproductive"
funds for servants and the like; but like Mill, gives
attention chiefly to the analysis and definition of capital.
He denies that it is intention which determines whether a
given portion of wealth shall be capital and shall be used
in paying wages. He quotes passages from Mill, and from
Fawcett, Mill's *alter ego*, in which the intention of the

owner is described as the decisive factor; and, following the more obvious meaning of these passages, conceives this intention to be applied directly to the money and potential money proceeds at the disposal of capitalists. To treat such a cause as decisive, he urges, "excludes the very cause which in real life governs both the quantity of wealth which is from time to time used as capital, and the particular mode of production in which it is used." That cause is "the existence or prospective existence of a purchaser." "The wealth or capital available for the maintenance of labour" is not the fund which limits wages; "the wealth available for the purchase of their work" is the real fund.*

This reasoning presents itself in two ways: negatively, as to Mill's discussion of the nature and limitation of the funds available for the immediate employer of labor; and positively, as to the real sources from which these funds are regularly replenished. The replenishment, according to Longe, comes from the purchases or the demand of the consumers who buy the articles made. Something has already been said as to this phase of the controversy; something more will be said of it when we take up, in a later chapter, the treatment of the wages fund at the hands of German economists.† The welfare of any particular set of laborers depends so obviously on the demand for the commodities which they make, that the same force is easily inferred to apply to laborers and to wages at large; and Longe could find a sufficiency of respectable company in this part of his reasoning. And the same may be said of the negative part,—of that which is concerned with the constitution of the wages fund, the relation of capital to wealth, and the significance of the capi-

---

* Longe, pp. 37–47.
† See Part I, Chapter V, pp. 106–109; and Chapter XIII, below.

tal of the immediate employers. Here Longe was on much-trodden ground; and what he said on these topics connects itself most directly with the turn which the controversy next took.

All the funds which serve to employ laborers are constantly treated by Longe in terms of money and of money value. This was a natural, an almost inevitable, result of those passages in Mill's *Political Economy* which were noticed in the last chapter. Mill's volumes contained the economic gospel of the day, alike for the faithful and the heretic. Longe had read and re-read the chapters which bore directly on his subject, and, not being versed in all the phases of economic discussion that bore on it more remotely, took Mill's words in their simplest and most obvious meaning. For him, the wages fund never appeared in any other light than that of funds or means in the hands of employers, available for paying immediate money wages. Hence he was easily led to deny that there was any fixity, or predetermination, in the fund; or any importance to it whatever. The farmer is limited as to his payments for wages "only by the amount of money for which his crops or stock will sell." Employers, we are told, really pay laborers *after* these have done their work; and laborers are maintained from what they have been paid on every preceding Saturday, "or from what they have inherited from ancestors." Coal is often bought when it is at the bottom of the pit, and the money is paid as soon as the coal reaches the pit bank : a case in which laborers, it is supposed, clearly need not get their wages from capital. So, many journeymen are paid by the fortnight or month, while the employers get the money some days before they pay their men.* The reader conversant with more recent discussions of capital and wages will

---

* Longe, pp. 48, 49, 53.

find here some familiar suggestions. To repeat, the presentation by Mill, the authority of the day, of the mode in which funds of capital were turned over to laborers, invited the sort of attack which Longe made.

Substantially the same view as that of Longe was adopted by another writer, whose position may be briefly referred to as another indication of the turn which the controversy was taking. Henry D. Macleod published in 1873 his *Principles of Economical Philosophy.** Like his other writings, this book had weight and value for the elucidation of the phenomena of credit and banking; but on the general principles of economics, Macleod had not much to say that gained or deserved a great deal of attention. As to the wages fund, he quoted with approval Longe's proposition that purchasers' demand determined the amount that would be paid in wages; but, for himself, laid most stress on the effect of credit in enlarging the sums that can be paid out to laborers. Here the conception of the source of wages as simply money funds appears in the most unequivocal form. " Thus we see that the true ' wages fund ' is not the actual amount of specie in the manufacturer's pocket, but the price which the consumers pay for the complete product. And how is this to be obtained before it is actually received ? By means of Banking Credits. This is the precise use and function of Banks which issue notes. It is to issue notes to form this ' wages fund ' in anticipation of the price paid by the consumers. And thus we see the gigantic importance of a solid banking system to the labouring classes. It multiplies the ' wages fund ' a hundredfold. . . ." †

---

* This book was mainly a new edition of the *Elements of Political Economy*, published in 1858.

† Macleod's *Principles of Economical Philosophy*, vol. ii, ch. xiii, pp. 126, 127. As to the direction in which such arguments as these of Mac-

Precisely the same point of attack as Longe's was also chosen by William Thomas Thornton, a writer who was of the inner circle among the reigning economists, a close friend of Mill's, well known by earlier publications, and in every way able to command an attentive hearing. Thornton published in 1869 * his book *On Labour : Its Wrongful Claims and Rightful Dues, Its Actual Present and Possible Future*. His predecessor Longe is not referred to in the book, and very likely was not known to Thornton ; yet both on the law of supply and demand as affecting wages, and on the determinateness of the wages fund, he might have got hints from Longe. The supply and demand discussion, which was much the more prominent in Thornton, we may still postpone for a moment, in order to follow without a break that as to the nature and limit of the wages fund.

Thornton never thought of denying that wages were paid from capital. Nor, for that matter, had Longe done so explicitly ; though some of his objections, carried to their logical outcome, must have involved such a denial. But Thornton, quite as explicitly as Longe, conceived this fund of capital to be money means wholly in the possession of the immediate managers and employers of the laborers. Naturally he concluded at once that, as such, it was not a fixed or inelastic fund. He was brief on this part of the subject, but none the less clear :

" Determinateness or indeterminateness is the one point of difference between those who affirm and those who deny the wages fund. . . . If there really were a national fund the whole of which must necessarily be applied to the payment of wages, that fund could be no other than an aggregate of smaller similar funds pos-

leod's are pertinent, compare what was said above, Part I, Chapters III and IV, pp. 63–65, 83–85.

* The preface to the first edition is dated Dec. 31, 1868.

sessed by the several individuals who compose the employing class of the nation. Does, then, any individual possess such a fund? . . . Of course, every employer possesses a certain amount of money, whether his own or borrowed, out of which all his expenses must be met, if met at all. . . ." *

and Thornton goes on to ask whether the employer may not spend more or less for a dozen different purposes,— on his family, on buildings, on repairs. The whole inquiry rests on the assumption that the money funds of the employers constitute the real and important capital applied to the payment of wages; and on such an assumption, he remarks, truly enough, that " it sounds like mockery or childishness to ask these questions."

To this attack, Mill surrendered. He reviewed Thornton's book in the *Fortnightly Review* for May, 1869, accepted Thornton's version of the question in dispute, and admitted that his objections were unanswerable. "The capitalist," says Mill, "starts at the commencement with the whole of his accumulated means, all of which is potentially capital." Doubtless Mill had in mind here the common definition of capital, as set forth in his own volumes: it depended on the intention of the owner. Thence he might have reasoned, looking merely at the money means of immediate employers, that there could be no wages fund distinct from any of the other possessions of the capitalist. Yet some thought of real capital, and of the irrevocable commitment of at least some part of it to other things than wages fund, seems to have remained in his mind; for the flexible element, which makes him concede that the wages fund is an indeterminate thing, is found by considering, not all the possessions of the employer, but certain available funds or uncommitted assets. How much he shall advance to laborers, how much expend

---

* *On Labour*, pp. 84, 85.

for himself and his family, is undetermined and free. "There is no law of nature making it inherently impossible for wages to rise to the point of absorbing not only the funds he intended to devote to carrying on his business, but the whole of what he allows for his private expenses, beyond the necessaries of life." Here again it is difficult to make out exactly what Mill was thinking of. It may be some version of the old doctrine of capital as fixed by intention ; or an echo of the Ricardian doctrine that all capital was resolvable into advances of wages ; or simply the naked case of the individual capitalist and his possible expenditure of money. At all events, it was the last mentioned that was uppermost. In the *Political Economy*, as we have seen, Mill had sometimes considered food, clothes, shelter, as constituting the wages part of circulating capital; sometimes had spoken of "funds" or "income" or cash. Here the latter view is taken unequivocally. The surrender of the rigid wages fund then becomes inevitable. The result is not satisfactory to one who would follow Mill's own advice of disregarding the outward mechanism of paying and spending, and attending to the realities of the phenomena.* Longe and Thornton had gone astray, in a direction which Mill himself, consciously or unconsciously, had pointed to in the *Political Economy*. Now he followed them into hopeless confusion between real capital and real wages on the one hand, and the money mechanism of nominal wages on the other.

The explanation of Mill's loose thought and hasty surrender is not far to seek. Personal regard for Thornton probably counted for something : he was disposed to make every possible concession to his old friend. But the main cause was a change in his interests and sympathies, which

---

* See above, p. 232.

led him to get quit of the wages fund discussion as promptly as possible.   In his later years, social problems, in their
bearing on the wider questions of philosophy and ethics,
engrossed his attention more and more.   By far the
larger part of the review of Thornton is given to the
ethical aspects of trade-unionism, the other topics being
passed over with a comparatively light touch.   He cared
much more for the right and wrong of trade-unionism, as
tested by some final standard, than for the mechanism of
market wages and the elasticity of the wages fund.

No doubt, too, another circumstance helps to account
for his ready acceptance of Thornton's version and refutation of his older doctrine.   He had himself never
stopped to consider that doctrine with much care.   We
have seen how briefly he had stated it in the *Political
Economy*, and how ambiguously he had applied it.   When
he was confronted by Thornton's objections, he had no
well-defined views of old standing to fall back on ; and
he was too much interested in the larger social questions,
perhaps was too old, to overhaul the whole theory of
wages and capital from its foundations.   On other topics
—thus on the law, or equation, of supply and demand,
which we shall presently consider—he had reached clearer
thought in his younger days, and, not being taken un-
awares, was able to weigh Thornton's objections more
critically.   On the wages fund doctrine, he had no accumulation of critical thought to draw on.

The law or equation of supply and demand, just referred to, occupied much space in this discussion.   As we
have noted, Longe and Thornton had found it necessary
to say something on the bearing of supply and demand
on wages and the wages fund.   Mill did the same ; though
he yielded less to Thornton here than on the nature and
elasticity of the fund.   The controversy branched off into

fields somewhat beyond the scope of the present inquiry; but some review of this phase of it may be advantageous.

Longe had begun by questioning whether the general law of supply and demand had anything to do with wages and the wages fund. He had no difficulty in showing that the writers then in vogue, and more especially Mill and Fawcett, supposed that law to be in point: they conceived of the immediate determination of wages as being a simple application of supply and demand. Ricardo long ago had set the example of distinguishing between market and natural wages: market wages being determined by the ratio of capital to population, and natural wages by their "cost,"—*i. e.*, by the price of food, or the quantity of labor given to the production of a given quantity of food. His successors had worked out a neat and harmonious formula, applicable alike to labor and to commodities: supply and demand determined marked or temporary rates, while cost determined natural or permanent rates. Mill had given precision to the phrases about supply and demand by putting the law in the form of an equation: quantity demanded varies with prices, and price must be such that quantity demanded equals quantity supplied.* Longe questioned the real working of the principle even in this version; but he maintained that in any case the wages fund theory alleged a relation between supply and demand very different from that set forth in Mill's equation. Under the wages fund doctrine, demand in relation to labor means quantity of capital offered, not quantity of labor demanded. The ratio or equation is the simple one of comparing a given quantity of offered capital with a given quantity of labor in the market, and not the more complex one of ascer-

---

* See the familiar passage in the *Political Economy*, Book III, ch. ii, § 4.

taining at what price the quantity demanded of labor will be equal to the quantity that happens to be supplied.

Thornton, like Longe, found it necessary to analyze the phrases about supply and demand which formed the whole of the philosophy of wages for Cobden and the public at large, and were used by the economists in a way not much less superficial.   Unlike Longe, who had taken up this topic very much by the way, Thornton took it up deliberately and systematically, and tried his hand at a complete restatement of the law of supply and demand. We need not follow the intricacies of his reasoning about supposed cases of horses at one price and another, of corn and gloves, Dutch auctions and so on.   With the application of the principle of marginal utility, this whole phase of economic theory has become much simplified.   Mill's equation of demand and supply is stated in better terms, and with fuller considation of all the elements involved, in the now familiar proposition that price depends on marginal utility.   Mill himself, in admitting the justice of some of Thornton's criticisms, pointed out that one important condition had not been mentioned in the *Political Economy*, which yet must be present if the equation of demand and supply is to fix price at a definite point. Quantity demanded must vary with price continuously. The same condition, it is clear, must be present if the modern version of the law of demand and supply is to bring a determinate answer.   If marginal utility is to fix price without a range of possible variation, each added increment of the article offered must have a less utility than the portion preceding it.   These are now commonplaces; they make Thornton's discussion antiquated, and leave Mill's significant only as showing that, on topics which he had stopped to think over with care, he reasoned with severe accuracy.

For the subject of the present volume, this general

discussion is pertinent because it shows both Mill, and Thornton following in the path which Longe had declared to be the wrong one : approaching wages and wages fund as a narrower problem within the larger one of demand and supply in general. And here Longe was right. Mill's equation of supply and demand assumes a demand, or quantity offered, which varies with the price of the thing on sale. Supply is supposed to be given ; demand, in the sense of quantity offered, is uncertain. The problem then is, at what price the whole supply will be carried off. But in the version of the wages fund doctrine which was then current, both supply and demand were fixed. Supply was the number of laborers ; demand was the quantity of capital, or of circulating capital. Bring the two together, and the average or general rate of wages must be the result.

This difference between the strict wages fund doctrine and the general law of supply and demand may be made more clear by considering another case of a similar sort, where also the usual formula of demand and supply was applied, and yet was inapplicable. The proposition that the value of money varies inversely with its quantity was traditionally presented by the classic writers as an ordinary case of the working of demand and supply. The permanent or natural value of money (*i. e.*, of specie) was supposed to be determined by its cost of production ; its market or temporary value, by demand and supply. Supply was the total quantity of money, due account being taken of "its rapidity of circulation," or the quantity in use for purchases at any moment. Demand for money consisted of all the commodities on sale. Clearly, demand here was a thing fixed from the start, not a thing varying as the rate at which the money was offered might be high or low. The value of money was determined in the simplest way possible : divide the total of money by the total of commodities. That the operation of demand

and supply as to money was peculiarly simple, had been pointed out often enough, most clearly by Mill himself. He had none the less presented demand and supply, or the play of forces that fixed the "market" value of money, as analogous to the play of forces that determined the value of individual commodities at any moment: whereas the two cases differ in essentials. Needless to say, we are not concerned here with the truth or untruth of the quantity theory of money. Its treatment by Mill and his contemporaries, whether right or wrong, shows that even on a subject which, like the theory of money, had received their deliberate attention, they made an indiscriminating use of the formula of supply and demand as the universal determinant of "market" values. Naturally, they did the same with regard to the wages fund, which had rarely received deliberate attention. In strictness, the theory of their wages fund was like that of general prices. Demand and supply, that is, capital and population, were both at any given time fixed: there was no play for a varying demand and no possibility of more than one point of equilibrium.

Mill, as we have seen, was brought to admit the indeterminateness and the elasticity of the wages fund, in the sense of money funds available for the direct employers. Hence he accepted, in some degree, the criticisms which Longe and Thornton made, in different ways, on his former off-hand application of demand and supply to the problem of market wages. He agreed with Thornton so far as to admit that here was a case where more than one point of equilibrium in the equation of demand and supply was possible, and where therefore no certainty existed that one rate or another should emerge from the forces directly in operation. It followed that workmen might get better terms,—higher wages,—by means of combinations and strikes, than they could get otherwise:

and thus Mill was led to the question which he had most at heart, the right and wrong of trades-unionism. The theoretical and more strictly economic questions as to demand and supply, like those as to the nature and limitation of the wages fund, received but a scant and unsatisfactory examination at his hands.

In truth, it may be questioned whether, under any form, an analogy can be usefully drawn between the immediate forces determining the general rate of wages, and the immediate causes determining the price of this or that commodity. Needless to say, a connection does exist between the causes that determine the wages of any one class of laborers and those that determine the prices of the commodities they make. Making allowance—often it must be a large allowance—for the friction caused by the position of employers as middlemen between laborers and consumers, we may say that the play of demand and supply in determining prices also determines proximately the share in general wages which shall go to one set of laborers or another. But this belongs to the problem of particular wages, not to that of general wages. As to general wages, Mill had come to the conclusion that the money funds which constitute the proximate demand for labor were indeterminate. We may go further, and admit that there is elasticity not only as to the money funds which go to hired laborers, but as to the consumable commodities which go to the laborers. Yet the variations which take place in the money wages or the real wages which may be turned over to laborers at large, present but a loose analogy to the changes in prices of commodities under the play of the motives analyzed in the doctrine of marginal utility. There is no sign of that continuous diminution of utility with each increment offered the purchasers, which is of the essence of the law of demand and supply as to commodities. In the concrete world, the expectations and calculations of the employing class, the manœuvres and combinations of laborers, a confused medley of causes acting in multiform ways, may bring about in any one season a greater or less of total wages, always within those limits of predetermination which have been elsewhere set forth.* Here we have phenomena of a sort that do not readily reduce themselves to any rule, or fit into any general law of value.†

Fairly weighed, Mill's review of Thornton thus marks no real advance in the discussion. The curious acceptance of reasoning by which the wages fund is supposed to be made up by the money means of the immediate employers, rendered it unfruitful as to the really difficult question at issue. The discussion of demand and supply added little to what Mill had said in the *Political Economy*, and certainly made no helpful application of old views or new ones on the topic in hand. Even on that question of the right and wrong of trade-unionism, which now chiefly

---

* Compare what was said in Part I, Chapter IV, pp. 82–94.

† Possibly, in an analysis of the succession of advances made to laborers over a long series of years, a general formula of demand and supply, or of final utility, may be applicable. Over a whole lengthened cycle of production, and in view of the total advances made during the cycle, it may be helpful to conceive of successive increments of capital as turned over to laborers, each with less and less utility for the capitalists as there are repetitions of the process. This mode of approaching the problem of the return to capital was suggested by Jevons, and has been followed with various modifications, by other writers since his time. But obviously it is applicable only to the problem of the final division of the proceeds of a complete productive cycle, not to the narrower question of "market" wages which is the essence of the wages fund problem. At best, I suspect that this mode of approaching the general problem of capital and interest, and so of wages, needs to be both amplified and qualified before it can yield a sufficient explanation of the realities of industrial life. Like the older formulæ of the classic writers, it brings a temptation to be content with large general principles, and a danger that their concrete application shall suffer neglect.

appealed to him, Mill simply applied the familiar formula of his utilitarianism. Had it not been for the brief and summary recantation of a form of the wages fund doctrine which he had never really maintained, this paper would have had no prominent place in his economic or philosophic writings.

The next important step in the controversy was taken by John Eliot Cairnes. A year or two after Thornton and Mill had threshed the matter over, and almost immediately after Mill's death, Cairnes published his volume on *Some Leading Principles of Political Economy, Newly Expounded.** As the title indicates, it is an attempt at a restatement and modification of more than one part of the economic theory. The rate of wages is the subject of the second book ; the passages pertinent to the present inquiry being partly in the opening chapter, which considers the theory of wages directly, and partly in the later chapters on Trade-Unionism, which apply and illustrate the theoretic conclusions.

As to the nature and constitution of the wages fund, Cairnes goes at the matter virtually in the same way as Longe and Thornton and Mill. The case of the individual employer and the means at his command are analyzed.

" Why does A. B. employ his wealth in productive operations ? and why does he employ so much and no more in productive operations ? . . . This point having been settled, he has yet to consider in what proportions the amount shall be divided between Fixed Capital, Raw Material, and Wages. What is to prescribe the respective quotas ? Manifestly, in the first place, the nature of the industry in which he proposes to embark his capital. . . . Now the

---

* London, 1874. The preface is dated March, 1874. Mill had died in 1873.

considerations which weigh with the individual capitalist are those which weigh with a community of capitalists; and we are therefore justified in concluding that the main circumstance governing the proportion which the wages fund shall bear to the general capital of a nation is the nature of the national industries." *

This clearly rests on the assumption that the fund for paying wages is held by the capitalists who directly employ labor, and that, in Thornton's language, it can be "no other than an aggregate of smaller similar funds possessed by the several individuals who compose the employing class of the nation." †

The same assumption is made more specifically when Cairnes goes on to examine further in what manner capital is divided into its three constituent parts of Fixed Capital, Raw Material, and Wages. A capitalist starts with £10,000; with £5,000 he can buy fixed capital and raw material, with the other £5,000 he can employ 100 workmen at £50 a year. This example might indeed be supposed, if it stood alone, to be merely illustrative, and not meant to give a literal account of the where and what of the wages fund. But Cairnes uses it as perfectly significant of the details and realities of things; for he proceeds at once to draw from the supposition as to employers' means in hand, a general conclusion of importance. Some simple arithmetic applied to the £10,000 shows that if laborers are plenty, a less proportion of the cash can go to wages, and a larger proportion will be needed to furnish the plant and materials required to keep the many laborers busy. The details of this odd bit of reasoning, and

---

* *Leading Principles*, Book II, ch. i, § 8. The first two of the extracts here quoted are separated by a page or two in Cairnes's text; but they are parts of a continuous thread of reasoning.

† See the passage as quoted above, p. 246. Cairnes later quotes the same passage from Thornton.

its validity, are not of great significance; what is important for the present subject is the use of the money illustration as a means of drawing large conclusions. Cairnes generalizes from it to the effect that the larger the supply of labor, the smaller the proportion of wages fund to other sorts of capital. The outcome of his reasoning is finally stated thus: "Our analysis accordingly issues in the following conditions as the determining causes of the Wages Fund, viz.: the total capital of the country; the nature of the national industries; and the supply of labor,"—a conclusion which rests simply on an analysis of the mode in which an individual employer would be likely to use his money means.

Cairnes, as was just noted, divided capital into three parts,—fixed capital, raw materials, and wages fund. He thus got rid of the phrase "circulating capital," which Ricardo and his followers had often used to denote that part of capital which was "destined to the maintenance of labor." But the change was one of language rather than of substance. Like his predecessors, Cairnes failed to keep clearly in mind the distinction between the real wages fund of commodities, and the money funds of the immediate employers; or rather, he neglected the former almost entirely. The threefold division was indeed made, in terms, with reference to the capital of the community at large; but when Cairnes proceded to any detailed reasoning as to the wages fund part, he gave attention solely to employers and to the money means they dispose of.

Reasoning so, how could Cairnes maintain that the wages fund was in any way fixed? that the employer could not borrow, or retrench on his personal expenditure? Within a few pages of the passages just quoted, in which the wages fund is described in terms of cash, he turned to Thornton's questions as to the determinateness

of the fund, and might fairly have been expected to answer
them directly.   He did not do so.   He then changed the
point of view; found it needful to enter on an explanation
of a larger and wider question,—the nature of economic
laws; and at last came back to answer Thornton by setting forth, not whether the wages fund was determinate,
but in what sense there was an economic law which made
it indeterminate within limits.*

As to the nature of economic law, and the kind of determination which it may be expected to bring about,
Cairnes wrote justly and truly.   "What an economic law
asserts is, not that men must do so and so, whether they
like it or not, but that in given circumstances they will
like to do so and so; that their self-interest or other feel-
ings will lead them to this result."   The application of
economic law in this sense to the wages fund was that the
habits and desires of capitalists would lead them to maintain accumulation and investment at a certain rate.   Individual capitalists might cut down wages and swell their
private expenditure; but, "the character of the wealthy
classes remaining on the whole what it is, increased accumulations in other quarters would neutralize exceptional
extravagance in some."   The disposition to accumulate
being thus fixed, a certain proportion of the sums invested
must (Cairnes italicizes the word) go to wages.   At the
root of the argument we find the theory of what Mill
called the effective desire of accumulation,—that, with a
given return to capital, accumulation will be maintained;
and so a determination and even predetermination of a
certain amount of capital to wages.

This is familiar doctrine : that high profits increase
accumulation, low profits check it.   But it does not apply
to wages *hic et nunc*.   Without stopping to inquire just

---

* See § 11 of the chapter just cited.

'how accurately and promptly accumulation in fact responds to a rise or fall in the return to capital, we may be sure that the process takes some years at least to work itself out. Clearly the old version was that this factor had nothing to do with "market" wages. At any given time, according to Ricardo and all the array of the English writers down to Cairnes's time, it was the ratio of capital to population that determined wages. If high profits were the result, more capital would be accumulated, and after a space wages would rise: but only after a space. Economic laws acting through the desire of capitalists to reap high returns,—"covetousness held in check by covetousness," as Cairnes himself elsewhere expressed it,—perhaps determined wages in a cycle of years. But here was no answer to Thornton's question: was the wages fund at any given time or at any given season determinate or indeterminate?

Thornton put his question by asking how the funds of capitalists Smith and Jones were determined. Cairnes also, when he tried to restate the doctrine, asked how the funds of A. B. would be distributed and used. But when he came to answer Thornton's question, he set up a different kind of "determination": one that was settled not once for all this season, but after a while through slow-working causes. Thornton would have admitted freely,—indeed did admit,—what Cairnes said about capital and accumulation and profits. He, too, maintained that in the end high profits stimulate accumulation and increase wages; and, conversely, that low profits check accumulation and in the end lower wages. But Thornton asked whether there was not flexibility in the funds immediately available for paying wages, and whether trade-unions could not squeeze from the employer something he would not otherwise give; and here Cairnes, with his rehabilitated wages fund, did not squarely meet the question.

Cairnes himself had in mind the trade-unions, and the application of his theory to their doings. Here the point of view just described is even more distinctly taken : the real limits to the action of trade-unions being found, not in any rigid wages fund, but in the fact, or supposed fact, that profits are at the minimum necessary to induce accumulatiou. At the very outset, to be sure, Cairnes notes incidentally that there are certain quasi-physical limits to the wages fund. "In order to maintain the stock of commodities of all sorts which in any civilized community goes to support the laboring population, a certain large proportion of the general wealth must exist in the form of fixed capital and raw material. The wealth available, therefore, for the remuneration of labor can not at the utmost be more than the balance which remains after those indispensable requirements have been provided for, under pain of complete failure of the fund." * This is not so far from a statement of the true question as to the wages fund proper : whether the tangible commodities that can go or will go to laborers are at any moment limited. By proceeding on this line Cairnes might have been able to give a direct answer one way or the other to Thornton's questions as to determinateness. But he passes at once to the other problem,—as to "the limits arising from the action of human interests operating under the actual circumstances of man's environment in the world." These "economic" limits are simply that "profits are already at or within a handbreath of the minimum": here is the effective obstacle to the endeavor of trade-unions to raise general wages.

When he got to this point, Cairnes said explicitly that the reasoning applied only to "the *average* rate of wages, as a *permanent* state of things" (the italics are his own).

---

* Cairnes, Book II, ch. iii, § 1.

For a while, trade-unions may secure a general rise in wages, even though profits be at the minimum : but after a lapse of time, and in consequence of a shrinkage of capital, they will find they have killed the goose that laid the golden eggs. Under favorable conditions, when the progress of industry makes a gain possible in one direction or another, they may secure a rise in wages at once, instead of waiting until a rise in profits brings greater accumulation of capital, and thus, eventually, higher wages. Either of these admissions assumes a wages fund that for the moment is *not* determinate.* By implication, Thornton's questions are answered just as he would have answered them; and the wages fund is rehabilitated by restating a doctrine as to the relation of wages and profits, and the effects of profits on accumulation, which had been preached by almost every English writer of the century.

It may, indeed, be maintained that there never was more than this to the wages fund doctrine : namely, Ricardo's teaching that profits were the leavings of wages, and his further teaching that accumulation was increased

---

* " A capitalist, for example, who has committed himself to an industrial enterprise by making large purchases of building and plant must find labourers to work for him or suffer heavy loss. . . . Under these circumstances, supposing the workmen on whom he relies to strike for higher wages, and that he has reason to believe they possess the resolution and are in command of funds sufficient to enable them to maintain a prolonged strike, it may be wisdom to concede to their demands. . . . It is evident, therefore, that workmen have, by means of combination and by accumulating sufficient funds, very considerable power of acting upon the rate of wages."—Cairnes, *Leading Principles*, Book II, ch. iii, § 3. This was all that Thornton maintained. Compare the passage cited above, at p. 257, about the employer with the £10,000, which he is supposed to assign in certain fixed proportions to plant, material, and wages. In the extract just given, Cairnes admits that the sum available for wages may be stretched without affecting the other parts of capital ; and, as the context shows, extends the admission to wages at large.

by high profits and diminished by low.   Historically, there may be ground for this contention.   We have seen that the whole doctrine of wages as determined by the ratio of capital to population was crystallized by Ricardo's handling of capital as resolvable into a succession of advances to laborers.   We have seen, too, that the rigidity or determinateness of the capital from which wages came was not often prominent in the minds of the writers who maintained its importance.   But none the less, the wages fund doctrine is a different and distinct one from that of the determination of wages by product, *via* capital.   It applies to wages in any one season ; and presents primarily the question whether at any given time there is an amount of capital available for paying wages which can or can not be increased.   That wages in the long run are determined by product, with enough deduction for interest to induce the accumulation of capital, is stoutly maintained by plenty of writers who sweep the wages fund out of the way with scorn.   It is virtually Cairnes's doctrine; and, while he insists on an advance from capital as an intermediate step in the settlement of wages by product, he adds nothing to what his predecessors had said as to the manner and degree of the determination of the advance of capital, or as to the position of employers and hired laborers in the social use of capital and in the social distribution of finished goods.

Before leaving this last stage in the old-fashioned way of reasoning on the subject, it may be pointed out how, notwithstanding his professed maintenance of the older doctrines, Cairnes had diverged far from them in his final conclusions.   He marks the last stage in a change of emphasis, so great as to be a change of opinion, which had been going on gradually and almost imperceptibly among the English writers since Ricardo's day.   Ricardo had laid it down first, that market wages depend on the ratio be-

tween capital and population; second, that if the result
of the momentary ratio were wages higher or lower than
was "necessary" or "natural," population would increase
or decrease until wages were again at the normal point;
third, that if the result of this process again were high
profits, accumulation of capital would be stimulated, until
at last a stage of equilibrium might be reached. In
Cairnes, we find that the second and third propositions
have changed places. The first step in the analysis remains practically the same, though the phrases are changed
a bit: wages depend on the ratio between the number of
laborers and that part of capital which constitutes wages
fund. The second step now is that if the process results
in higher or lower profits than are needful to induce accumulation, capital will grow more or less rapidly, and
its return will be brought back to the normal level. Capital gets a certain minimum return: wages get the rest.
The third step is that which Ricardo had put second: the
Malthusian theory of population, regulating the supply
of labor, and eventually bringing wages to the point fixed
by the standard of living. The two writers, at either end
of the line, agree in giving scant attention to the step
which they put third in order. Ricardo said little of the
accumulation of capital and the likelihood of its responding to a high or low rate of profits: he conceived that
wages adjusted themselves to their natural rate more
quickly than profits to their point of equilibrium.* Cairnes,

---

* Ricardo generally dismissed the question as to profits in a footnote,
as in the *Essay on the Influence of a High Price of Corn*, *Works*, p.
377 ; or briefly referred in his text to the fact that of course accumulation
would be checked long before profits got to zero. *Works*, p. 67. The
chapter in the *Political Economy* entitled " The Effects of Accumulation
on Profits " (chapter xxi) is chiefly given to other subjects than its title
indicates : to some criticisms of Adam Smith, and to the relation between
gross profits and interest.

on the other hand, makes but brief and off-hand mention of the supply of labor as determined by the principle of population; while the increase or decrease of capital, in correspondence with the rise or fall of profits above the normal point, is presented and emphasized at length. In Ricardo, profits appear as the residuary legatee; in Cairnes, wages.

This change in emphasis appeared gradually. Torrens and M'Culloch had approached the later point of view when they confronted laborers' combinations with the same objection as Cairnes's: an enforced rise in wages would check accumulation. Mill stood half-way, on this subject as on others. He gave much space to the effective desire of accumulation, and the rate of return on capital as a measure of that desire; and he presented the tendency of profits to a minimum in a manner to imply that accumulation responded rapidly and easily to changes in the rate. Elsewhere, and more commonly, he remains on the Ricardian ground: wages are the element that is stationary, and profits vary. In Cairnes, the assumed fixity of wages at last becomes only a remoter possibility, not dwelt on at all in the treatment of concrete questions. This final abandonment of a doctrine fundamental in Ricardo's reasoning on distribution brought with it a complete change of front, and new vistas on every aspect of the social questions: a change of which all the consequences in economic theory have not yet been fully worked out.

CHAPTER XIII.

THE WAGES FUND IN GERMANY.

WE may now conveniently consider the treatment of the wages fund doctrine by the economists of Continental Europe; and among these, chiefly by the Germans. Chronologically, this phase of the history of the doctrine should have an earlier place; for an unmistakable departure from the lines of reasoning traditional among the English was made by Hermann before the days of the younger Mill. But the insular condition of social and political speculation in Great Britain in the middle of the century, and the stagnation of economic thought in particular, prevented any breath of influence from reaching English thinkers. The Germans went their way, unnoticed by their English-speaking contemporaries, until, in very recent times, links of connection were formed, and the international exchange of thought has rebegun.

Outside of Germany, there is, before our own days, practically nothing on the subject. The French never were much influenced by Ricardo; and consequently that simplification of the theory at Ricardo's hands, by which wages were assumed to be paid once for all from a specific quantum of capital, never appeared among them in emphatic form, and never received great attention. They commonly said that wages depended on capital; but with less emphasis and less definiteness of statement than among English writers. To go through the hasty and uncertain versions of the relation of capital to wages, which are to be found from Say to Bastiat and Cherbuliez, would be to repeat, with even less satisfactory results, the story of inconsequent thinking which we have found in the English successors of Ricardo. Among Italians, also, nothing of interest or importance appears; and we may turn at once to the Germans.

Hermann has already been referred to as the writer who began the breach with the English theorists. Before his time it is difficult to find much that is promising in German economic thought, beyond the work of popularizing and spreading the views of Adam Smith. Hermann was an incisive and original thinker; and his reasoning on wages and capital is as unquestionably the source of the treatment of this subject in German text-books, as Ricardo's on international trade is of the handling of that subject among the English. He was, moreover, one of the few Continental writers who, before the present movement in economics began, had read Ricardo with care, and had been affected by his example of rigid analysis and unrelenting reasoning; and he approached the subject, unlike Jones and Sismondi, in a mood to develop rather than to question the classic doctrines. The first edition of his *Staatswirthschaftliche Untersuchungen* was published in 1832. The second and enlarged edition of 1874 served rather to amplify his reasoning than to add anything substantially new. The high intellectual quality of the book and the independence of its thought are beyond question; and the German economists are certainly not without justification in their admiration of Hermann's work and in their willingness to accept his doctrines.

As to wages, Hermann objects to the doctrine then current in England on several grounds. First, the number of laborers paid directly out of the income of consumers is too large to be overlooked; and Hermann notes with approval that Adam Smith had made "revenue" as well as "stock" a source from which wages are paid. Next, the proportion of wages fund to other capital is not defined in the current statements. This objection had been sporadically presented in England before Hermann made it; but neither there nor in Hermann's reasoning is it given the prominent place which it received in later times. The radical objection is the last one. Capital, after all, is not the real source from which wages are paid. That real source is the income of those who buy the products made by the laborers, or, briefly, the income of consumers. Here is the objection accepted as conclusive by Hermann's followers in Germany, and serving as the basis of their own statements of the causes determining wages.*

To understand the views of any writer on the whole range of subjects of which the wages fund doctrine is a part, it is needful to consider his views on the nature and functions of capital at large, and more particularly on the place in the analysis of capital of finished commodities consumed by laborers. Unfortunately, on this vital topic we find Hermann speaking with uncertain sound. Not that he had failed to give careful thought to the analysis of capital. To the word "capital" he gave that larger significance which has already been referred to.† Virtually all wealth he regards as capital: classifying it as con-

---

* *Staatswirthschaftliche Untersuchungen*, first edition, pp. 280–285 ; second edition, pp. 474–477. It is significant of the change in social conditions in the interval between the two editions (1832–1874) that in the first Hermann says the wages fund doctrine is practically harmful, because it encourages arrogance among the employers, who are taught to think themselves the real payers of wages, and so entitled to favors and bounties ; while in the second he finds it harmful because it teaches laborers to look on employers as the real wages-givers, and so lures ignorant workmen into hopeless strikes.

† See above, Part I, Ch. II, p. 39.

sumer's and producer's capital, according as it is or is not yet in the hands of those who are to derive enjoyment for it. This suggestive distinction has been permanently incorporated into most German text-books; while his description of the mode in which circulating capital (a part of producer's capital) constantly passes into commodities for immediate use, and so into consumer's capital, anticipates much modern thought as to the steady ripening of inchoate wealth into enjoyable commodities. Clearly Hermann meant by consumer's capital what has been described in these pages as enjoyable wealth; while producer's capital signifies what has here been described as simply capital. For a consideration of the fundamental relation of capital to wages, it would be necessary for Hermann to set forth clearly what place he would assign to the enjoyable commodities constituting the real reward of laborers: whether they are to be regarded as producer's capital or as consumer's capital.

But on this topic he did not fully work out his conclusions. In agricultural operations he classes food for laborers as part of circulating capital, *i. e.*, as producer's capital.* Elsewhere he clearly implies that all consumable commodities of a perishable sort, whether used by laborers, by capitalists, or by idlers, are not part of producer's capital at all.† In discussing wages, he speaks of the employers' capital as a fund which could act but once in paying wages, and which would be dissipated unless constantly replaced from the sale of the product,—a statement which implies that this capital is at least the immediate source from which the laborer's wages are first derived. Here are doctrines not clearly formulated and

---

* *Staatswirthschaftliche Untersuchungen*, p. 307, 2nd edition.

† See the analysis of *Nutzkapital* at p. 221, and of *flüssiges Kapital* at p. 283.

not entirely consistent with each other; defects which illustrate once again the difficulties which beset the thinker in this tangled subject.

We are compelled, therefore, for our guidance in following Hermann's views, to rely on the comparatively brief passages in which he advances directly the doctrine that consumer's income is the real source of wages. This, as we have seen, was virtually the doctrine put forth by Longe, at a much later date, though with much less consistency of statement. Something has already been said in explanation and criticism of it; but in view of the prominent place it has had in the theoretic literature of Germany, something more may be added.

The difficulty with a view like Hermann's is that it does not clearly distinguish between particular wages and general wages,—between the causes which affect the wages of one class of laborers as compared with another, and the causes which determine the wages of all laborers. The nature and extent of the consumer's demand for the products made by a particular set of laborers have an obvious effect on the wages of these laborers; and the inference is easy, however unwarrantable on closer thought, that all wages depend on consumer's demand or income. The transition is made the more natural by the habit of considering capital in terms of money, and the capitalist employer as the possessor of a fund of cash which represents the apparatus of production controlled by him. Even before the time of the younger Mill, the English economists, whom Hermann followed and criticised, frequently spoke of it as a money fund. Ricardo had set the example of reducing all capital to terms of money; his immediate successors did more, and spoke of wages capital as if it consisted of cash and nothing more. Hermann saw that the wages fund, in this sense, so far as it existed at all, was constantly replenished from the sale of the disposable product; and he was naturally led to regard those who bought the product as the real payers of wages. And, to repeat, the wages of any particular set of laborers do depend precisely on this. Their money income and their share of the goods available for consumption are settled by the terms on which their products sell in the market. The appearance of the capitalist employer as a middleman between them and the purchaser does not alter this situation, so long as the competition between capitalists is free. What the employer can pay the individual laborer, or the group of individual laborers, and what he will pay if competition is free, depends on what the consumers pay him.

Bearing in mind that the wages fund doctrine is worth discussing, or replacing by something else, only as an attempt to discover the causes determining general wages, we find very great and very obvious difficulties in the way of applying Hermann's reasoning to the wider question. At bottom, he presents the old question whether demand for commodities is demand for labor; and on that question the reasoning of the classic writers was in essentials so simple and so sound that there is no escape from answering, as they did, in the negative. We may intelligently measure the remuneration of an individual section or class of society in terms of money, and so may seek the measure of particular wages in the *Zahlungsfähigkeit*, or money demand, of those who buy the laborers' product. But for society as a whole, and for laborers as a whole, consumable commodities are the only measure of income,—money and exchange being but devices for sharing this real income among the different members. The ultimate source can only be the output of real goods from the labor of society,—the steady flow of enjoyable things which issues from the exertions of men. This is the total consumer's income,—the source from which all of us, whether laborers or idlers, get remuneration or tribute or alms. It is clear that Hermann did not mean to lay down the proposition that wages come from consumer's income in this sense. He had in mind the money payments of those who buy goods from the employer, and so recoup him for his outlays. But these purchases are of importance only in determining the share of real wages or real consumer's income got by a particular group of laborers : they play no part in the causes determining wages at large.

The same fundamental difficulty emerges from another point of view. Laborers are themselves consumers, in many countries the largest and most important body of consumers. They buy commodities with their wages; and their demand, according to Hermann's reasoning, is an ultimate source of wages. Wages are thus an important source of wages,—reasoning which runs so obviously in a circle that we must be surprised to find it unnoticed by a mind as acute as Hermann's. If it be objected that there are consumers, like rent receivers or pensioners, who are not laborers, the situation is not bettered. Unless we suppose the laborers to produce only commodities bought by these separate consumers, and to buy among themselves no commodities made by other laborers, we still find that consumer's income includes in its constituent parts a larger or smaller element of wages, and that an undefined portion of the source of wages is simply wages.

Hermann's doctrine, ineffective as it is in grappling with the question of general wages, nevertheless has found its way into almost every German book on general economics. On the one hand, the confusion between money and real wages; on the other, the natural disposition to fasten attention to the dealings between the immediate employers and their hired laborers,—make its acceptance easy of explanation. Moreover, in Germany economic discussion has always been, much to its advantage, more concrete than that of Ricardo's followers in England; and the liberal space given to an enumeration of specific causes affecting the wages of different sets of laborers, indicates an attitude toward the whole subject such as would make natural the ready acceptance of an apparently straightforward and practical explanation of wages as determined by consumer's demand. At all events, hardly a book on economics from a German hand since the time of Hermann can be found in which his lead on the subject of wages is not more or less closely followed.

While Hermann himself, so far as spirit and method are concerned, did not diverge far from the classic school, his views on wages seem to have gained acceptance in proportion as the breach with the English writers became wider. In Rau's treatise, which expounded economic principles to two generations of German students on the familiar English lines, we still find the old doctrine that wages depend on the quantity of capital. In later editions Rau referred to Hermann's doctrine in his notes, and there admitted, with caution, that the latter had rightly divined the ultimate source of wages; but the classic theory maintains its place in the text in the dignity of large type.* In Mangoldt's *Volkswirthschaftslehre*, which, though not published until 1868, represents the methods and traditions of an earlier date, the subject is discreetly given a wide berth. Apparently, Mangoldt was not disposed to commit himself either to the old doctrine or to Hermann's modification.† But in a book like Roesler's on Wages, which, though it made no deep impression on German thought, reflected the drift of things at the time

---

* Rau's *Lehrbuch*, eighth edition (1868), § 195.

† It is due to this subtle and independent thinker to say that his *Volkswirthschaftslehre* was printed posthumously, from a manuscript not left in finished state.

of its publication (1861), Hermann's views appear with marked emphasis. We are told, in italics, that the employer's capital is indifferent to the laborers, who draw their wages solely from the consumers, the employer being merely a middleman.* Roscher's *Political Economy*, in which the independent German movement first took shape in a general text-book, also accepts Hermann's view. Roscher's statement is sententious, in accordance with his general practice; but it is none the less clearly an adoption of Hermann's view.† The year of his first edition (1854) may be noted as a date after which Hermann's doctrine appears in almost every German book on general economics.

The next important and independent step, with effects clearly traceable in the theoretic parts of current German treatises, was taken by a writer still active among us, Professor Lujo Brentano. Shortly after the publication of Thornton's book *On Labour*, and of Mill's review of Thornton in the *Fortnightly*, Professor Brentano printed in the *Jahrbücher für Nationaloekonomie* a paper on the theory of wages as developed by English economists.‡ Some further discussion of the subject was undertaken by him in the second part of his book on the English trade unions (*Zur Kritik der englischen Gewerkvereine*, 1872) ; and it is again considered briefly in the volume on *Die Arbeiterverhältnisse gemäss dem heutigen Recht* (1877). The later publications add little to the theoretic matter of the paper

---

* C. F. H. Roesler, *Zur Kritik der Lehre vom Arbeitslohn* (1861), p. 141 ; compare also p. 87. Roesler follows Hermann closely on other doctrines, especially in regard to the separate productivity of capital

† Roscher's *Nationaloekonomie*, §§ 165, 166. The rendering of these passages in the English translation of Roscher is far from satisfactory.

‡ *Die Lehre von den Lohnsteigerungen mit besonderer Rücksicht auf die englischen Wirthschaftslehrer. Jahrbücher für Nationaloekonomie*, 1 Folge, vol. xvi, pp. 251–281 (1871).

in the *Jahrbücher*, which deserves careful attention, as being, after Hermann, the most influential of German contributions to the theory of wages.

Professor Brentano's paper divides itself into three parts. First comes a sketch, admirably done, of the history of the wages fund doctrine among English writers; then a consideration of that doctrine; and, finally, an effective criticism of Thornton's theory of wages. It is the second part, on the wages fund doctrine, which chiefly concerns us here. With it goes a discussion of the theorem that demand for commodities is not demand for labor. That theorem had been used by the classic writers, and especially by Mill, chiefly as an answer to the notion that the luxurious expenditure of the rich was beneficial to the poor; but Professor Brentano rightly treats it as a simple corollary of the doctrine that wages are paid from capital, and as significant in its relations to that doctrine.

Like Thornton, Professor Brentano is on one point more conservative than some later critics of the old doctrine. Wages he admits to be paid in the first instance from capital. "There must be a stock of accumulated products of previous labor—that is, of capital—sufficient to feed the laborers engaged in production." But, like the English writers of earlier and later date, Brentano does not linger over the why and how of this need of an "accumulation" of real commodities. The point of view is soon shifted to that of the advance of capital by employers to hired laborers, without notice of the difference between this and the advance from an accumulated stock of products. In the book on English trade unions, the importance of capital as the proximate source of wages is again admitted; but it is urged that it is only a vehicle which serves to convey wages to the laborers from their real source. It is on the fixity of the fund, and the ultimate source whence it is replenished, that he professes to differ with Mill and Mill's teachers. He points out with truth that the predetermination or fixity of the wages fund was never laid down emphatically by Mill in the *Political Economy ;* and, at all events, he reaches unreservedly his own conclusion that there is no such fixity. The capital which employers will turn over to laborers is an elastic quantity. It can be swelled by the use of credit, or by trenching on the funds which the employer had meant to use for his own consumption ; and it accommodates itself readily to changes in the ultimate source of wages. As to that ultimate source, Brentano expressly accepts Hermann's views : the source lies in the income of those who buy the laborer's product.

The essential thing to note in Brentano's ingenious and able discussion is, that the capital which is described as the proximate source of wages is still conceived as wholly in the hands and at the disposal of the immediate employer of labor. It is still a " fund," though one which can be swelled in one way or another. The best illustration of this limitation of his analysis is to be found in the treatment of the mode in which the capital at the disposal of employers can be enlarged.

As was noted a few moments ago, he examines Mill's statement of the proposition that demand for commodities is not demand for labor. Mill had asked how, even with a high demand for velvets, they could be produced, or a demand for labor could set in, unless there were food, the product of former labor and therefore capital, wherewith to support the laborers who make the velvet. Brentano's answer to Mill is a simple *tu quoque.* In an advanced community there can never be any difficulty in securing or augmenting capital ; for, according to Mill's own doctrine, the distinction between capital and non-capital lies only in the mind of the owner. An increased demand for velvets would cause some owners to change their minds, and so transform part of their possessions into capital; thus an effective demand for labor would appear. This turns the tables on Mill very neatly; for Mill had expounded his doctrine as to the determination of capital by the mere intent of the owner, in language which perhaps fairly warranted Brentano's use of it. But that doctrine itself is tenable only in the limited sense which has already been indicated.* In the long run, unquestionably it is true that, under a *régime* of private property, the disposition of the owner decides whether wealth shall be used for immediate enjoyment, or for producing further wealth, that is, as capital. At any given moment, however, tools, implements, and materials are of necessity capital; while finished commodities and food exist in a quantity which, whether rigidly fixed or not, certainly cannot be augmented *ad libitum* by a mere change of intention.

Brentano had in mind more or less clearly the case of the individual capitalist, who can sell his house or his diamonds or his factory, and can use the money-proceeds in hiring laborers; so transforming, by a mere change of intention, his luxuries or fixed capital into wages-capital. Mill perhaps had a similar possibility in mind; at all events, his language, not only in the passages referred to by Brentano but in plenty of others, looked to the funds and means of the direct employers of labor. As to the funds of an individual capitalist and employer, it is mockery, as Thornton said, to ask whether they are fixed or predetermined. Brentano could have no difficulty in disproving the fixity of the wages fund from this point of view. But such an inquiry can tell us nothing as to the constitution and limits of the total money funds which the whole class of active capitalists have at their

* See Chapter III, pp. 62, 67, and Chapter XI, pp. 225–227.

disposal for the hire of laborers; still less can it tell us anything as to quantity or the predetermination of the consumable commodities from which laborers get their substantial reward.

We have but another phase of the same difficulty when Brentano refers, as others had done before him, to the possible use of credit as a means of swelling the sources from which wages are paid. He remarks that the capitalist will always be willing to grant larger wages, provided he can get them back through higher prices paid him by the consumer; and, if it happens that he does not himself possess the funds for the larger payment, he simply borrows them. Of the individual employer this is unquestionably true; and of the process by which a particular set of laborers may get better terms for themselves it is an accurate account. But it is hardly necessary to point out, after what has already been said, that a stretching of credit can not possibly affect the supply of commodities from which real wages must come, nor serve to increase wages at large. This mode of approaching the problem of general wages is as hopeless as that which makes the wages fund expansible by a change in the intentions of employers. When Brentano, in his book on trade unions, gives a statement of the wages fund doctrine, preparatory to a refutation of it, he defines the fund as "the property [*Vermögen*] of a country which can by possibility be used, either directly or as a means of obtaining credit, for the payment of wages." * Here the word *Vermögen* is used with the same connotation of money available for paying wages that appears in the traditional use of the word "funds" by English writers. The refutation of the doctrine in this form does not advance matters more than the advocacy of it did.

---

* *Zur Kritik der Englischen Gewerkvereine*, pp. 200–203.

If the negative part of Brentano's reasoning is thus unsatisfactory as to the real difficulties of the subject, the positive part is no more conclusive. It is true that Hermann's theorem is cited in terms, and is accepted: consumer's demand and income, we are told, are the real source of wages. But Brentano does not fail to see the difficulty arising from the fact that laborers themselves are consumers. A rise in wages, he points out, may be secured partly at the expense of other wages, and so may be nugatory for laborers as a class. It may be secured also, in part or in whole, from the incomes of other classes,—from those of employers or investors or rent-receivers, and so may represent a substantial change in distribution to the advantage of the receivers of wages. All this is true; and followed out to its last consequences, would bring the writer face to face with the problem of the elasticity of the total money funds and the total real funds which may go to laborers as a whole. But Brentano does not proceed to this stage. He accepts Hermann's theory as a needed correction of that version of the wages fund doctrine which had been brought into renewed prominence by the attacks of Longe and Thornton; he hints at the deficiencies of Hermann's solution, so far as general wages are concerned; and then remarks that after all wages at large are an abstraction, a vague and indeterminate generality, and that the only thing worth discussing is the concrete rise or fall in the wages of specific sets of laborers. This is not an unnatural conclusion, in view of the unsatisfactory character both of the old views and of the substitutes offered by writers like Thornton and Longe. It is obviously natural, more especially, to a writer who, like Brentano, had given detailed study to the history and doings of trade unions, and thus had been brought into contact with the effective causes that bear on the fluctuations of particular wages; causes which, as has been pointed out

elsewhere,* have little to do with the general flow of the
real wages fund.

The final conclusions reached by Brentano are thus
sensible enough, so far as application to practical questions goes. The source of general wages is elastic; there
is no iron-clad obstacle in the way of an advance in wages
for any particular set of laborers; such an advance does
not necessarily mean a corresponding loss to other laborers; a general simultaneous advance for all laborers is
not indeed theoretically impossible, but is not worth discussing because outside the practical possibilities of real
life. All this is true; and if there is ambiguity as to
the cause of the elasticity of wages,—whether of general
or particular wages—it does not affect the truth of the
conclusions as to the limits to trades-union action. But
the theoretical basis of the whole does not go deep.
There is no complete statement of the function of capital
in the production or distribution of wealth, or of the relation between the operations of the individual employer
and the source of real wages.

Hermann and Brentano are the two writers who have
taken the lead among the Germans in the discussion of
wages; and the result of their combined labors has been
to push aside, in the text-books and hand-books of the
Germans, the simple formula of the older English writers,
and to leave nothing very distinct in its place. It would
carry us beyond the scope of the present inquiry to examine the variations of the theory of wages as they appear
in the different text-books of recent years.† In most of
them a " relative " truth in the wages fund doctrine is ad-

---

* See pp. 101–108, *infra.*

† For a brief review of the treatment of the topic in some of the well-
known German books, see the *Quarterly Journal of Economics*, October,
1894, where the substance of the present chapter was published, with
some further details and examples.

mitted, or at all events something is said as to the importance of capital for the immediate payment of wages; and
then there is some further reference, more or less explicit,
to Hermann's proposition as to consumer's demand as the
ultimate source or determinant of wages. On this topic,
as on others, the theoretic views of the German economists of the last generation mark a transition stage.
The clear-cut doctrines and unqualified statements of the
Ricardian school in England were found inconclusive and
unsatisfactory. But nothing very precise and definite
took their place. The old sharply-defined conclusions
were sometimes rejected without attempt to put anything
in their place; sometimes the edge was taken from them
by qualifications and corrections which made it difficult
to say how much was really left. This tentative mode
of expounding the subject was unquestionably better than
the bold and uncompromising dicta of M'Culloch, and in
many ways was preferable to Mill's exposition, with its
emphatic elaboration of the Ricardian deductions. But it
could not lead to anything definitive; and certainly on
the wages fund it served rather to bring out the deficiencies of the English writers than to substitute any new
doctrine of substantial value.

CHAPTER XIV.

CONTEMPORARY DISCUSSION.

IT is not the object of the present volume to follow the discussion of the wages fund doctrine at the hands of the many writers of our own time who have expressed their views on the never ending controversy. The varieties of opinion are endless ; on no topic in the range of economic theory would it be so difficult to extract any consensus of opinion. But, to understand the stage at which the discussion stands, it will be advantageous to follow two main trains of thought which have become conspicuous and important during the last twenty years.

After the weakness of the old doctrine had been made plain by Thornton's and Longe's criticisms, Mill's recantation, and Cairnes's attempt at rehabilitation, the attack was continued by a series of English-speaking writers of whom President Walker was the acknowledged leader. Not only was it continued ; but it was carried farther than by Longe or Thornton. Not the rigidity and predetermination of the wages fund, but the significance of the payment of wages from capital in any form was doubted or denied. The initial step in distribution was thus declared to be, not the payment of wages from capital, but the division of shares in the current product of labor. On the other hand, a new mode of approaching economic theory was advocated in an entirely different quarter, without immediate reference to the old controversy, yet with important and unmistakable effects on it. The Austrian school developed a new theory of value, and from that a revised statement of the relation of capital to wages.

The most significant presentations of the first-mentioned train of thought, in which the payment of wages out of capital is absolutely denied, came from two American writers. The most unqualified was that of Mr. Henry George; the most influential and weighty that of President Francis A. Walker. An examination of their arguments will show how far the revolt from the old doctrines proceeded, and how much need there was for a complete revision of this part of economic theory.

George's * attack on the old views was the later of the two in point of time; but it was the more extreme and uncompromising; and its consideration will most advantageously open this stage of the controversy. *Progress and Poverty*, published in 1879,† has for the subject of its first book "Wages and Capital," and there handles the wages fund doctrine without gloves. The aim of the book is to show that all the evils of the social body arise from private ownership in land, and are to be cured by the virtual confiscation of land on the part of the state. As a preliminary to this result, it was necessary to dispose of current explanations of existing difficulties, and among

---

* I trust I shall not be thought discourteous if I do not always use the conventional prefixes in speaking of living writers, such as Mr. George, President Walker, and others referred to in this chapter. So far as Mr. George is concerned, I am glad to express my respect for his nobility of purpose ; while the stimulating effect of his writings on economic discussion during the last twenty years is too obvious to need mention.

† The preface informs the reader that the book was completed in March, 1879, but that the views maintained in it were set forth in a pamphlet on *Our Land and Land Policy*, published in San Francisco in 1871. I have not seen the earlier pamphlet, and do not know how far it presented the wages theory of *Progress and Poverty*.

them the explanation of low wages as caused by relative scarcity of capital.

The arguments against the wages fund doctrine are twofold, negative and positive. They are meant to prove both that the old doctrine is false in itself, and that another doctrine is sound.

The first argument to show that the wages fund doctrine is false is its incompatibility with an unquestionable fact,—the co-existence of a high return to labor and to capital. George points out that in new countries both interest and wages are high. High wages, according to the wages fund theory, denote a plenty of capital. High interest denotes a scarcity of capital. Therefore, if the theory be sound, high wages and high interest can not exist together. If in fact they do exist together,—and every one knows that sometimes they do,—the theory must be false. The same dilemma is presented with regard to the fluctuations of wages and interest in times of depression as compared with times of activity. When there is industrial activity, wages and interest are both high; yet if plentiful capital be the cause of the high wages, how can interest be high also ? The converse case appears in times of industrial depression, when we have low wages, and yet an indication of a plenty of capital in the low rate of interest.

This would be promptly answered on the part of a writer like Cairnes by the suggestion that " capital " was used in different senses in the two conjunctions. Plenty of capital with reference to wages meant plenty of " circulating " capital, in the phrase of the older writers ; or plenty of the wages fund part of capital, in the language of Cairnes. It is quite possible that capital itself should be relatively not plentiful, and yet that a large part of it should be " circulating capital," or wages fund. Cairnes so explained those conditions in new countries which

George presented as inconsistent with the old-fashioned reasoning. In a country like the United States a larger part of capital is in the form of wages fund, a smaller in the form of plant and material.*

This is a fair answer to a question like George's, even though, as an independent explanation of the high earnings of laborers in new countries, it does not cover the whole case. George at all events meets it indirectly rather than directly. This reply to his objections can not be maintained, he avers, as to the second part of his argument,—that high wages and high interest come together in " good times."

It is not improbable that the ordinary upholder of the classic doctrine would have been somewhat taken aback even by the first part of George's attack. Doubtless he would have found it still less easy to give a prompt answer to the objection in its second form. For in this reasoning as to capital in good times and in bad times, the term " capital " is used with that vagueness which was so characteristic of the usual statements of the wages fund doctrine: the quantity of capital being noticed as having a bearing both on wages and on interest, with no great discrimination as to the how and why in either case. In fact, looking simply at the surface phenomena of money wages and of the money market, it is easy to see that capital means different things in the two cases. In relation to money wages, it refers to the total money funds turned over by employers to the hire of laborers; in the other, to the money funds in the hands of lenders, chiefly for short-time loans, and offered by them to the active managers of business. It is quite conceivable that the one sort

---

* Cairnes made the suggestion in answer to Longe, and not directly with reference to any such contention as was made by George.—*Leading Principles*, Part II, ch. i, § 7.

of fund should be large as compared with the laborers, while the other should be small as compared with the borrowers. At best, this sort of consideration gives attention only to the surface phenomena,—to money wages on the one hand, and on the other to the bargaining between one class of business men and another. Neither real wages nor the substantial return to capital at large can be brought into clear light by such reasoning.

There is another side to this particular phase of the slow-dragging discussion. George evidently had in mind that opposition between wages and profits which all the followers of Ricardo descanted on: high wages made low profits, and low profits high wages. The connection of this theorem with the wages fund doctrine has been touched on already.* The manner in which it led George to think he had found a dilemma is not far to seek. A thinker of George's slender training, absorbed in his own panacea for the cure of all social ills, could not be expected to construe with accuracy Ricardo's involved expressions. Wages, like other words, was used by Ricardo in a peculiar sense: he meant by the word not money wages, not even real or commodity wages, but wages as representing the product of so much labor. When Ricardo said wages were high, he meant that wages got the product of much labor; when low, the product of little labor. So understood, it follows very simply that high wages make low profits, and it by no means follows that high wages, in the sense of high commodity wages, make low profits. Ricardo's proposition, moreover, applies only to the relations between laborers and capitalists in what may be called a completed cycle of production: it applies to the total of the advances made to a given series of laborers in the succession of seasons over which their pro-

---

* See Ch. IX, pp. 168–172.

ductive labors extend, as compared with the total of finished commodities produced by this series during the cycle.
It has nothing to do with that part of the advances which
happens to be made to the laborers of any one season;
while just this is the narrower question of the wages fund
and of market wages. Here, as on other topics, Ricardo's
definite and narrow proposition, stated in the obscure
fashion of its author, had been mechanically repeated by
the writers of the next generation, and had been applied
to all sorts of cases with which it had nothing to do.
George was hardly to be blamed if he used the much-
abused formula against those who understood its real
bearing no better than he.

We may turn now to the positive part of George's reasoning: that which undertakes to show that wages are
paid from product.

Here the basis of the argument may be stated in
George's own words. "The fundamental truth, that in
all economic reasoning must be firmly grasped and never
let go, is that society in its most highly developed form is
but an elaboration of society in its rudest beginnings, and
that principles obvious in the simpler relations of men are
merely disguised and not abrogated or reversed by the
more intricate relations that result from the division of
labor and the use of complex tools and methods." Now
the first laborers, in the simplest state of society, must
have been supported from the product of their own labor;
here is the key to the problem; all laborers are paid from
the product of their own labor.

In this sort of reasoning, George doubtless walks in a
well-trodden path. Ricardo had reasoned from the primitive fisherman and huntsman to the fundamental principles of value and exchange; and in very modern speculations on the same topic, the analysis of the simplest case
is supposed to supply the key to all the phenomena. To

give such reasoning validity, it must be shown that there is no essential difference between the conditions of the simple case and the complex. In George's deduction, the primitive workmen,—the gatherer of shell-fish or of berries,—gets a consumable commodity in the interval between meals; the laborer of the great civilized community does work which may not result in enjoyable goods for years. The element of time enters in the one case, not in the other; the difference is world-wide.

Too much space should not be given to the various turns which the reasoning took at George's hands. We are told that laborers always produce something: hence it is inferred that they produce what they live on. We are given a vivid description of " butter churned but a few days before, vegetables fresh from the garden, and fruit from the orchard "; as if all these commodities had been produced by present labor. We are told that the laborers always add to the wealth of their employers before pay-day comes around; which is supposed to show that they are paid from what they produce.* In truth, the

---

* The following passage may be cited, as characteristic both of the swing of George's style and the quality of his matter:

" Keeping these principles in view we see that the draughtsman, who shut up in some dingy office on the banks of the Thames, is drawing the plans for a great marine engine, is in reality devoting his labor to the production of bread and meat as truly as though he were garnering grain in California, or swinging a lariat on a La Plata pampa; that he is as truly making *his own* clothing as though he were shearing sheep in Australia or weaving cloth in Paisley, and just as effectually producing the claret he drinks at dinner as though he gathered the grapes on the banks of the Garonne."—*Progress and Poverty*, Book I, ch. i, p. 25.

The statement in the first half of this neatly-balanced sentence would be denied by no economist ; but the insertion, in the second half, of the two words " his own " (which George does not put in italics) gives an entirely different turn to the matter. The draughtsman makes bread and wine, doubtless ; but his own bread? or the claret he drinks at dinner?

vogue of *Progess and Poverty* is not due to any solid and consistent reasoning, or to any novelty in principle. It is a consequence of the tide of social unrest, on which an earnest man, made eloquent by faith in a gospel of his own, has been carried to a commanding position and not undeserved fame. As to the wages fund doctrine, George's attacks are chiefly significant of the ease with which the old statements could be shaken, and of their failure to put in any clear light the basis of truth and fact on which the doctrine might rest. At all events his share in the controversy had little visible effect on the development of economic theory. Though effective in shaking the hold of the old doctrines among masses not usually touched by theoretic controversy, his writings exerted no great influence on trained students; a result due in part to the thinness of his thought, but perhaps quite as much to the ruthless sweep of the social remedy which he finally proposed.

A much deeper influence on the course of thought has been exercised by the other American writer whom we have associated with George,—President Francis A. Walker. This distinguished soldier, scholar, and adminis- trator is justly regarded with respect, and with something more, by his associates in these various fields of activity. So far as economic science is concerned, whether or no all of the doctrines and measures advocated by him shall prove to stand the test of time, no one can deny that his independence and vigor powerfully stimulated discussion at a time when something very like stagnation had been

---

The reader who cares to follow some interesting details of George's rea- soning, may compare the passage which descants on the fresh butter and vegetables, with another, in the preceding chapter, which sets forth that " it is not the last blow, any more than the first blow, that creates the value of the finished product."—*Progress and Poverty*, Book I, ch. iii, p. 58, and ch. iv, pp. 66, 67.

reached in English-speaking countries, and that his writings in many ways mark the beginning of a new and fresher stage.

President Walker's views on the wages fund doctrine were matured at a comparatively early date. They are set forth in an article in the *North American Review* for January, 1875 ; and are repeated in the book on *The Wages Question*, published in 1876. They appear again in his contributions to more recent periodical literature, especially to the *Quarterly Journal of Economics*, and in the various editions of his text-book on political economy. The later publications handle the wages fund doctrine in a somewhat perfunctory and indeed contemptuous manner, the assumption being more or less explicitly made that it had already received its *coup de grace*. Hence the earlier discussions are the more significant; and, among them, the two chapters of the volume on *The Wages Question* may be selected, as containing the fullest and most careful statement of the author's views.*

First in order, as the case is presented in that volume, comes a statement or argument that may be readily accepted, but hardly bears on the real problem in hand. "An employer pays wages to purchase labor, not to expend a fund of which he may be in possession." And again : "The employer purchases labor with a view to the product of the labor; and the kind and amount of that product determine what wages he can afford to pay. . . . It is, then, for the sake of future production that the laborers are employed, not at all because the employer has possession of a fund which he must disburse. . . . Thus it is production, not capital, which furnishes the

---

* *The Wages Question*, New York, 1876 ; chapters viii and ix.   I refer to these chapters generally, and will not encumber the notes with detailed references.

motive for employment and the measure of wages." So much is unquestionably true; and as to that not uncommon version of the old view, by which the individual employer is supposed to have funds irrevocably committed to the hire of his laborers, it is valid and unanswerable. But the argument here is mainly as to the motive which influences the employer ; and it may be readily admitted that the attainment of a product at a profit is his motive, without any admission one way or the other as to the nature or limitation of the funds which pay wages or form the measure of wages.

Next comes another point. An objection that might come from an upholder of the old view is stated and refuted. " It may be said : we grant that wages are really paid out of the product of current industry, and that capital only affects wages as it first affects production, so that wages stand related to product only in the first degree and to capital in the second degree only; still, does not production bear a certain and necessary ratio to capital ? " This question Walker rightly answers in the negative, pointing out that production is affected by other things than the volume of available capital. The land, the natural resources, the industrial quality of the laborers, are important factors. So much is clearly true; and if it be granted that wages are primarily determined by product, it must follow that they are affected by capital only as one among many factors. But the adherent of the old view would never make the supposed admission, or resort to the supposed reply. The kind of connection between wages and capital which is to be disproved is the direct and immediate one. Wages depend, according to the old view, not on capital *via* product, but (if on product at all) then on product *via* capital ; and the connection with the capital link of the chain is not to be brushed aside as lightly as this. To assume that wages are paid in the first instance from product, disposes of the whole question at issue.

This assumption becomes clearer in an illustration presented in the next paragraph. " Given machinery, raw materials, and a year's subsistence for 1,000 laborers, does it make no difference with the annual product whether those laborers are Englishmen or East Indians ? " Clearly the question is to be answered in the affirmative ; the quality of the laborers does affect the product. But the adherent of the wages fund doctrine would point out that, by supposition, there was but a year's subsistence on hand; and he would suggest that this was the " capital " important for the purposes of his doctrine. Until a new stock of subsistence could be got,—which presumably would require a year,—the laborers, whether Englishmen or East Indians, could get no more than there was to be had. Assuming that the capital, of all sorts, was owned by a set of employers, and that the only way for laborers to get the subsistence on hand was by bargain with the employers, the rate of wages during the first year would be a simple matter of division. These assumptions, as to the ownership of practically all wealth by one class, were made rather by implication, than in so many words, by the classic writers ; but they should fairly be accepted for the purposes of their reasoning, and make it difficult, as to the first year's wages in such a case as Walker supposes, to find a flaw in that reasoning. The growth of capital, after the first year, under the influence of high profits, might make probable a new supply of subsistence and other things, and an eventual adjustment of wages to product. But this is very different from the direct determination of wages by " current product," which is assumed as the basis of Walker's argument, and is by no means proved as the result of it. Whether a case like that here supposed, with its fixed year's subsistence, is typical of the real course of production and distribution in modern communities, or even instructive in their analysis, is another matter. So far as the wages fund doctrine goes, the example is of the sort that serves to strengthen more than to weaken it.

The assumption of the thing to be proved, which appears in this argument as to the industrial quality of the laborers, is made again in the next chapter : where it is pointed out in more detail and with more emphasis, that the nature of the soil, the possibility of a stage of increasing rather than diminishing returns from land, the course of invention, the growing division of labor, may result in changes in product connected but loosely with changes in capital. Thence it clearly follows that these things directly affect wages, *if* product directly determines wages. Such reasoning, to repeat, may be set aside, as not pertinent to the case ; and we may concentrate attention on the arguments which really touch the points at issue,—the relation of capital to wages, the extent to which advances are made from capital, and the exact mode in which wages are paid out of product or capital.

President Walker's attempt to deal with this crucial question begins with the proposition that, while " wages are to a very considerable extent, in all communities, *advanced* out of capital," they " must in any philosophical view of the subject be regarded as *paid* out of the product of current industry." What is meant by a " philosophical view " is not quite clear. It can hardly mean that wages, while in fact paid out of capital, are to be philosophically regarded as paid out of something else; though such an interpretation might be consistent with some of the speculations presented by philosophers of all ages. It may mean that wages are paid of product, not indeed for the time being, but in the long run. Yet in this sense there is nothing essentially inconsistent with the wages fund doctrine. We have seen that Cairnes's conception of profits as always within a handbreadth of the minimum, and as certain to be kept there by prompt accumulation consequent on higher profits, means simply that wages are determined, in not a very long run, by product: while yet Cairnes holds them to be proximately determined by the capital available for paying wages. It must be said that Walker appears not to be fairly conscious of this turn of the older reasoning, and sometimes speaks in a manner to imply that he too believes wages to depend on product in the indirect way there stated. Thus in the second of the two chapters now under consideration, we are told that " it is the prospect of a profit in production which determines the employer to hire laborers ; it is the *anticipated value of the product* * which determines how much he can pay him,"—a phrase which might be interpreted to mean in substance very much what a writer like Cairnes would lay down on the theory of wages.

But Walker at bottom means something different from this : " current product " is the phrase which he prefers in describing the source whence wages are paid ; the advance from capital is an accident ; and we must inquire further as to his conception of the advance from the one source and the payment from the other.

" In all communities wages are, by the very necessity of the case, advanced to a very considerable extent out of capital. . . . The tiller of the soil must abide in faith of a harvest, through months of ploughing, sowing, and cultivating ; and his industry is only possible as food has been stored up from the crop of the previous year. The mechanical laborer is also removed by a longer or shorter distance from the fruition of his labor. So that almost

* The italics in this passage, and in others quoted later, are not President Walker's.

universally, it may be said, the laborer as he works is fed out of a store gathered by previous toil, and saved by the self-denial of the possessor." Much seems here to be conceded to the old-fashioned economists. Almost universally, laborers are supported by the product of past labor; and the source whence they get their support is conceived to be food and other tangible things of a previous season's making.

But this admission is at once limited: "*to the extent of a year's subsistence*, then, it is necessary that some one should stand ready to make advances to the wage-laborer out of the products of past industry." And only subsistence need be provided: "this by no means involves the payment of his entire wages in advance of the harvesting of the crop or the marketing of the goods." Here we have the beginning of a shift in the point of view: the "marketing of the goods" appears as the last stage in production. Almost at once, thereafter, it is questioned whether wages are, after all, largely advanced out of capital; for the laborer does not get his money until after he has done his work for the employer, or indeed after the employer has sold the product. The employer may "realize" on his product before he pays wages to the workmen. Railways and steamboats are instanced as collecting cash daily, *i. e.*, securing their "product," while paying wages monthly. "Quite as common, probably, even yet in countries which we may call old, as weekly payments are monthly payments; and here the probability that the laborer may receive his wages out of *the price of this marketed product* increases with the quadrupled time given the employer to dispose of it."

Observe the gradual transition here. First, we have the tiller of the soil, who gets his food,—his real wages,— from the labor of the past. Here the securing of a consumable commodity is regarded as the last stage in completing the product. Next, we have the harvesting of the crop, without precise statement as to when this harvesting brings a " product " and yields wages : whether at the stage when bread is finally got, or at that when the crop of grain is sold. Last, we have the money view full fledged : the " marketing " of the goods and the " price " of the product are described as yielding wages. It is the old story in the wages fund controversy : sale and money receipt are confounded with the final attainment of food and other enjoyable goods, and the fund whence wages are paid is conceived as money or cash in the hands of the in- dividual employer.

The railway company is said to pay wages out of prod- uct because it takes in cash before pay-day; though clearly its real product is the transporting of goods or men from one place to another, and so ordinarily no more than the advancement of productive operations by one small stage. The manfacturer who sells pig iron (say), pays his laborers out of the price of the product; yet the pig iron can not become a product, in the sense of being eaten and enjoyed, of satisfying any human want, until a long succession of further steps are taken with it. Presi- dent Walker might fairly argue that, for polemical and negative purposes, he was justified in using " product " in- differently in the two senses here noted ; because those who had long maintained and expounded the wages fund doc- trine so often confined themselves to the money view of capital and product. But for progress in getting at the truth of the matter, reasoning which confounds these two things leaves matters in as ill plight, at the least, as they were before.

One further case, much made of by Walker, may be considered, because it presents the same question in a somewhat different way. Among the facts of concrete industry which he finds inconsistent with any necessary or universal advance of wages out of capital, are cases of partial advances of wages by employers. In the South and West of the United States, at the time of his writing, he notes that "the employer advances to the laborer such provisions and cash as are absolutely required from time to time; but the 'settlement' does not take place until the close of the season or of the year, and final payment is often deferred until the crop is not only harvested but sold." Here the provisions and cash first turned over in part payment are apparently regarded as coming from capital; while the cash paid when the crop is sold, comes from product. Yet it is obvious, if we once get beyond the money point of view, that the cash advanced out of capital is spent on finished, consumable commodities; and the cash paid out of the product, or crop sold, is spent on like commodities; that in either case these commodities constitute the real wages, whose amount and determination it is important to ascertain. What we need to know is whether these consumable things, whenever secured, and whether bought with money on hand before or after the sale of the crop, are to be regarded as product or capital; whether they are the current product of the laborers who buy them and enjoy them; whether they are rigid or flexible in amount. These essential questions President Walker nowhere touches.*

---

* The same sort of case is described in more detail as to farmer's accounts, chiefly in New England, at an earlier date. Here President Walker finds the hands charged with "advances of the most miscellaneous character. There are charges for grain and salted meats from the product of the previous year, for cash for minor personal expenses, for bootmaker's bills, grocer's bills, apothecary's bills, doctor's bills, and even town-tax bills, settled by the employer, for the use of teams for hauling wood for the laborer or breaking up his garden in the spring. Yet in general the amount of such advances does not exceed one-third, and it rarely reaches one-half, of the stipulated wages for the year." The

The proposition that wages are paid out of product, supported in this unsatisfactory way, became the starting-point of President Walker's theory of distribution, set forth in his text-books, now so much in vogue in English-speaking countries. It simplifies the perplexing problems so temptingly; it is so obviously true of the individual employer and of those direct wages which he pays his men in money, and which every one first thinks of when questions about wages confront him in concrete life,—that we need not be surprised if the theories of distribution which rest on it, presented as they are with rare skill in exposition, are found eminently teachable and a welcome substitute for the older beclouded views. But they do not really solve the problems in hand. Certainly, so far as the wages fund doctrine was concerned, this attempt at revision settled nothing. There is indeed a sense in which it is true that real wages, like real interest and real rent and real business earnings, are paid out of current product. But as a first step in the theory of distribution, the proposition that wages are derived from current product gives an inaccurate picture of the ways and processes of production; while the determination of wages as a residual share is even more unreal than its supposed payment out of product. President Walker's service in the wages fund discussion, and in economic theory at large, has been rather that of compelling a thorough overhauling of old views than that of substituting a new economic system of solid and permanent value.

Nevertheless, the general theory of distribution set

---

remaining two-thirds or one-half, we are given to infer, are not advanced by the employer, but paid out of product. It is hardly necessary to point out that, whether grocers' bills are settled by the employer before pay-day or by the laborer after, the real source of wages is the 'same,— the stock of goods held by such dealers, which in neither case are the laborer's product.

forth by Walker gained an acceptance and influence probably greater than that of any writings in the English
tongue since the days of the younger Mill. The text-
books in which they were set forth came into very wide
use ; and the virtual adherence of a large circle of eminent
economists was a proof of more solid success. Jevons in
England had reached similar general views at a somewhat
earlier date, and readily fell into line.* Professor Sidgwick, the weight of whose opinion was deservedly great,
adopted the same mode of approaching the theory of distribution, and the same general conclusions as to wages.†
Followers were many, and dissidents few, in English-
speaking countries. In France, where the old rigid views
had never had much vogue, the new ones were welcomed
by a considerable and influential circle; though sometimes with a certain Gallic courtesy in the admission of a
degree of truth on both sides, which made it difficult to
classify the French writers in one way or the other. The
controversy waxed hot in Italy, where the books both of
Cairnes and of Walker were translated, and a long series
of books and of articles in periodicals maintained the
views of the old school and of the new. Among the Germans less attention was given to the controversy; not
because the old views held their own with any tenacity,
but because, in this case, the Germans were singularly
neglectful of an important phase in the development of
economic thought. On the whole, the trend of the discussion for a decade or more was such as to justify President Walker in the assumption that there was nothing left
of the wages fund doctrine, that the payment of wages

---

* Jevons's *Theory of Political Economy*, second edition, p. 292. See
also the Preface, p. xlviii ; and Jevons's *State in Relation to Labour*, p.
94. Compare what is said of Jevons in later parts of this chapter.

† Sidgwick's *Principles of Political Economy*, Book II, ch. viii, § 5.

from current product was an established theorem, and that the problems still unsolved were concerned with the details of the share in this current product which went to laborers.*

Meanwhile another current of thought was being brought to bear on the wages fund discussion, from a very different quarter, and with very different objects and results. The speculations which are associated with the Austrian school, while directed mainly to the phenomena of value and exchange, have also led to important attempts at the reconstruction of the theory of capital, and these again, explicitly or implicitly, to a reconsideration of the theory of wages.

We are concerned here only with that part of the general theory of value developed by the new school which bears on capital and wages. The value of all economic goods,—to recall summarily the essentials of the new views,—is defined as their "importance" to the person whose wants they are to satisfy; and the exchange value of goods is made to depend on the play of such subjective importance in the minds of those who sell and buy. The diminishing importance of successive increments of any one commodity leads to the theory of final or marginal utility; and final utility becomes the main force acting directly on exchange value. It is probable that in this train of speculation, undue attention has been given to suppositions of fortuitous barter, in which the seller has possession of articles which might be used by himself; whereas too little attention has been given to the conditions of an advanced division of labor, in which the pro-

---

* A convenient summary of the views of a series of writers, and especially of modern French and Italian economists, is given in Professor Aldo Contento's *La Teoria del Salario nel Concetto dei Principali Economisti* (Venice, 1894).

ducers and sellers practically want none of the articles they make, and in which final utility to buyers alone has effect on the exchange values of commodities. It is part of the same defect that the consequences of the changing quantities offered by producers under the stress of competition, have been unduly thrust in the background. But these are matters not material for the present inquiry. For this, the essential thing is that value is conceived as affected primarily, not by the cost of articles, but by their importance, or final utility, as means of satisfying human wants.

The direct satisfaction of wants being thus the starting-point in the inquiry, it was inevitable that attention should be turned to the fact that a great mass of goods do not serve directly for such satisfaction. Inchoate goods, not ready for enjoyment, have in themselves no importance or utility. They serve wants only by being converted into commodities capable of yielding direct satisfaction. Hence they find their place in the revised theory of value as having a " derived " importance and utility, dependent on the importance and utility of the enjoyable commodities which they serve to make. This train of thought led naturally to the consideration of the interval of time that must elapse for the conversion of inchoate goods into completed commodities; and this again to the relation of present labor to present product, the functions of capital, and that whole series of inquiries as to the nature of civilized production, which had been so long and so unhappily divorced from the discussion of the wages fund.

Some of the more significant steps in the development of this train of thought may now be mentioned ; with a view not to sketch the history of the new doctrines, but to point out how they have tended to give a new course to the discussion of wages. At the outset there was no hint of connecting them with the old-fashioned theory of wages; and the unexpected manner in which they finally came to connect themselves with the old views, is one illustration the more of the slow and faltering steps by which even the shrewdest of men must feel their way to the results of a departure from familiar lines of thought.

The first careful and deliberate statement, in the terms of the new doctrine, of the relation of dependence between enjoyable and inchoate wealth seems to have been made by Gossen. The work of this erratic genius bore little fruit at the moment, and perhaps had no marked influence on the subsequent course of thought; but it may be referred to as an indication of the mode in which the remodelled theory of value gradually connected itself with the subject of wages and capital.* Gossen worked out the theory of subjective value, of diminishing subjective value with the increase of quantity, and so of final utility; and applied to these topics the mathematical treatment to which they lend themselves so naturally. What is more pertinent to our subject, he divided goods into different classes, according to their availability for the satisfaction of human wants. The classes were three: (1) consumable goods ready for enjoyment; (2) goods not having all the adaptations necessary for enjoyment, as wheat and rye, which need to be made into bread, or a carriage, which needs a horse and driver before sufficing for final satisfaction; (3) goods

---

* Hermann Heinrich Gossen, *Entwickelung der Gesetze des Menschlichen Verkehrs*, Braunschweig, 1854. As to Gossen's position in the attempts to apply mathematical methods to economics, see the generous notice in the second edition of Jevons's *Theory of Political Economy*, Preface, pp. xxxv–xlii. As to his position in the development of the psychological theory of value, see the notes in Pantaleoni's *Principii di Economia Politica*, pp. 38, 96, 105; where, however, the cordial recognition of Gossen's merits leads to some undue depreciation of later thinkers of the same school.

which serve to make other goods, but never themselves minister to enjoyment, as tools and machines, and fuel consumed to make power. This classification, whether or no advantageous for the inquiries which Gossen conducted, would not be satisfactory for an investigation of the successive steps in production : for the carriage (which is ready for use) and the wheat (which still needs to be ground) are put together by Gossen, yet stand in different stages; while the fuel and the wheat may belong close together. But Gossen was concerned only with the dependence of the various incomplete goods, for their effectiveness in satisfying wants, on the finished commodities; for this purpose his divisions may be helpful, and at all events they brought out clearly the chain of connection. A point most essential for the theory of wages and capital was, however, not touched by him : the interval of time between the successive links in the chain. The idea of a succession in time between the several classes of goods seems not to have been in Gossen's mind, and certainly was not made prominent by him. This first step in the psychological theory of value thus did not bring into view that aspect of it which connects it with the theory of wages and capital.

It is curious that the next writer who followed the methods of Gossen in general economics, while again contributing virtually nothing to the direct application of the new reasoning in the theory of wages, yet also promoted that application indirectly. Jevons, in his *Theory of Political Economy*, of which the first edition appeared in 1871, worked out, independently and originally, the reasoning as to the general dependence of exchange value on final utility, and essayed with equal originality the application of mathematical methods to economics. In addition, he said some things that were true and important, even if not entirely novel, on the theory of capital. But the theory of final utility did not lead Jevons to consider the different ways in which inchoate goods and enjoyable commodities satisfy human wants ; and he was thus prevented from making any satisfactory application of his new methods to the problem of general wages, or at least that part of the problem of general wages with which the wages fund discussion is concerned.

While no classification of goods according to the nearer or remoter fruition of enjoyment appears in Jevons, an essential function of capital is there grasped and stated with a directness which is refreshing after the long series of vague generalities among his English predecessors, and which had its strong effect on later thinkers of the same school.   Jevons lays it down that capital is nothing but subsistence : it serves only to feed laborers over a lengthened process of production.   The element of time is its essence.   He states in italics that its effect is " to allow us to *expend labour in advance.*"   Not only is this fundamental fact emphasized, but the further fact is noted (though not so fully) that there is connection between the supply of capital, the march of improvement, and the length of time over which the period of production extends.   " Whatever improvements in the supply of commodities lengthen the average time between the moment when labor is exerted and its result or purpose is accomplished, such improvements depend on the use of capital.   And I would add, that this is the sole use of capital."   Here the conception of an average duration of the period of production, and the function of capital in the lengthened course of production, are clearly set forth.*

This is not new doctrine ; but it is stated with fresh and needed emphasis, and indeed is soon carried almost too far.   We have seen that the analysis of capital as a

* *Theory of Political Economy*, ch. vii, especially pp. 243, 245, 248.

succession of advances of food to laborers was at the basis of Ricardo's reasoning as to value and as to distribution. It was set forth more or less distinctly by most of his followers. But it had been often buried under other matter, and obscured by deductions that were half true or applications that were false; and it had hardly ever been brought into clear connection with the wages fund doctrine. Thus it needed to be simply and emphatically restated and reapplied. But Jevons did no more. than restate it, and took no further steps in its application. Indeed, he may be said to have stepped back; for not only did he lay it down that all capital is subsistence, —which is true if properly explained,—but he came perilously near to saying that all which is not subsistence is not capital,—which requires still more explanation to be intelligible and true. " I would not say that a railway is fixed capital, but that capital is fixed in the railway. The capital is not the railway, but the food of those who made the railway." * Elsewhere Jevons approaches the subject from a different point of view, and with a result substantially the same: maintaining that all forms of wealth, whether completed or uncompleted, whether in consumer's hands or not, are equally capital.† His views, in truth, were not fully developed. He did not affect, in this volume on the theory of economics, to have reached definitive conclusions on the subject at large. He was concerned chiefly with advocating a new method and a new point of view: the method of mathematics, and the point of view of final utility. On capital, he had no well-matured opinions, and thus did no more than to redirect attention to its connection with the lapse of time between the beginning and the end of productive exertion.

---

* *Theory*, p. 264.

† Compare what was said on this topic in Part I, Chapter II, p. 39.

This failure to mature his conclusions appears strikingly in what Jevons says specifically of the wages fund doctrine. That doctrine he professes to reject ; yet with qualifications which, while professing to save something, show that he did not really see what was good in it and what bad. He sets forth in general a residual theory of wages. The laborers are paid from product and get what is left after interest and rent are provided for. He qualifies this by noting a temporary stage during which the wages fund theory applies. Such temporary application of the wages fund, however, has nothing to do with that lapse of time between the beginning and the end of production which he emphasized in his earlier analysis of capital. It has to do with a much briefer period. During the early stages of new enterprises or new industries, involving risks and uncertain profits, he finds that the anticipated outcome of the enterprise, rather than the actual product secured, will determine wages. This anticipated result will determine how much capitalists will then pay out to laborers. Only during this temporary stage of risk and uncertainty, he conceives the wages fund to be in operation. But when stable conditions are reached, and it is known what the outcome of a business enterprise is to be—and such is assumed to be the usual and normal state of things—the laborer will receive " the due value of his produce after paying a proper fraction to the capitalist for the remuneration of abstinence and risk." *

---

* *Theory*, pp. 292, 294, 295. The significant parts of these passages may be quoted : " It is the proper function of capital to sustain labour before the result is accomplished, and as many branches of industry require a large outlay long previous to any definite result being arrived at, it follows that capitalists must undertake the risk of any branch of industry where the ultimate profits are not known. But we have now some clue as to the amount of capital which will be appropriated to the payment of wages in any trade. The amount of capital will depend on the

This curious and indeed unique version of the applicability of the wages fund is completely divorced from what Jevons had said, a few pages before, of the function of capital and its relation to time in production. As a statement of the final outcome of distribution, it is much the same as what would be laid down by either Cairnes or Walker,—in fact, by any writer who believed the return to capital to be sharply fixed by a minimum reward for abstinence. It is not very material, for this ultimate result, whether wages are conceived to be paid from capital or from product. But as to the process whereby the result is brought about, if at all, it is very material to remember that laborers in fact are not paid from what they produce, but from that capital which, in Jevons's own language, serves to sustain them through the period over which their exertions are spread. Evidently Jevons had in mind, in this sally on the wages fund, the case of individual laborers and their immediate employers, and the determination of money wages by the money value or exchange value of the product. He thought of the doctrine as referring solely to these proximate relations between capitalists and laborers. It has been sufficiently shown how much warrant he had, in the writings of the economists who had set it forth, for this conception of its scope. His general reaction—certainly a healthy one—from what he

---

anticipated profits, and the competition to obtain proper workmen will strongly tend to secure to the latter all their legitimate share in the ultimate produce." In the early stages of a new industry (Atlantic cables are instanced), much will be paid in wages, if capitalists make a large estimate of probable profits. "At this point it is the wage fund theory that is in operation. . . . The wage fund theory acts in a wholly temporary manner. Every labourer ultimately receives the due value of his produce after paying a proper fraction to the capitalist for the remuneration of abstinence and risk." The question at once suggests itself, is not capital as much needed when wages are normal as when they are abnormal, to perform the function of sustaining labor?

called "the maze of the Ricardian economics" disposed
him to fling aside once for all a mechanical doctrine such
as, in the current and authoritative versions, the wages
fund theory was. On this topic, as on others, his impa-
tience with the self-satisfied English political economy of
his day led him to flat denial rather than to careful sift-
ing of the true from the false. At all events, he contributed less than might have been expected, in view of
his own conclusions as to capital, to the satisfactory statement of the relation of capital to the present reward of
laborers.

Thus neither Gossen nor Jevons, who were the most
important forerunners of the new mode of approaching
economic theory, linked together the two chains of thought
which were to lead to a fresh consideration of the theory
of wages. Gossen pointed out that incomplete commodities derive their utility from those complete and enjoyable.
Jevons, while following Gossen in the theory of final
utility, and taking another forward step in the emphasis
he laid on the element of time in its connection with
capital, gave no attention to the relation between inchoate
wealth and consumable commodities.*

The gap between the two lines of thought was 'soon
closed. In 1871, the same year in which Jevons published the first edition of his *Theory*, Professor Carl
Menger published his *Grundsätze der Volkswirthschaftslehre*,
which contains, more or less explicitly, the characteristic

---

* In any attempt to trace the general development of the new theory
of value, it would be necessary to refer to the contributions of Léon
Walras. But I have found nothing in either edition of Walras's *Élé-
ments d'Économie Politique Pure* which bears on the present inquiry.
There is some brief mention of the wages fund doctrine (see Leçon
32 in the second edition, pp. 359–364), but it is directed mainly to
Mill's simple statement in the *Political Economy*, which Walras, like
Cairnes, finds to be only a statement of the problem, and no solution.

doctrines of the Austrian school, and is rightly regarded by its members as the main source of their inspiration. With every allowance for the suggestions contained in the works of previous writers, such as Gossen, Walras, and Jevons, it must be admitted to be an original and powerful book. How far the general doctrines set forth in it will prove a complete substitute for the older views, how far will serve only to correct and qualify them, remains still to be seen. For our subject, however, the situation is comparatively simple : and what Menger contributed toward its elucidation can be stated in brief terms.

At the outset Menger distinguishes between different classes of goods. Things consumable and enjoyable are " Güter erster Ordnung," as bread; those not quite in the stage of enjoyment are of the second order, as flour, fuel, stoves; those of the third order are still farther removed from enjoyment, as grain and flour mills; and so on. He adds that the precise classification of goods, as being in the first, second, or third order, is not essential. The lines of demarcation can not be rigidly drawn ; the classification is no more than an aid for the clearer explanation of a difficult subject. Thereafter he speaks, as a rule, simply of goods of lower order or of higher order : those of lower order being nearer the stage of completion and enjoyment, those of higher order more remote from it.*

The next step is in a direction already pointed out by

---

* *Grundsätze der Volkswirthschaftslehre*, ch. i, § 2. It should be mentioned that Menger includes among goods of higher or lower order the kinds of labor appropriate or trained for the use of the several classes of goods : the miller's labor being classed with the mill, the baker's labor with the bread. I have never been convinced that it is expedient thus to fit human labor into the same scheme of value as the product which it makes : the attempt to do so being the result of an unnecessary striving after formulæ of universal application.

Gossen: the value of goods of higher order is dependent on that of the goods of lower order which they serve to make.

Then comes the step important for the present discussion. Time must elapse before goods of higher order can be converted into goods of lower order. Menger criticizes Adam Smith for having ascribed the progress of the arts and the growth of wealth to the division of labor alone. The great cause of material progress he finds in the development of an extended chain of labor, by which enjoyment, instead being secured without delay, is the result of the orderly and progressive advance of goods of higher order to the later stage of consumption and enjoyment. Whether or no this criticism of Adam Smith is entirely just (Menger himself notes incidentally that an " appropriate division of labor " must concur to make effective the process described by him), the passage gives due emphasis to what we have called the successive division of labor, and so to the true relation between present work and present exertion.* Later this whole train of thought is still more fully developed. The succession of stages in production is sketched : first, the present, when goods of the first order are on hand and available; then a second period, during which goods of the second order can be advanced to the stage of completion ; and so on. The conception of a general production period is also defined, —of the average length of time elapsing between the beginning and the end of the whole series of laborious acts by which the present supply of enjoyable commodities has been produced. Chiefly concerned, as he is, with the value of inchoate goods as derived from that of finished commodities, Menger does not enlarge on the element of time and the extension of the production

---

* *Grundsätze*, ch. i, §§ 4, 5.

period; but the essential truths are none the less clearly set forth.*

On capital Menger does not seem to have fully matured his thought, and certainly had not fully settled his choice of phraseology. It is said that the function of capital is to provide for present needs, and to make possible the devotion of present labor to the satisfaction of future needs; and that " capital " should refer to the stores of goods available for the use of the present and the future, enabling mankind to secure the gain which accrues from an extension of the period of production. This would indicate that the line of thought suggested by Jevons was uppermost in his mind. We are told explicitly that the division of goods into those of higher order and of lower order does not coincide with the division between capital and not capital.† Many years later, Menger expressed himself again on the meaning of capital, but again with very brief statement of his own views; intimating only that the true conception was to be found rather by the analysis of the various ways in which property was made to yield income, than by a consideration of the intrinsic uses of economic goods.‡ Whether or no his views on

---

* *Grundsätze*, ch. ii, § 1, *c*; ch. iii, § 3. Menger not only points out in general that " Vorsorge," or planning for the future, distinguishes the activity of civilized man, but, in a note at p. 136, remarks that the longer the period over which the acts of production are spread, the greater the final productivity. This, however, is but briefly intimated; it remained for his successor, Professor Böhm-Bawerk, to develop the thought.

† See the extended footnote in Menger's *Grundsätze*, pp. 130–131.

‡ In an article " Zur Theorie des Kapitals " in the *Jahrbücher für National-oekonomie, Neue Folge*, vol. xvii, pp. 1–49 (1888). The article undertakes a critical review of the various conceptions and definitions of capital; repeats what was said in the *Grundsätze*, that the distinction between capital and other wealth is not the same as the distinction between inchoate and enjoyable wealth; and suggests that the way to a solution of the question is by considering " das werbende Vermögen über-

this part of theory, if developed in detail, would have much affected the trend of thought, must be uncertain. The question proximately is one of phraseology, and so far not essential. On the crucial question of the relation in time between inchoate wealth and consumable commodities, Menger set forth clearly the important truths.

Finally, this phase of economic theory received its fuller development at the hands of a disciple of the Austrian school who may be fairly ranked with the leader. In 1888 Professor Böhm-Bawerk published the *Positive Theory of Capital.** Here again, however unmistakable and considerable may be the indebtedness to previous writers, we have the marks of vigorous independent thought; combined, moreover, with a skill in exposition not found in the leader of the school, and conducing not a little to the powerful impression which the volume made on economists the world over.

Much of the analysis of industrial operations which is contained in the *Positive Theory of Capital* has been accepted in the first part of the present essay; and it will therefore not be necessary to give so full an account as would otherwise be called for. On the other hand, we are not concerned with the refinements of the theory of interest which it aims to establish. That theory must indeed have a bearing, on the causes that determine wages in the end, and on the final outcome of distribution. The essential truths which it involves can be stated in much simpler terms than its author thought well to use; and so stated, would probably be found to involve a less radical depart-

---

haupt," and the " Ertragserscheinungen jeder einzelnen Kategorie des werbenden Vermögens in ihrer Eigenart." This points to a different sort of inquiry and conclusion from that followed in Böhm-Bawerk's *Positive Theory of Capital*, which was in press when Menger's article appeared.

* The English translation appeared in 1891.

ure from familiar ideas than we are told to expect. But as far as the immediate relations between capital and labor are concerned, it is not necessary to follow the ramifications of the reasoning by which the exchange of present goods for future is explained. The mode in which the particular subject of the present inquiry has been dealt with by this brilliant writer is comparatively simple, and can be described in brief terms.

The relation between present labor and present product; the successive stages in production; the yield of consumable commodities as the outcome of a lengthened series of exertions,—all is set forth methodically and in detail, in such manner as to make this part of economic theory henceforth an established and unquestioned possession of the science. The increase in the productiveness of labor with the advance in the arts of civilization is indeed linked perhaps too closely with the lengthening in time of the general process of production. We are told that, as a fact of experience, the greater the length of the period of production, the greater the final outcome in consumable commodities; while yet each prolongation of the period brings a less increment of commodities than that which preceded. This supposed close and regular connection between the period of production and the final yield of enjoyable wealth becomes later an essential postulate of the theory of interest: it being assumed that the extension of the period of production will always increase the final output, yet always increase it in diminishing ratio. It has been elsewhere intimated that we have here an unduly rigid version of the direction which is likely to be followed by progress and invention.* But so far as the relation of present labor to its product is concerned, it is not material whether we admit unreservedly, or qual-

* See Part I, Chapter I, pp. 9-10.

ify carefully, the proposition that the longer the time over which labor is spread, the greater will surely be the final yield. It suffices to have it established once for all that in civilized industry there is always the long interval between labor and fruition.

Next, capital is defined as the "future goods" of the community,—as the wealth not yet available for consumption. This is the community's real capital; whereas its real income consists of the utilities derived from completed consumable things. Whether or no the definition so chosen be found acceptable — and to the present writer, as has already appeared, it seems in its central idea convenient and consistent *—it has the merit once again of bringing into clear light the real course of production in modern communities, and of getting rid of the difficulties which arise from considering capital in its relations to money wealth or to individual income.

Last among Böhm-Bawerk's contributions to the questions closely connected with the wages fund doctrine, we have the conception of the general subsistence fund. The total possessions of the community are reduced to a common basis by the description of all wealth as available

---

* I say, in its central idea; because there is a difference between Böhm-Bawerk's definition and that adopted in the first part of this volume (see Part I, Chapter II). Those enjoyable commodities which, like dwelling houses, are durable sources of direct satisfaction, are considered by Böhm-Bawerk to be capital, in so far as the utilities which they yield are available in the future. They are partly present goods, but partly future goods. To my mind, they, or the utilities they yield, are simply income, in so far as no further exertion is needed to bring them to the enjoying person. Consistently with his reasoning, Böhm-Bawerk maintains that these "future goods" yield interest precisely as other future goods, such as machines and materials, yield it. This seems to me doubtful. If there were no other "capital" than durable sources of immediate satisfaction, the phenomenon of interest as we have it in the modern world would probably not emerge.

sooner or later for enjoyment or subsistence. Omitting the land and other natural agents, all goods, whether now enjoyable or not, are conceived as serving in due time to satisfy wants. The machine ripens into the consumable commodities which, so long as it lasts, it helps to produce: some of the utilities it yields are thus available at an early date, some not till the distant period when it is finally on the point of being thrown away as old metal. Materials reach the stage of fruition more quickly and evenly. Goods whose more obvious physical manipulation has ceased, and which are awaiting purchase in dealers' hands, are nearly ready and available. All, however, are alike as containing more or less ripened utilities, and serving to provide for the wants of the community over a longer or shorter space in the future. They thus constitute in the aggregate one indistinguishable subsistence fund on which the community draws for the present and future; while present labor can do no more than advance commodities in their due order through the successive steps in production.

This is not an entirely novel conception. Indeed, its author does not present it as such. He remarks that it has some resemblance to the old theory of the wages fund. Like that, it emphasizes the stock of wealth already produced as the source whence laborers are maintained and rewarded; though with a clearer conception of the nature and function of capital than had been reached by any of the older writers. It is clearly unlike the old view, in that it has regard to the whole period of production, and not to any one season.* On the other hand, it has more

* In noting the points of resemblance and difference between his own theory and that of the wages fund, Böhm-Bawerk summarizes the latter after the manner of Jevons and Cairnes: as containing simply the truism that wages depend on the ratio between the number of laborers and the amount paid them in wages. *Positive Theory*, Book VII, ch. v, p. 419.

than a family resemblance to Ricardo's analysis of capital as a succession of advances to laborers,—a resemblance to which the author does not call attention, but which is none the less clear. It thus proceeds, in some part, on old lines; with yet a mode of statement of its own, and certainly an important advance in the understanding of the complex course of industrial operations.

The application of this conception to the theory of wages is not fully worked out, and criticism and comment must therefore be tentative. So far as its application to wages as a separate item in distribution is concerned, there is an obvious difficulty in the fact that the general subsistence contains the income not only of laborers, but of the whole community. So much is expressly pointed out by the author himself. It is true that this difficulty is sought to be avoided; but not with signal success. The fund is assumed at first, for the purposes of abstract reasoning, to yield advances to laborers alone. We are promised at a later stage an exposition of the manner in which other shares of distribution will then emerge.* But that exposition is never fully carried out with regard to the subsistence fund. What we find, is that analysis of the exchange of present goods for future, and of the consequent emergence of interest as the inevitable result, which had already been set forth in essentials even before the discussion of the subsistence fund was reached. The causes which determine interest can probably be stated in simpler terms than we find in the elaborate analysis of the superiority of present goods over future, and the equally

---

The off-hand manner in which the doctrine was often stated by its upholders, may give fair ground for such a version : but, as we have seen, there was more than this in it, and a more substantial resemblance to the doctrine of the *Positive Theory* than Böhm-Bawerk would imply.

* *Positive Theory*, Book VI, ch. v, especially the footnote at p. 320 ; and Book VII, ch. v.

elaborate attempts to apply to them the psychological theory of value. In any case, these refinements go but a very little way toward explaining just how the total subsistence fund and its ripening instalments are diverted to one and another class in the community. No doubt, for the explanation of the fundamental forces which shape distribution, a sound theory of interest is essential. This, however, even supposing it to have been reached by our author, does not suffice for the purposes of that investigation of the machinery of distribution which is the essential part of the wages fund problem.

But, to repeat, the conception of the subsistence fund is advanced briefly by Böhm-Bawerk, and its application to the direct questions of wages is avowedly not completed. Criticism is therefore both difficult and likely to be unjust. No attempt is made to consider the concrete mode in which the fund reaches laborers. Still less is any attempt made to consider separately the special case the great and preponderating class of hired laborers, and the dealings with them on the one hand, and with the idle investor on the other hand, of the active manager of industry. Such a more detailed and concrete examination of the machinery of distribution is an essential part of the discussion of the wages fund question and all that hangs thereby.

We must be content, therefore, to accept as it stands the contribution which Böhm-Bawerk has made to the general position of the laborer in relation to past and present product. So far as he goes in his treatment of the relation in which the real reward of laborers stands to the capital and the total possessions of the community, it would be difficult to find a flaw in the analysis. The marshalling of the possessions of the social body ; the mode in which these constitute a stock available for the needs of the present and the nearer future ; the advance of present supplies to laborers who produce for future needs; the diversion of part of the inflowing real income to other classes than laborers; the determination of the share that goes to laborers by the play of motives among those who own the existing stock,—on these topics economic theory will gain by following the main trend of the exposition which has finally resulted from the labors of the Austrian school. It is not all new; but it is freshly and luminously stated; and it is deserving of all praise.

CHAPTER XV.

THE results of the prolonged inquiry may now be summed up: both the positive conclusions reached in the first part of the volume, and the outcome of the historical and critical chapters of the second part.

We began, in the first chapter, with the proposition that all laborers, and all the members, of any community in which the successive division of labor has been developed far, are supported chiefly by the product of past labor. When once attention is fastened on real wages, the enjoyable and consumable commodities which satisfy human wants; and when the mode in which production is carried on in any but the most primitive communities is considered,—it becomes clear that present labor does not produce present real income.

Whether labor is to be regarded as paid from capital or not, depends on what is meant by the term capital. The most consistent and significant meaning of that term is, wealth not yet in enjoyable shape. In this sense, labor clearly is not paid from capital: for by definition things yielding satisfaction or constituting real income are not capital. But real income is constantly emerging from capital. Labor is steadily putting the finishing touches to wealth not yet in enjoyable form, and so advancing it to the stage where it becomes a source of real wages as well as of real interest and real rent. Considering any but the shortest period in production, the resources from which the community must look for support and enjoyment exist at any one time mainly in the form of capital, not in the form of enjoyable wealth.   Income now earned or now acquired has its real source in the continuous flow of consumable commodities which is steadily emerging from the capital of the community.   Such was the result of the second chapter.

The third chapter considered the special case of hired laborers, and the relation between the capitalist employer and his workmen.   If all laborers were independent,—if all were owners or tenants of land, or artisans carrying on production at their own risk and charge,—no ground would exist for saying that their share of enjoyable wealth and real income came from the available total by a process differing in essentials from the process by which others secured their income.   But in fact, in most modern communities, a very large number, often the larger number, among those who earn their living by manual labor are not in this independent situation.   They are dependent, for their share of real income, on being hired by some one else.   With the advantages or disadvantages of this situation our inquiry is not concerned.   As the industrial situation stands, ownership of wealth is in fact unequally divided; the greater part of the capital and of the steadily accruing wealth of the community is owned by a comparatively small number of active capitalists; and the money rights derived from the sale of the endless variety of marketable commodities flow first into their hands.   Hired laborers are dependent for their money income, and therefore for their share of real income, on a bargain with those owners of capital.   The body with whom hired laborers deal directly, consists of their immediate employers only; but the body whose dealings are really decisive as to the extent to which laborers shall be hired, is much larger. It includes the middlemen, merchants, bankers, who form so influential a contingent in the ranks of the active managers of industry. In a larger sense, and in the long run, it may be said to include also the idle investor, who invests his money means,—his claim on the community's possessions, —by putting them in the hands of the managing class, and who gets from that class a stipulated income. At all events, hired laborers are dependent on a wages fund (if one chooses so to call it) which is in the hands of the capitalist class. Their money income is derived from what the capitalists find it profitable to turn over to them.

This is a wages fund doctrine, and a conclusion as to the relation of capital to wages, quite different from that reached in the first two chapters. It bears not on the permanent and unalterable relation of real capital to real wages, but on the relations of certain kinds of laborers to the capitalists of our modern communities. It would not be applicable to a society in which all workmen were independent producers, or in which the centralized administration of production was secured by coöperative methods; still less in a society organized on a collectivist or socialist basis. It explains some of the phenomena of modern advanced communities, and applies to them the more, in proportion as the *régime* of employing capitalists and hired laborers is the more fully developed.

The remaining chapters of the first part gave some further applications and illustrations of the main conclusions reached in the first three. On the one hand, the much-debated question as to the elasticity of the proximate source of wages was examined in its double aspect,—as to the source of the real wages of all laborers, and as to the sources of the money wages which hired laborers get from employers. In either case, there were found to be wages funds which were roughly predetermined, yet were so elastic, and elastic within such considerable limits, that the predetermination served chiefly to illustrate the nature of the reasoning applicable to questions of general wages, and could not give guidance as to any concrete difficulties or practical problems.

In the concluding chapter of the first part, it was then pointed out that, in its relations to other economic questions, whether practical or theoretical, the whole wages fund controversy was of comparatively little significance. Practical questions,—on strikes, trade unions, combinations,—invariably arise as to particular wages, not as to wages at large; while it is only to the questions of wages at large that general reasoning as to wages and capital can apply. So far as the deeper problems of distribution are concerned, it appeared again that these have little to do with the general wages fund. More particularly, the residual theory of wages, which has been much associated with attacks on the old wages fund doctrine, has no real connection with the questions as to the sources either of real wages or of any other sort of real income. In fact, the wages fund doctrine, or what there is of truth in it, has to do rather with production than with distribution. It serves to describe the process by which the real income of the community emerges from a prolonged process of production; and it serves to describe in what manner the hired laborers of advanced industrial communities get their share of this accruing real income. It thus describes important parts of the machinery of production and of distribution. But it can tell us little as to the forces which move that machinery,—as to fundamental causes which make the real income of the community large or small, or which determine the share of that real income which in the long run shall go to wages or interest or rent. Its truth has been misconceived, its importance exaggerated.

In the critical and historical chapters of the second part, the long and often wearisome controversy has been followed from Adam Smith to the present time. For near a century, indeed, there was little in the way of controversy. Adam Smith pointed out that, with the division of labor, the relation between productive exertion and its enjoyable result becomes indirect, and prolonged in time ; and he laid it down that wages are therefore paid from capital. In this very first stage of the discussion the confusion appeared between money wages and real wages— between the payment of the hired laborer from the money resources of the employers, and the derivation of real income from social capital. Adam Smith explained at length that money was but "the wheel of circulation," and that the true source of all income was consumable goods; but he failed to examine what was the relation of consumable goods to capital.

His successors did not go farther. For one reason and another, they failed to do more than repeat the vague and general proposition that wages depended on capital. The main cause of this unsatisfactory treatment was the emphasis which, after Malthus and Ricardo had made their influence felt, was given to "natural" wages, to the standard of living, and to the principle of population. This caused questions as to "market" wages to be dismissed with brief mention, and so to receive no more careful examination than had been given this topic by Adam Smith. The formula that wages depended on the ratio between capital and population was handed on from writer to writer with no important variation and no real development, throughout the period of the ascendency of the English school.

The unsatisfactory and ambiguous character of the accepted formula is clearly shown by the mode in which it was applied at the hands of John Stuart Mill. By this authoritative writer the lengthened period of production is referred to in the briefest terms, and the dependence of labor on "capital" in the sense of real capital is rather implied than expressed. On the other hand, "capital" in relation to wages is usually described as funds, sums, money resources, and spoken of as if it were all in the hands of the direct employer. The latter meaning was fastened on by the critics who first began to question the soundness of the traditional view. Longe and Thornton began to ask whether the funds which employers could turn over to laborers were predetermined, and so were led to deny the rigidity of the wages fund. Cairnes tried to answer them; but, while continuing to speak chiefly of employers' resources and money funds, he never fully faced the question whether those funds were or were not predetermined. In the end, this almost exclusive attention to employers' funds and laborers' money wages, led to a denial not only of the rigidity of the wages fund, but of the payment of wages out of any fund of capital at all. It was maintained that wages were paid from current product, not from capital.

In the closing chapter we have compared this last turn in the wages fund controversy itself with the new mode of approaching economic theory which is associated with the Austrian school, and which has served, unexpectedly and undesignedly, to bring once more into the foreground the mode in which real income emerges from social capital. The examination of these two currents of thought has brought into bold relief the question which underlies the whole controversy. The two propositions,—the one, that labor gets its reward from a product that is its own, or at least is current product; the other, that present labor represents in the main a future result and gets its immediate reward from products of the past,—both have directed attention to that relation in time between exertion and result, which had been so lightly passed over in the older literature of the subject. It is not too much to hope that on this topic, at least, there may be substantial agreement among economists. It has been said that the controversy over the wages fund is a barren one; and so it is, as an effort to settle the causes which finally determine wages and shape distribution at large. But as a mode of describing the methods and sequence of production, the concrete structure of society in its economic aspects, the manner in which a prolonged and complicated series of exertions brings at last the flow of real income, the place which capitalists have in the distribution of income,—on these topics something can still be gained from the discussion. The inquiry here undertaken as to the true relation of wages to capital, and the summary of the historical development of the old doctrine, may put into truer light old views and modern criticisms, and may be helpful for that restatement of economic doctrines on which the present generation is so busily engaged.

INDEX.

(See also the Table of Contents.)

327

THE END.